Praise for

# THE VAULT OF WALT

"Jim's vast knowledge of Disney has constantly amazed me and he understands how the Disney Studio, Theme Parks, and Disneyana all tie together. Jim is an excellent Disney Heritage writer and speaker, and it's about time he put together this collection of stories he has gathered over the years."

—Disney Legend (2005) Tom Nabbe, Disneyland's original Tom Sawyer

"Jim's story telling has always mesmerized me. Now some of his Disney tidbits are in a book! Let me put it this way. Chatting with Jim is a delicious nine course meal. Hours with his book will be a mouthwatering feast."

—Author and actress Margaret Kerry, original reference model for Tinker Bell in Disney's *Peter Pan*

"No one knows more hidden nooks and crannies in the vast history of Disney animation than Jim Korkis. I'm delighted that he's gathered his fact-filled columns in this book."

—Disney Authority Leonard Maltin, author of *The Disney Films* and host and consultant of *Disney Treasures* DVDs.

"Disney history is full of unexplored byways, and no one has done a better job of mapping many of them than Jim Korkis. Even the most knowledgeable Disney buffs will be surprised and delighted by what they find in his book."

—Disney history expert Michael Barrier, author of *The Animated Man: A Life of Walt Disney*

"Disney stories are insightful as well as fun, and no one tells them better than Jim Korkis. Jim truly loves his material, and so will you. I heartily recommend his new book and I guarantee you'll love every page."

—Artist and writer Floyd Norman, whose career at Disney spanned from Walt's era through Eisner's reign.

# THE VAULT OF WALT

### Unofficial, Unauthorized, Uncensored Disney Stories Never Told

# THE VAULT OF WALT

Unofficial, Unauthorized, Uncensored
Disney Stories Never Told

JIM KORKIS

Visit us on-line at:
www.ayefourpublishing.com/vaultofwalt

Printed in the United States of America.

First Printing: 2010

ISBN-978-0-615-40242-0

*This book, as always, is dedicated to my father and my mother, John and Barbara Korkis, who passed away less than a decade ago but whose unconditional love, constant support, common sense and good humor continue to inspire me to this day.*

# FOREWORD

Some years ago our son Walt brought to my attention an article on the Mouse Planet website. It was that rare thing; an honest, well written piece that was so authentic, so true to my dad's spirit, so unprejudiced and non-judgmental that as I read it I could see the twinkle in dad's eye, hear his laugh.

I immediately wrote the author Wade Sampson a letter of appreciation. Some weeks later I received a reply and learned that Wade Sampson was actually the pseudonym of Jim Korkis, who worked for the Walt Disney World Company as a Coordinator at the Learning Center and was well known and respected as a Disney Historian. Since that time I looked forward eagerly to "Wade's" ongoing output, learning some things I didn't know, but always delighted with what he chose to write about and his obvious understanding and even affection for his subject.

Jim does not put my father on a pedestal, but he does like him, and I do not think that disqualifies him from having objectivity in his opinion of him. I find myself in the same position.

I am so pleased that many of his writings are now bound together in this book. Dad's personality, character and values are displayed in the selections Jim has offered here.

I have not hesitated to correspond with Jim whenever I think of something that might interest him, or to add some insights into something he has written about. Dad did not hide anything about his life. He loved to talk about it. But he never really talked about religion, and his feelings about prayer, and I learned from Jim's article how deeply these feelings went.

I look forward to his continued exploration of dad's life and times. Something interesting and illuminating always seems to turn up, some little event and angle that adds to the story of his very good life.

**Diane Disney Miller**
July 2010

*Diane is the eldest daughter of Walt and Lillian Disney and a noted philanthropist. Among many other achievements, she was instrumental in the creation of The Walt Disney Family Museum in San Francisco that opened in 2009.*

# INTRODUCTION

What's all this?

Unauthorized, unofficial, uncensored Disney Stories? Is all that really true?

Yes, that's true but don't expect to find scandals, rumors, urban legends and fanciful assumptions in these pages. The history of Disney is so rich that despite all the books that have been written about the subject, many great stories were never told. These are just a few of those fascinating "lost" stories and the facts behind them.

Sometimes these stories are missing simply because there was no more space in a book to explore these interesting little tangents. Often, they were missing because the author had no clue that these stories even existed or had no access to the necessary research to tell the story.

Think of this book as a Disney History companion filling in some of those nooks and crannies that may only be mentioned in a brief sentence or two, if at all, in other Disney history books. These chapters truly are the forgotten but fascinating Disney stories.

Each individual chapter is a self-contained story so feel free to open the book to any page and begin reading. These chapters were originally written to be read one at a time and savored so don't feel the need to gorge on the new information all at once. Think of the book as a box of chocolates with different delights and maybe some tasty hidden surprises to enjoy during a pleasant afternoon.

Some of these stories appeared in a preliminary draft form under my writing pseudonym of "Wade Sampson" on the www.mouseplanet.com website every Wednesday for several years. However, all of these chapters have been rewritten extensively with new information and quotes added and all corrections made.

---

Who is Wade Sampson and why use a pseudonym? Without going into lengthy details, I found myself in an untenable situation where I was not allowed to share Disney heritage without severe reprisals. Most of the people in the Disney historical community were well aware "Wade Sampson" was my writing pseudonym and the true nature of the very real necessity for me to adopt a pseudonym in a vain attempt to protect myself from unjustifiable retaliation. I thank them all for being so discreet in keeping that secret for so long. However, they never knew the true origin of the name.

The name "Wade Sampson" is actually an extremely obscure Disney reference and only Disney Archivist Dave Smith and Disney historian Michael Barrier were able to immediately recognize it without prodding.

1971 was the year Walt Disney World opened, Roy O. Disney passed away, and some felt marked the beginning of the end for Walt's dreams. That same year, a novel was released entitled *The Rat Factory* by J.M. Ryan. This comedic tale is a colorful account of a young artist named Ambrose who works at the Sampson Studios in Hollywood in the Thirties and his various exaggerated struggles. The studio produced popular animated cartoon characters including Ricky Rat, Dizzy Duck and Halfwit Hog. These well beloved icons were the creation of the fictional Wade Sampson, a thinly veiled and often unflattering surrogate for Walt Disney.

The author, J.M. Ryan, was in fact a pseudonym as well. The novel was written by John Richard McDermott who worked as an artist at the Disney Studio on Hyperion in the Thirties. Intertwined in an improbable storyline were McDermott's memories and perspectives of working at the Disney Hyperion Studio. I assumed the pseudonym as an intriguing nom de plume with several different layers of Disney connections. It is my hope that my columns over the past few years have somewhat redeemed the name and character of Wade Sampson as portrayed in the novel.

This secret is being revealed here and now because there is no longer a necessity for me to hide my true identity. I do feel that Wade Sampson is much a nicer and smarter writer than I am but I will continue to try to live up to the high standards that he has established.

---

Primarily, most of the stories in this book relate to the time when Walt Disney was alive because of my affection, respect and fascination for Walt.

As you read the fact-filled stories throughout this book, please do not be fooled into thinking that these are the definitive versions. It has been my experience that there is always something more to be told about any story. Even if I have spent decades exhaustively researching a topic, too many times I have discovered as soon as I commit the article to print that suddenly another previously unknown anecdote or quote or perspective about the story will magically appear to taunt me for not discovering it earlier. Fortunately, some of those gems were found at the last moment before this manuscript was sent to the publisher and so could be included in these articles.

Was performer Spike Jones inspired to create his wacky music arrangements from performing in Donald Duck's gadget band on radio? Was *The Aristocats* originally supposed to be a two part live action episode of the weekly Disney television series? Did Warner Brothers legendary director Chuck Jones, who co-created classic characters like Pepe Le Pew the skunk and the Road Runner and Coyote, find he couldn't succeed at the Disney Studios? Did Walt really intend to introduce Smell-O-Vision to the story of the Founding Fathers at Disneyland?

You really won't find these stories anywhere else and certainly not with the wonderful quotes from people who actually lived the stories. The book is divided into four sections: Walt Disney Stories, Disney Film Stories, Disney Parks Stories and The Other Worlds of Disney Stories.  Hopefully, that will make it easier for you to find what you want to read.

If you have half as much fun reading these stories as I had writing them, then I had twice as much fun. I hope you enjoy and share these stories with others.

**Jim Korkis**
a/k/a Wade Samspon
July 2010

# TABLE OF CONTENTS

## Part Three: Disney Park Stories

## Part Four: The Other Worlds of Disney Stories

## About the Author                       453

## Acknowledgements                       457

PART ONE:  THE WALT STORIES

On my book shelves, I have over three dozen different biographies of Walt Disney. Some are scholarly tomes. Some are barely a hundred pages in length because they were meant for children. Some are done in a comic book format. Some are in a foreign language. In addition, I have dozens of different biographies of Walt that have appeared over the decades in magazines and newspapers.

None of the stories in this section appear in any of those other sources, except, on very rare occasion, in a brief sentence or two.

Having interviewed animators, Imagineers and associates of Walt for over thirty years, I am continually surprised at how much more there is to discover about this amazing man.

Everyone seems to have different perspectives and different stories about Walt. It is like the classic story of the blind men and the elephant. Each blind man is led to experience an elephant for the first time. One feels the trunk and assumes the elephant is like a tree branch. Another feels a leg and immediately believes that an elephant is like a pillar. Yet another feels the ear and feels the elephant must be like a big leaf fan. They just see a small part, never the whole picture, and as a result make some odd assumptions.

Even over four decades after his death, new information and insights about Walt Disney are unearthed nearly every day. I wanted to write about some of the stories not covered elsewhere and to share that "lost" information with others to help keep the stories alive.

Besides the many interviews I have done and decades of locating crumbling, yellowing documents from letters to newspapers to magazines to unpublished material, I have been fortunate to have had my own personal experiences where I have been able to do things like examine part of Walt's famed miniature collection up close and in particular the Granny Kincaid Cabin where he personally crafted many of the miniatures.

I have also been fortunate to have established a friendly relationship with Diane Disney Miller, Walt's sole surviving daughter. She has been gracious and generous to pre-read some of my articles and to supply her own personal insights and memories and, where necessary, make gentle corrections. Surprisingly, even Diane didn't know some of the material I uncovered about her father.

In these articles, I have tried as much as possible to let people speak for themselves. I apologize if some of the quotes seem too lengthy or frequent but for some of these people, especially those who have passed away, this is their only chance to tell their own stories. In particular, I have made every effort to allow Walt to share his own thoughts in his own words through interviews, speeches, publicity material and letters.

Hopefully, these stories will give you a richer understanding of Walt Disney as a son, a brother, a husband and a father. He was an amazingly complex and an amazingly simple man. Walt was once asked how he would like to be remembered. He replied, "I'm a storyteller. Of all the things I've ever done, I'd like to be remembered as a storyteller." Here are some Walt stories about that still memorable storyteller.

## THE MINIATURE WORLDS OF WALT

Strangely, for a man who always had big dreams, Walt Disney took some of his greatest delight in the world of miniatures. For decades, he both constructed and collected a huge variety of intricate tiny objects. Sometimes those small objects inspired some much larger ideas including attractions at the Disney theme parks.

It is believed that Walt first seriously worked with miniatures when he helped build a Lionel train layout for his nephew, Roy E. Disney in the early Thirties, working intently on the surrounding landscaping and structures for the train track.

However, Walt's fascination with the magical power of tiny worlds was really launched in 1939 when he saw the famous Thorne exhibit at the Golden Gate International Exposition in San Francisco. Using miniature furnishings and accessories gathered by her uncle during his world travels, Mrs. James Ward Thorne had created exquisite rooms decorated to represent European and American interiors of different eras. It was said that the rooms were so perfectly crafted that viewing them was like becoming miniaturized and then entering another time. Needless to say, they captured Walt's imagination completely.

In the late Forties, Walt merged his love of trains with his love of miniature making to build a small-scale railroad, the "Carolwood Pacific" that steamed around the backyard of his home on Carolwood Drive. He was especially proud of the bright yellow caboose, with its diminutive oil lamps, brass doorknobs and actual working spring latches.

Walt painstakingly crafted a pint-sized potbellied stove for the caboose as well. "I had a pattern made up, and it turned out so cute with the grate, shaker and door, and all the little working parts, I became intrigued with the idea," Walt wrote. "I had a few made up: one was bronze, another black, and I even made a gold one! Then we made more and started painting them in motifs that fitted the period at the turn of the century."

Each of these five and a half inch tall stoves had a different design, and eventually about one hundred were made. Walt gave some to friends, and even sent some to an antique gift shop in New York where, to Walt's delight, Mrs. Thorne herself purchased two to add to her renowned collection, the same collection that had inspired Walt's hobby. They sold for twenty-five dollars each and Walt made no special effort to market them or make a profit. He was just curious to see if there was any interest and by 1957, the supply was depleted.

"It has been fun making them and others appreciate them, too, so all in all, I feel well repaid," said Walt.

Actor Richard Todd, who performed in several of Walt's British live action films, recalled visiting Walt's home and seeing "cabinets full of the objects he loved: tiny things, miniatures of all sorts in china, wood or metal. He gave me a tiny potbellied stove that he had made himself, a beautiful little thing about six inches high, painted in white, green and gold."

Walt began seriously collecting miniatures during his European travels, bringing home countless tiny objects of glass, wood, china and metal. In a letter to a friend in 1951, Walt wrote: "My hobby is a life saver. When I work with these small objects, I become so absorbed that the cares of the studio fade away…at least for a time."

When Walt's collection was inventoried in the mid-Sixties, the listing was over a thousand items including paintings and books like the *Holy Bible, Tennyson's Poetical Works, A Miniature History of England* and eighteen volumes of the plays of William Shakespeare. There were musical instruments like three banjos, a mandolin, a guitar and an organ, crafted by conductor Frederick Stark. A set of dueling pistols were near a leather case inscribed "The Colt Story in Miniature" that had fourteen six-shooters. There were eleven classic cars including a 1915 Model T Ford, 1903 Cadillac, a 1904 Rambler and a 1911 Rolls Royce. Walt also displayed a model battleship and steamboat.

However, just collecting these tiny treasures was not enough for Walt. He wanted to create an entire miniature world. In the early Fifties, he asked animator Ken Anderson to draw twenty-four scenes of life in an old Western town. Walt planned to carve tiny figures and build the scenes in miniature. When he had made enough, he would send them out as a traveling exhibit.

Walt told Anderson: "I'm tired of having everybody else around here do the drawing and the painting. I'm going to do something creative myself. I'm going to put you on my personal payroll, and I want you to draw twenty-four scenes of life in an old Western town. Then I'll carve the figures and make the scenes in miniature. When we get enough of them made, we'll send them out as a traveling exhibit. We'll get an office here at the studio and you and I will be the only ones who'll have keys."

Walt immediately put advertisements in newspapers and hobby magazines seeking vintage miniatures of all kinds for his tableaus. Fearing prices would soar, Walt asked his two secretaries at the time, Kathryn Gordon and Dolores Voght, to use their names in the advertisements rather than announcing that Disney was looking for these items.

Several newspapers and hobby magazines carried the ad: "WANTED: Anything in miniatures to a scale of 1 ½" to the foot or under. Up to and including early 1900's. Give full description and price. Private collector. K. Gordon (and her address)."

Besides pixie-sized furniture, Walt collected miniscule tableware including delicate Limoges and Havilland tea services, small Toby jugs, sky-blue Wedgewood pitchers as well as washing bowls of Willowware, Bennington crocks and jars. Sparkling wine and perfume bottles, drinking glasses smaller than thimbles, several sets of silverware fit for fairy queens, silver tea services and a candelabra as delicate as a cobweb completed the collection.

Walt spent countless hours carefully constructing the first of his tiny tableaus. The first scene, entitled "Granny Kincaid's Cabin" was based on a set from his live-action feature, *So Dear to My Heart* (1949). To build the chimney, Walt picked up pebbles at his vacation home, the Smoke Tree Ranch, in Palm Springs.

Inside the cabin, a hand-braided rag rug warmed a floor of planks not much larger than matchsticks. A china washbowl and pitcher, guitar with strings thin as cat whiskers and a small family Bible sat on the table. A tiny flintlock rifle hung on the wall, and a spinning wheel with flax sat in the corner. The scene looked as if Granny herself had just stepped briefly outside. Granny would not be seen, however. Viewers would simply hear a recording of her voice describing the cozy scene, for Walt had recorded a narration by actress Beulah Bondi, the famous character actress who played the part of Granny in *So Dear to My Heart.*

"The interior of Granny's cabin was completely dressed up with miniatures. Walt made the rocking chairs and the rest himself. He then said, 'Let's make up a cross section. Let's have Grandmother rocking, Bible in hand, with a diorama behind her depicting the outdoors. Granny would say, 'Oh hello there, I'm just reading my Bible.' She'd chat for a while, then return to her reading'," revealed Imagineer Wathel Rogers although the figure of Granny was never constructed.

The cabin was exhibited at the Festival of California Living at the Pan Pacific Auditorium in Los Angeles from November 28 to December 7, 1952. A press release announced that it represented the beginning of Walt's new miniature Americana exhibit, entitled "Disneylandia."

"This little cabin is part of a project I am working on, and it was exhibited as a test to obtain the public's reaction to my plans for a complete village," Walt explained in a 1953 interview. With the public's positive reaction as encouragement, Walt once again returned to his workbench and the miniscule hammers, screwdrivers, clamps and magnifying glasses that were part of a miniature-maker's craft.

Gradually two more small tableaus took shape. One was a frontier music hall stage complete with a one-eighth scale, three-dimensional, tap-dancing vaudevillian, called "Project Little Man." Disney Imagineers filmed actor and eccentric dancer Buddy Ebsen performing tap-dance routines against a grid pattern for live action reference. Sculpted by Charles Cristadoro and connected to a series of cams and gears like a music box, the little figure moved and was considered the beginning of audio-animatronics. Walt was disappointed with the lack of range of expressions on the carved face of the character and explored using plastics instead to make it seem more realistic.

In June 1951, Walt and his team of designers and technicians began work on a third miniature display—a traditional barbershop quartet crooning *Sweet Adeline*. The scene would include a barber, customer in a chair and two more patrons waiting. Again, live actors were filmed for reference. "We got as far as building the guy in the chair and the barber," Imagineer Roger Broggie recalled. "Then the whole job was stopped!"

Walt became convinced that only a limited audience would be able to view these tableaus and they would be unable to generate the necessary income to pay for their continued maintenance. Disneylandia grew to become Disneyland. As Broggie recalled, Walt said, "We're going to do this thing for real!"

In 1953, the sales pitch for Disneyland that Roy O. Disney took to New York to raise money for the building of the theme park included a description of this never-built land that would have been located between Tomorrowland and Fantasyland:

> *Lilliputian Land. A land of Little Things…a miniature*
> *Americana village inhabited by mechanical people nine inches*
> *high who sing and dance and talk to you as you peek through*
> *the windows of their tiny shops and homes. In Lilliputian*
> *Land, there is an Erie Canal barge that takes you through the*
> *famous canals of the world, where you visit the scenic wonders*
> *of the world in miniature.*

*Here a little diamond-stack locomotive engine seventeen inches high steams into the tiny railroad station. You sit on top of the Pullman coaches like Gulliver, and the little nine inch engineer pulls back the throttle taking you on the biggest little ride in the land. And for the little people who have little appetites—you can get miniature ice cream cones, or the world's smallest hot-dog on a tiny bun.*

While Lilliputian Land, like many of Walt's other original ideas for Disneyland, was never developed, Disneyland did showcase a small sized Storybook Land in Fantasyland.

Walt had been influenced by his visit to Madurodam, a tourist attraction in the Netherlands that showcased landmarks in miniature size, and his initial idea was to create scale replicas of world-renowned landmarks. Eventually Walt's idea evolved into miniatures of equally beloved landmarks, famous locations from his classic animated features. A majestic Cinderella's Castle overlooks a small world that includes Geppetto's Toy Shop, Mr. Toad's mansion and the Seven Dwarf's Cottage with nearby glittering, jewel-filled mine. Each structure was built with the same meticulous attention to detail that Walt lavished on his own miniatures.

Imagineer Ken Anderson, who designed Storybook Land, said he quickly discovered that it was "one of Walt's favorite rides. He'd make frequent visits to the model shop at the Burbank studio to provide comments and his expertise on the miniature models."

Walt also considered a plan to put Lilliputian-sized replicas of famous American landmarks like Thomas Jefferson's home, Monticello, and George Washington's home, Mt. Vernon, on what would eventually become Tom Sawyer Island. Some early

Disneyland souvenirs even show these tiny landmarks dotting the landscape. The decision was made to turn the Island into the domain of Mark Twain's adventurous young rascals, Tom Sawyer and Huck Finn, instead and the miniature buildings were never built.

Walt's interest in miniatures didn't wane after the opening of Disneyland Park. While designing the Ford Pavilion with its soaring Magic Skyway for the 1965 New York World's Fair, something was needed for the Rotunda entry area to show that Ford was an international company. Walt suggested a miniature village. Soon, Imagineers had designed the "International Gardens"—a series of buildings on a scale of a half-inch to one foot that recreated world-renowned landmarks from eleven countries. Soon, scenes of Colonial America and "Merrie Olde" England, golden-hued Aztec temples in Mexico and the half-timbered houses of Medieval Europe invited visitors to imagine themselves small enough to walk the twisting lanes.

Still fascinated with the entire process of miniature making, Walt personally supervised the work. One day as he was visiting the Imagineers' workshop, he saw six-foot, eight-inch tall Imagineer Jack Ferges crawling around under his desk. As Ferges later remembered, "Walt said, 'What are you doing?' I said 'I just dropped the entire city of Copenhagen.' Walt laughed so hard, he had to sit down."

Eventually, shelves were built on two walls and enclosed by glass doors in Walt's office suite at the Disney Studio to showcase his amazing miniature collection. For Walt, good things did indeed sometimes come in small packages.

## SANTA WALT

On the Disney weekly anthology television show, the episode entitled *Holiday Time at Disneyland* originally ran December 23, 1962 and has been rerun many times over the decades. The show starts with Dickensian Christmas carolers singing in front of the Sleeping Beauty Castle at Disneyland. Amazingly, it is snowing in Anaheim, California. The lively bell ringer turns around to face the audience and it is a smiling Walt Disney.

Later, Santa Claus himself shows up and worries that the snow might not be good for the special Disneyland holiday parade. Walt has Tinker Bell magically turn off the snow. Two children excitedly run up to Santa Claus and Walt for an autograph on their Disneyland souvenir guidebook.

"Sure, you can have our autographs," says Walt filled with Christmas spirit. "You go first, Santa." After Santa signs his autograph, Walt prepares to sign and the kids grab the guidebook and run off mumbling under their breath, "Who's that other guy?" Walt is amused and tells Santa, "It is your day, Santa, so make the most of it. I've got 365."

Walt Disney wrote in *Reader's Digest* (December 1941) that "One reason the Christmas season appeals to me is that it makes us suspend business-as-usual routine and let our minds soar for a while. Christmas seems to release even the most solemn of us from the Scrooge realism that occasionally besets all of us."

Despite that proclamation, Walt's wife Lillian claimed that he didn't care as much for the holiday season as people thought because he couldn't go into the studio to work. Lillian recalled, "Walt didn't like holidays because he couldn't work on them. Everybody took off for the day, at the Studio. Christmas didn't mean a great deal to him. When he got through with the festivities he went to his room and read, usually. He never wasted time. He liked to set up the children's toys as he did the train one year. But he couldn't just sit and visit with people."

Walt's daughter Diane Disney Miller has stated that "(Dad's) not sentimental about Christmas. He's more sentimental about family relationships like birthdays...about his own birthday. He feels very sentimental about that and you don't dare slight him or forget because he would be very deeply hurt. If you mention it, he's fairly assured you will remember. But if he thinks that you don't remember, when it has arrived he just feels a little bit slighted."

However, that is not to say that Walt disliked Christmas. The joy of Christmas for Walt was in giving to others, especially his family, and not about receiving presents for himself. Walt found more delight in the simplest of gifts than in the lavish presents from his peers in the motion picture industry. It was a philosophy that came from his financially challenged childhood. "My parents were conservative people and there were few extra dollars for such frivolities in those days. I always got some sensible, modest present for Christmas. One time Roy bought me a shiny gyroscopic top with its wonderful spinning ability," Walt once told an interviewer.

Every December over a twenty-five-year period, Walt Disney wrote a news filled Christmas letter to his younger sister, Ruth Beecher, in Portland, Oregon, detailing the family events and what was going on at the studio. On December 8, 1947, he wrote: "I bought myself a birthday-Christmas present—something I've wanted all my life—an electric train.

Being a girl, you probably can't understand how much I wanted one when I was a kid, but I've got one now and what fun I'm having. I have it set up in one of the outer rooms adjoining my office so I can play with it in my spare moments. It's a freight train with a whistle, and real smoke comes out of the smokestack—there are switches, semaphores, station and everything. It's just wonderful!"

Walt was so excited that he also asked to see whether her son, Ted, might like a train set for Christmas. He made the same offer to his niece, Marjorie Davis and her son, Geoffrey, and his brother Herbert's grandson, David Puder.

Traditionally on Christmas morning, a huge tree appeared in the Disney's two-story living room. Walt would have spent much of the night decorating it while Lilly filled the stockings and laid out the multitude of gifts. Many of them were toys of Mickey Mouse and other Disney characters. Aside from the children's toys, there was no evidence of Walt's studio life in the Disney home. He didn't have framed cels on the wall nor did he display a Mickey Mouse toy by his phone or wear a Donald Duck tie.

Walt did strive to maintain the Santa Claus myth as long as possible for his two daughters. In the December 1938 issue of the magazine *Woman's Day* in an article by Munro Leaf, the author wrote: "After Walt Disney found out at the age of six that there wasn't any team of reindeer waiting up on the roof while a fat man slid down his chimney, he had fun pretending to his parents that he still believed the whole works."

Leaf asked Walt if he believed in Santa Claus today and Walt responded, "Certainly, yes. When my little daughters confront me with the question, I shall say without a twinge, 'Of course there is.' Long Live Santa Claus!"

Their daughter, Diane Disney Miller remembered, "They always used to be very insistent upon observing the Santa Claus myth. Mother would fill our stockings in the middle of the night on Christmas Eve. They were hung outside our bedroom doors. I think we probably had them outside the doors because it was easy for mother to get to them. She probably arranged it that way."

Diane also remembered a special memorable gift from Santa when she was in elementary school:

> One Christmas, Santa Claus brought us [Diane and her
> younger sister Sharon] a playhouse and I just knew that Santa
> Claus did because it just appeared Christmas morning out
> in our backyard. It was this darling little playhouse. It was
> designed at the Studio and the Studio carpenters put it up. It
> was a little one room, about the size of a good-sized closet.
> It had little leaded glass windows and one of those little
> mushroom chimneys on it, though there was no fireplace, and
> a sink with running water. It had a little tank inside the cooler
> that you filled then you could turn on the faucet and the water
> would come out. It had a little cooler all stocked with little tiny
> canned goods. You know, the small cans that you can buy. It
> had a telephone in it that would connect with our phone in the
> kitchen.
>
> And I talked to Santa Claus on it that morning. We had a big
> fat butler at the time and it must have been him that I talked
> to. He asked if the house was all right and I said, 'Yes, Santa,
> fine.' I was afraid to speak. My eyes were probably as big
> as saucers, because I knew it was Santa and I knew he had

*brought the house. Some way, he had managed to keep me out of the house all day before Christmas. The Studio carpenters had come up and given their time to put the house up for us. I still have pictures and I have a few things of the little house.*

*It was so dear and I knew Santa had brought it. And a little boy next door was sort of cynical about it. I said to him, 'Well, Morgan, look what Santa brought.' He said, 'Santa Claus? You're crazy. There were men up in your front yard all day yesterday putting the house up.' I said, 'Morgan, you're a liar. I was out in the front yard playing all day long and there were no men.' I was so positive. I remember it. I just couldn't have been more positive that Santa had brought that house. It was really a wonderful thing. We have some pictures of it.*

Lillian Disney, in the *McCall's* article "I Live With a Genius" (February 1953), also recalled that little dwarf cottage: "After *Snow White* came out, it was so successful we felt flush about buying presents for the kids. The studio carpenters had spent days building a replica of the dwarfs' house for them. Then they (Diane and Sharon) started playing train with the boxes the things had come in."

During the making of *Snow White*, Walt saw the ink and paint staff working overtime very diligently during the holiday season to finish the cels for *Snow White* and so he jumped into his car and raced over to Hollywood and bought up every lady's compact he could lay his hands on.

When he returned to the studio, he quickly donned a fake white beard and red cap and burst into the ink and paint corridor as Santa Claus, distributing the gifts to each one of the girls. All of Walt's money was tied up in the production and he couldn't afford to give them a cash bonus at the time.

For thirty years later they were still talking about the night Walt played Santa Claus for them.

It was a tradition that Walt carried on for many years. Disney Legend Joyce Carlson remembered that during her time in the ink and paint department, "At Christmas time, we'd have a little party and he'd bring little compacts, face powder, nylons, cosmetics and he'd go around to all the girls and you could pick what you wanted."

Author Bob Thomas recalled that Walt enjoyed playing Santa Claus for his friends so much that he maintained a file of hundreds of children of his personal friends, members of the press, studio workers, film executives, and more. Each child got gifts of Disney character merchandise, primarily one large important item plus a few little ones, all individually wrapped.

Walt's secretaries were the real Santa's elves responsible for putting together all these packages for the children. Beginning early in November, they were often kept busy right up to a few days before Christmas in a special room in the studio warehouse. Walt dropped in daily to inspect the packages and make sure that his directions were being carried out. The gifts continued until the child reached the age of twelve, then he or she was dropped from the list and received a Disney Christmas card instead each year.

Diane wrote that Christmas in the Disney family household was one always filled with joy:

> When we were tiny, we were too young to enjoy a lot of
> toys. Like I see pictures of our first Christmas and I was
> surrounded by toys. Mechanical toys, dolls and stuffed
> animals of a towering size and all things like that. Toys of

*every conceivable shape and kind. And there I was sitting,*
*surrounded by the mechanical ones, and hitting at them as*
*they moved and performed.*

*Dad gave us (Diane and Sharon) each a watch when we were*
*seven years old that was inscribed on the back with his name*
*and the date. Mine said, 'To Diane From Daddy'. Other*
*Christmases, it was antique jewelry, which he liked. When*
*he gives gifts he wants to give gifts you can remember him*
*by. He's afraid that he's going to be gone and forgotten. He*
*loves to give us jewelry. And every Christmas he's given us a*
*little piece of jewelry. On Christmas it was usually something*
*antique. He loves antique jewelry. Nothing expensive or*
*elaborate but a little pair of antique gold earrings. He gave*
*Mother once some seals in the forms of a necklace and then*
*at a later Christmas there were some seals hanging from a*
*bracelet. Seals used for sealing wax and things like that.*

Walt told a reporter for *Good Housekeeping* magazine
(December 1933), "When you ask me what I want for
Christmas – Christmas is so much fun I hardly care, just so
there's something to open up from somebody...one thing I
don't want is shirts, but I'm shy on polo ponies. I wouldn't
mind a couple of those."

Unfortunately, Walt missed celebrating his final Christmas
by just ten days. Walt checked into St. Joseph's Hospital on
November 30, 1966, and during much of the time was heavily
sedated and in pain. He already had one lung removed on
November 7th but the cancer had metastasized and Walt had
started to deteriorate much faster than his doctor expected.

Walt's last filmed introduction for his weekly television
program was filmed on October 6, 1966. It was for the show

*A Salute to Alaska* that was to be shown in February 1967. Walt barely moves during the introduction and looks a bit pale. The famous film where he describes the Epcot project was filmed roughly three weeks later on October 27, 1966. He only appears briefly at the beginning and at the end of that film where he sits most of the time.

Once he entered the hospital, Walt was too ill to even dictate his yearly Christmas letter to his younger sister, Ruth. One of his personal secretaries, Tommie Wilck, sent her Walt's best wishes and the assurance that he would write her a Christmas letter when he felt better. "When Walt is back in his office, I'm sure you'll get a more up-to-date and personal note from him. In the meantime, he sends his love."

On December 14, 1966, Walt's daughter went Christmas shopping to get something nice for her father who had lost a great deal of weight like a nice cashmere sweater, one of his favorite items of clothing. She picked up a few things and wanted to bring in a Christmas tree to her father's hospital room but felt it wouldn't be allowed.

Walt never got his Christmas gift that year. He never left the hospital. He passed away the morning of December 15, 1966.

## HORSING AROUND: WALT AND POLO

*"The secret of success if there is any, is liking what you do.
I like my work better than my play. I play polo, when I have
time, and I enjoy it, but it can't equal work!" said Walt Disney
in an interview that appeared in the San Francisco Chronicle
(December 31, 1933).*

In the Thirties, polo was a very popular and expensive activity, especially among members of the entertainment industry even though it is an unbelievably intense physical sport. This was an era when actors tried to emulate off-screen the macho characters they portrayed on the silver screen. While some of them were athletic, most of them were ill prepared for the demands of the difficult and challenging game of polo.

Actor Spencer Tracy loved to saddle up his polo ponies and for a time in the Thirties, played every free moment off the movie set. Studios pleaded with him not to play because of fear of injury, so Tracy played under aliases until he quit when his friend Will Rogers died.

Polo was also used for social networking in the Hollywood community. The famous Beverly Hills Polo Lounge was created at this time and remains a popular and somewhat exclusive social gathering location today for Hollywood notables.

In the Thirties, there were more than twenty-five polo fields in Los Angeles, including such popular spots where Walt Disney played as the Uplifters Polo Field (now bulldozed and replaced with a street) and the Riviera Polo Field (now the home of the Paul Revere High School). The Riviera adjoined a golf course and there were three or four polo fields and many celebrities kept stables there.

In Hollywood, the strongest champion of the sport was humorist Will Rogers, who was introduced to the game in 1915. During the Twenties and Thirties, Rogers popularized the sport among the elite in Hollywood, from Hal Roach to Darryl Zanuck to Walt Disney.

Walt had a personal friendship with Rogers. In fact, at one time, he was negotiating with Rogers to appear in Walt's first full-length animated feature film. *Snow White* was not the first choice of a feature project for Walt. He had developed several possibilities including *Alice in Wonderland* featuring a live-action Mary Pickford as Alice interacting with animated characters.

When that project fell apart, Walt considered using the same basic concept but with Will Rogers as Rip Van Winkle interacting with animated characters. Rogers' untimely death put an end to that project. Previously, Walt had sent some of his top Disney animators including Grim Natwick, Art Babbitt and Bill Tytla to Rogers' Santa Monica ranch to sketch the popular comedian in action.

The popularity of Mickey Mouse in the early Thirties brought great success and attention to Walt. However, it also brought great stress. Managing and expanding his studio as well as the many demands being made on him in other areas from merchandising decisions to publicity requests in addition to the tension at home where his wife Lillian struggled through two miscarriages resulted in Walt suffering one of his infamous nervous breakdowns.

Walt's doctor suggested that Mickey Mouse's father take up some form of exercise to help relieve the stress. Walt tried wrestling, boxing, and golf, but each attempt only frustrated him further rather than releasing tension. Walt had always loved horses, so he took up horseback riding and joined a local riding club.

Always a multi-tasker, Walt decided to combine his love of horseback riding with his desire to integrate with Hollywood society by taking up the then popular sport of polo. At the time, Walt quipped that to him polo seemed to be just "golf on a horse."

In the beginning, Walt enlisted Disney Studio personnel, including Jack Cutting, Norm Ferguson, Les Clark, Dick Lundy, Gunther Lessing, Bill Cottrell, and even his brother Roy to participate.

They studied the book *As To Polo* by William Cameron Forbes (1929) and had lessons and lectures by Gil Proctor, a polo expert. Eventually, they did practice in the San Fernando Valley at the DuBrock Riding Academy from six a.m. in the morning until they had to report to work at the Disney Studio at eight a.m.

Walt built a polo cage at the studio so that during lunch breaks, the men could sit on a wooden horse and practice hitting the wooden ball into a goal. He even installed a dummy horse in his backyard so he himself could get in early morning practice before heading to the DuBrock Riding Academy.

"My sister and I grew up in a large playroom surrounded by framed head portraits of dad's horses and cases full of trophies. That is as close as we came to having a horse of our own and the shed on our back lot that was a sort of tack room for his polo saddles. It was always locked. So was the polo cage down

at the bottom of what we called 'the canyon'. I always wanted
to get into that cage and play on that horse, but was told that it
was off limits because of Black Widow spiders," remembered
Diane Disney Miller, Walt's daughter.

Finally, the Disney team started participating in matches
with similarly inexperienced teams at the stadium on Riverside
Drive.

Walt and Roy would play regularly with their employees on
Wednesday mornings and Saturday afternoons. In addition,
Walt and Roy joined the prestigious Riviera Club where such
Hollywood luminaries as Spencer Tracy, Leslie Howard, Darryl
Zanuck and others held court on the playing field. During this
time, Spencer Tracy became a close friend of Walt's, and Tracy
and his wife were often invited to Walt's home.

"Many of dad's friendships came from polo. Some years
ago, I was surprised to hear Bill Cottrell tell Rich Greene that
he felt that Spencer Tracy was, perhaps, dad's best friend.
Dad's friendship with Will Rogers was very important to him.
He cherished being a part of the lunches that Mrs. Rogers
would serve after a game.    Other long lasting polo friends
were Carl Beal, who my mother told me was dad's best friend
on the occasion of Carl's death from leukemia when I was
quite young, so it made an impression on me. Robert Stack,
who was a teen-ager at the time, Russell Havenstrite, a wealthy
oil man and eventual neighbor, and many others who played
and loved the game were good friends as well," recalled Diane
Disney Miller.

In 1934, Roy Disney bought four polo ponies. At one point,
Walt had nineteen horses in his stable. Polo players needed
several horses because the horses would get hurt or tired and

if a player didn't have a good horse to get him to the ball, he couldn't hit it. Seven of Walt's ponies were named June, Slim, Nava, Arrow, Pardner, Tacky, and Tommy. However, purchasing good polo ponies was an expensive situation.

"Don't fall over dead when I tell you I have six ponies now. After all, it's my only sin. I don't gamble or go out and spend my money on other men's wives or anything like that, so I guess it's okay. Anyway, the wife approves of it," wrote Walt to his mother.

Roy Disney was a fair player but Walt was highly aggressive. Walt was neither athletic nor coordinated. Director David Swift who at the time was an animator stated, "He wasn't much of an athlete. I don't know how he played polo. I didn't see how he could stay on a horse and swing a mallet at the same time."

Unlike other young boys, Walt never really participated in sports. For most of his childhood, his spare time was filled with a morning and afternoon newspaper delivery route that was very demanding of his time and energy. While other young children played sports after school and on the weekends, young Walt worked and never developed some of the sports coordination skills of others.

Walt compensated for this lack of sports experience and coordination by being a focused competitor. Actor Robert Stack, who was a teenager at the time, remembered that Walt would "run right over anybody who crossed the line. Walt was a good polo player—and he loved the game... And I have a couple of trophies at home with Walt's name on them. We hadn't won the world's championships but we had an awful lot of fun."

Walt's wife, Lillian, would spend most of her Sundays sitting on the sidelines, munching a bag of popcorn while Walt played. "He would stop and buy me a big package of popcorn and I'd sit and eat popcorn and watch him play polo," she laughed.

A program from 1937 declared: "Benefit Polo Game Sponsored by Santa Monica Charity League and Santa Monica Junior Chamber of Commerce: May 9, 1937 Riviera Country Club." The first match was the Mickey Mouse Team against the Hollywood Team. The Mickey Mouse Team: James Gleason, Robert Presnell, Happy Williams and Walt Disney. The Hollywood team included J. Walter Ruben, Mike Curtiz, Paul Kelly and Dr. Percy Goldberg. Walt Disney captained the "Mickey Mouse Team" when it came to polo matches. However, many Disney fans may be unaware there was also a "Donald Duck Team."

Disney producer Harry Tytle was quite a polo player in college but in the depths of the Depression there were few jobs for polo players. However, he did get to play with Will Rogers in August 1935 which turned out to be Rogers' last game.

He also knew Harold Helvenston, who was a professor of dramatics working at the Disney Studio at the time. One night at dinner, through the kindness of Helvenston, Tytle met some Disney employees, including George Drake and Perce Pearce, and found himself hired as a messenger boy at the Disney Studio in the traffic department.

Once at the studio, Tytle was introduced to Walt as a polo player and was invited to play with Walt at the Victor McLaughlin Arena. Walt must have liked the competitive spirit of the young man because Tytle soon found himself playing with Walt at the Riviera Country Club against Spencer Tracy and his family. Tytle, who didn't have the artistic skill to compete with other aspiring animators at the studio, worked briefly in many different departments at the Disney Studio.

However, he still had time to teach polo to a group of editors and cutters from other studios, played polo for the Junior Chamber of Commerce and formed the "Donald Duck Team." The "Donald Duck Team" (including team members like Mel Shaw and Larry Lansburgh) played a wide area as far off as Arizona. They once took the group down to Mexico City in 1938 and won their match.

Tytle thinks the team won because they were constantly being underestimated since they had a portrait of Donald Duck emblazoned on their shirts. "A clever touch suggested by Walt," remembered Tytle in his autobiography.

Walt's enthusiasm for polo inspired a popular Mickey Mouse cartoon. *Mickey's Polo Team* was released on January 1936 and was directed by Dave Hand, whose attention was already focused on his directing responsibilities for *Snow White*.

There isn't much of a storyline in the cartoon. It is just an interesting premise for physical gags of a polo game between four popular Disney animated characters against a team of four Hollywood celebrities. The spectators in the stands are a mix of Disney animated characters and Hollywood celebrities. Clarabelle Cow kisses Clark Gable, Edna May Oliver sits next to Max Hare, and Shirley Temple cheers next to the Three Little Pigs among other celebrity caricature cameos.

The Mickey Mouse team consists of Mickey, Donald Duck, Goofy and the Big Bad Wolf. The Hollywood team of movie stars is composed of Charlie Chaplin, Oliver Hardy, Stan Laurel and Harpo Marx. While modern audiences may struggle to identify the caricatures of some of the then-famous stars in the cartoon like Eddie Cantor, W.C. Fields or Harold Lloyd, even the most astute and knowledgeable classic films buff might have trouble identifying the referee.

The referee is a caricature of Jack Holt, who was a popular silent screen star who made the transition to talkies primarily in Westerns. In fact, Holt was the father of famous Western movie cowboy star, Tim Holt. Jack Holt was well known as a "manly man" and a strong supporter of polo as terrific physical exercise. He played at the Riviera alongside Walt Disney but is unfortunately largely forgotten by modern audiences.

This cartoon was made at the height of the Disney Studio's involvement in playing polo. However, this was not the version that Walt originally intended. There was to be considerable footage devoted to a caricature of Will Rogers. It was Rogers' death in an unfortunate plane accident in August 1935 while *Mickey's Polo Team* was in production that resulted in his caricature being removed from the cartoon.

The cartoon generated its own little controversy that has been forgotten over the years. The January 11, 1938 edition of the *San Francisco Examiner* ran a photo of Walt in Los Angeles looking pensive as he flipped through some papers. The caption stated: "Disney Faces Accuser in Court":

"Disney to answer charges of John P. Wade, writer and actor that 'Mickey's Polo Club' (sic), was taken from a scenario submitted by Wade. 'Mr. Disney told me the script could not be used. Then, several months later, I saw the film,' Wade testified. Disney contends the idea was his own."

*Time* magazine for January 24, 1938 revealed the outcome of this particular court action where Wade sued for a share of the film's profits. "Alleged plagiarism that the gag of the horses riding the riders had been lifted from author Wade's skit: 'The Trainer's Nightmare.' In court, attorneys for Cartoonist Walt Disney identified the device as a variation on 'the reversal gag' easily traced it to Aesop."

Said Superior Court Judge Thomas C. Gould, dismissing the suit and plagiarizing *Ecclesiastes*: "...it appears there is nothing new under the sun."

By 1938, Roy Disney was becoming worried that the combination of Walt's aggressiveness on the filed and the inherent danger of the sport itself might rob the Disney Studio of its visionary leader. In fact, Roy himself had quit the sport that year and was getting rid of his polo ponies and urged Walt to do the same. Walt resisted that suggestion to hang up his mallet even after he had seen matches where fellow horsemen had suffered severe injuries.

Always pushing himself, Walt eventually wanted to play with the better players. There was a South American team (known as "The Argentines") who were practicing on a field at the Riviera and Walt wanted to practice with them.

Actor Robert Stack remembered, "Any time the Argentineans would come in they would bring their horses with them. The reason they came, most of these great polo players came was to sell the horses and make a lot of money which they did. You could see some of them red-hots in our [movie] profession, and I think Walt was among them, bidding these fantastic sums for these magnificent horses."

Even then, it was almost impossible to tell Walt "no" so Walt took the field. One of the players hit the ball just as Walt, who was on his horse, was turning around and the ball hit Walt hard enough to knock him from the saddle. Walt had four of his cervical vertebrae crushed and was in tremendous pain. Instead of seeing a doctor, he went to a chiropractor, who manipulated Walt's back. Sadly, the injury might have healed if Walt had been placed in a cast.

Instead, it resulted in a calcium deposit building up in the back of his neck that resulted in a painful form of arthritis that plagued Walt for the rest of his life. In his later years, Walt required a couple of shots of scotch and a massage from the studio nurse in order to get home at night. When the neck and back pain flared up, Walt was often unpleasant in his interaction with his staff. When he went into St. Joseph's Hospital for the final time, no suspicion arose when employees were told Walt was just taking care of an "old polo injury."

In 1938, Walt sold off his ponies and resigned from the Riviera Polo Club. Walt loved to saddle up and socialize with Hollywood's elite on the polo fields but it left him with a painful physical injury that influenced his moods for the rest of his life. Unfortunately, it was an unhappy ending to this interesting interlude in his colorful life.

## WALT'S SCHOOL DAZE

Walt and his younger sister, Ruth, both graduated from Benton Grammar School in Kansas City, Missouri, on June 8, 1917. It was the only graduation Walt had from any school.

Walt graduated from seventh grade, and he surprised his parents by delivering a patriotic speech to the graduates. In later years, his sister remembered the speech was "something about national or international affairs."

During the graduation ceremonies, Walt drew cartoons in his fellow students' yearbooks. Even then, he was well known as the boy who was going to grow up to be a cartoonist. The principal quipped to Walt's fellow students, "He will draw you if you like." Along with the diploma, the principal gave young Walt a seven dollar award for a comic character he had drawn.

In May 1963, Walt received a Distinguished Alumnus Award from the Kansas City Art Institute from which he had never graduated. He had taken only a few Saturday morning children's art classes there. He had also received an honorary high school diploma from the Marceline School Board three years earlier in 1960, since he had only attended one year of high school.

"Gosh. This goes along with my honorary high school diploma. I had honorary degrees from Yale, Harvard and the University of Southern California before word got out that I didn't have a high school diploma. Now I have six high school diplomas," Walt said with a laugh in 1963 at the ceremony.

Walt received honorary degrees from both Yale and Harvard Universities on successive days in June 1938. Neither degree was a doctorate. They were both Masters of Arts.

After the Harvard ceremony, Walt told reporters, "I'll always wish I'd had the chance to go through college in the regular way and earn a plain Bachelor of Arts like the thousands of kids nobody ever heard of who are being graduated today."

While Walt is rightly respected as an effective educator, he had a very limited formal public school education. When the Disney family lived in Marceline, Missouri, Walt's dad, Elias, decided that Walt could not attend school until his younger sister, Ruth, was old enough to go as well, because it seemed to be the most practical thing to do. In that way, Walt could look after his little sister and they could share the same classes.

"My birthday came in the middle of the term and you had to be a certain age, so they just said, 'Well, we'll just wait and send him when Ruth can go.' And it was the most embarrassing thing that can happen to a fellow that I had to practically start in school with my little sister, Ruth, who was two years younger," said Walt in later years.

Walt's mother, Flora, was a former grammar school teacher who had taught in the Central Florida area. She home schooled the children in the subjects of basic arithmetic, reading and writing. She was a good, patient teacher, and Walt loved being home schooled by her.

At age seven, Walt was enrolled in the two-story red brick Park School that held close to two hundred children. It was a standard basic education from McGuffey Eclectic Reader.

Walt was not an attentive student and was always finding other things that captured his interest, especially cartooning.

His teacher, Miss Brown, arranged the children's seats according to their achievement in class. Walt was placed in a chair near the back door, and the teacher labeled him the "second dumbest" in the class because he wouldn't pay attention. Miss Brown complained repeatedly, "He was always drawing pictures and not paying enough attention to his studies."

When the Disney family moved to Kansas City, Walt was enrolled at Benton Grammar School. He had to repeat second grade since the teachers felt he hadn't been provided a sufficient education in Marceline. This, of course, meant Walt was almost two years older than most of the other children in his class.

Walt's subjects included grammar, arithmetic, geography, history, natural science, hygiene, writing, drawing, and music. Walt was known to be a voracious reader, especially enjoying the works of Robert Louis Stevenson, Horatio Alger (who was famous for his many stories of young men who rose from rags to riches by hard work and honesty), Sir Walter Scott, Charles Dickens, and Mark Twain.

Supposedly, Walt read everything that Mark Twain wrote. Walt also enjoyed Shakespeare, but only the parts with battles and duels he later told an interviewer. He also loved the adventures of Tom Swift, a young boy who loved science and technology, and who first appeared in print in 1910.

However, for the most part, Walt was a mediocre student. His worst subject reportedly was algebra. In Walt's defense, he didn't have much time to study or sleep at home since he was also handling a newspaper route that required him to get up at three in the morning each day to deliver the morning newspapers, and to rush home after school to deliver the afternoon edition. So, he sometimes caught up on his sleep in class.

"I often think of the days I spent at Benton," Walt wrote in 1940 to one of his former teachers, Daisy A. Beck. "I don't know whether you remember or not but I participated in several athletic events and even won a medal one year on the championship relay team. Do you remember the time I brought the live mouse into the classroom and you smacked me on the cheek? Boy! What a wallop you had! But I loved you all the more for it. And I can still plainly see the kids marching, single file, into the classrooms to the rhythm of the piano in the hall. I remember how [Principal] Cottingham would break in on any classes if he had a new story and all work would cease until he had his fun. He had his faults, but I think of him as a swell fellow."

One time, during a geography lesson, Principal Cottingham discovered Walt not paying attention to the class lesson but instead hiding behind a big geography book drawing cartoons. In front of the entire class, the principal reprimanded Walt with the stern prediction: "Young man, you'll never amount to anything."

Walt didn't take offense nor held a grudge. He always sent Mr. Cottingham and his family Christmas cards and autographed animation cels once Walt finally amounted to something. He even arranged for the entire Benton School student body to ride buses to downtown Kansas City and see *Snow White and the Seven Dwarfs* when it came out in 1938.

In fourth grade, Walt's teacher, Artena Olson, assigned the class to draw a bowl of flowers. Being very imaginative and creative, Walt drew human faces on the flowers, and he gave the flora hands and arms instead of leaves. He was reprimanded by his teacher that flowers do not have faces and hands and the assignment was to draw a still life.

In fifth grade, on Abraham Lincoln's birthday, Walt dressed up as the former President, complete with homemade stovepipe hat, crepe hair whiskers and his father's frock coat, and came to school having memorized the Gettysburg Address.

"He made this stovepipe hat out of cardboard and shoe polish," remembered his classmate and friend Walt Pfeiffer. "He purchased a beard from a place that sold theatrical things. He did this all on his own. Walt got up in front of the class and the kids thought this was terrific so Cottingham took him to each one of the classes in the school. Walt loved that."

After graduation, Walt enrolled in Chicago's McKinley High School in the fall of 1917. He would attend high school for only a year before volunteering as a Red Cross ambulance driver in France. Instead of continuing high school upon his return, Walt started his first animation studio, Laugh-O-Grams, and his formal public school education was at an end.

The first elementary school in the United States to be named after Walt Disney was in 1956 at Tullytown, Pennsylvania (now called Levittown). The second was in Anaheim, California in the spring of 1958 and Walt caused a commotion at the dedication when without warning, he spontaneously declared that school was out for the day and had busses take all the children to Disneyland.

The third was built in Marceline, Missouri in 1960 to replace the Park Elementary School that Walt attended as a child. That year, Disney artist Bob Moore designed and coordinated the installation of a series of Disney character murals for the school. Walt also gave the school a Mickey Mouse flag; a flag that flew at Disneyland Park; a fifty-five foot cast aluminum flagpole from the most recent Winter Olympics where Disney provided the entertainment; and school material like playground equipment and a filmstrip projection system. The fourth Walt Disney Elementary School was in Tulsa, Oklahoma in 1969.

It is ironic that a boy who struggled in school and as he said "getting through the seventh grade was one of the toughest trials of my whole limited span of schooling" ended up being universally acclaimed as a major educator and influenced and encouraged so many young minds.

In December of 1955, the *Journal of the California Teacher's Association* interviewed Walt and the interviewer came away with the following impression: "His impact as an educator may not be so widely appreciated. Yet he has done-and is doing-notable and lasting things in the field of education. His record and his plans establish him as a remarkable public educator. And like all successful people, he remembers his 'good' teachers."

Walt's favorite teacher was his seventh-grade teacher. She was a young woman with auburn hair named Daisy A. Beck. She taught at Benton School in Kansas City, Missouri. By all accounts, she was an attractive, outstanding teacher whose encouragement of Walt's wanting to draw was just another example of the support she demonstrated to all her other students, especially in sports, where she felt winning wasn't everything but making a best effort was.

As Daisy Beck's niece Helen recalled, her aunt shared with her the following anecdote: "All [Walt] did was sit and draw and she recognized his talent. Now, a lot of teachers at that time didn't. So, she kept saying, 'Walt, you've got to know more than just drawing. You've got to have something in your brain. When you get through with your arithmetic, I don't care how much you draw. You can draw any pictures you want, anything —when you're through!' I don't think he was a very good student by any means, but Auntie always said that he had a great mind."

Walt's affection for Beck didn't end at graduation, and in later years, after they reconnected, they continued to exchange letters up to her passing away, and Walt eagerly shared each new letter he received with Disney storyman Walt Pfeiffer who had been Walt's best friend and classmate during those Benton school years.

Beck also took the time to understand what Walt's life was like outside the classroom with his early morning and late afternoon paper route. "If he was sleepy and had fallen asleep, she just let him sleep," said one classmate. "She understood why the boy was so tired."

Walt's only participation in school athletics came as a result of the fact that Beck was coaching the school's track team. As Walt recalled in a 1940 letter to his favorite teacher, "I often think of you and the days I spent at Benton. I can plainly see you ... coaching the athletic teams for the annual track meet. I don't know whether you remember it or not, but I participated in several events and even won a medal one year on the championship 80-pound relay team. I was kept rather busy with my paper route and I didn't have much time to train, but I did manage to get in on a few events...."

In 1955, Walt took a moment to share in a letter his memories of Daisy Beck:

*"The teacher I remember best, with affectionate respect, is Miss Daisy A. Beck. She taught the seventh grade in the old Benton Grammar School in Kansas City, Missouri. She later became Mrs. W.W. Fellers by marriage and she retired years ago after a rich full life of devotion to the hundreds of youngsters who moved through her classroom. And now she has passed on.*

*"But persons like Miss Daisy A., as we called her, never retire from your memory. She remains as vivid today as she was in the days of her patient concern for a laggard boy more interested in drawing cartoon characters on textbook margins than in the required three Rs.*

*"She gave me the first inkling that learning could be enjoyable-even schoolbook learning. And that is a great moment in a kid's life. She had the knack of making things I had thought dull and useless seem interesting and exciting. I never forgot that lesson.*

*"Getting through the seventh grade was one of the toughest trials of my whole limited span of schooling. You've got to be good to teach the seventh. You have to know a lot about human nature in the bud. How to get into stubborn resisting young minds and how to make the classroom compete with everything that tends to lure a kid's attention to the world outside.*

*"That's the kind of teacher Daisy A. was. I had little inclination toward book learning and very little time to*

*study. When I was nine, my brother Roy and I were already
businessmen. We had a newspaper route for the Kansas City
Star, delivering papers in a residence area every morning and
evening of the year, rain, shine or snow. We got up at 3:30
a.m., worked until the school bell rang and did the same thing
again from four o'clock in the afternoon until supper time.
Often I dozed at my desk, and my report card told the story.*

*"But Miss Daisy A. wasn't discouraged. She knew our
circumstances. She never slacked what she considered
her teacher's responsibilities. I think I must have been a
special challenge to her patience. She never scolded. And
I don't believe she ever shamed any of us youngsters with
discouragements.*

*"Once only she lost patience with me. That was for a prank.
I had rescued a field mouse from a cat and had brought it to
school. Attached to a string, it had crawled to a nearby desk. A
girl's shriek brought the teacher on the double, and boy, did I
get it! She smacked me on the cheek so hard I felt it for several
days. I deserved it. In a way, it was educational, too. One of
my first 'true life adventures,' you might say.*

*"It was always my inclination to think in pictures rather
than words. I was already dreaming of becoming an artist-a
newspaper cartoonist, at this point. I spent many study
hours drawing flip-over figures on textbook margins-like the
McGuffey readers-to entertain classmates.*

*"Miss Beck understood this, too. She was not only tolerant
about these extra-curricular activities, but actually
encouraged them. She saw what she regarded as potential*

*talents in other kids, too, and did everything she could to bring them out.*

*"The point is, she tried to understand all of us as individuals. But she never favored or pampered any of us. She managed somehow to promote our personal inclinations without neglecting the formal grade requirements.*

*"She knew that the good students, the apt ones, who got their lessons easily would get along well without much urging or coaching. It was the laggards, like myself, who most needed encouragement. So with great patience and understanding, and incredible faith, she lavished her teaching genius upon the least promising of her charges.*

*"Other teachers at Benton who often come to mind were Miss Katherine Shrewsbury and Miss Ora E. Newsome, art teachers, Miss Ethel Fischer, and by no means least, J. M. Cottingham, the principal, who acknowledged that I never had to visit his office in punishment. That, I must admit, was sheer luck.*

*"To sum it all up, the outstanding teacher of my youth instilled in us a permanent sense of wanting-to-do rather than having-to-do."*

## GOSPEL ACCORDING TO WALT

Walt Disney was a strongly religious man who truly believed that good would triumph over evil and that it was important to accept and help everyone no matter how different they were. He had a great respect for all religions.

Walt Disney's own name owes its existence to religion and the church. He was named after Reverend Walter Parr. Parr preached at the St. Paul Congregational Church in Chicago that the Disney family attended at the turn of the century. When St. Paul's needed a larger church, Walt's father, Elias, who was earning his living as a carpenter volunteered to build a new church for the congregation and he put up a plain, serviceable structure with a tall, sloping roof.

Elias was close friends with Parr and would occasionally step into the church pulpit to deliver the weekly sermon when Parr was out of town or indisposed. Elias's wife, Flora, would play the organ for the Sunday services. Parr baptized the young Walt Disney in the church on June 8, 1902.

Elias Disney has been portrayed as stern and straight-laced man although there is evidence that he was also a sociable, caring man who sometimes demonstrated a sense of fun with his fiddle playing on Sunday afternoons. However, one of the things that Elias took very seriously was religion.

He didn't believe that adults should indulge in alcohol or tobacco and disapproved of things he believed were frivolous including candy for children and some books. He lectured his sons that if they were determined to read before falling asleep that instead of wasting their time on the popular books of the day, they should have their noses in a Bible. Each day in the Disney household began with a prayer session around the breakfast table.

This strong religious upbringing had a definite effect on the young Walt but not what his father would have suspected. As an adult, Walt did not attend church.

"He was a very religious man," said his daughter Sharon, "but he did not believe you had to go to church to be religious.... He respected every religion. There wasn't any that he ever criticized. He wouldn't even tell religious jokes."

Walt's daughter, Diane Disney Miller, recalled:

*"Dad drove us to Sunday School every Sunday for some years. It was the Christian Science Church, because mother was dabbling in all that for awhile. Then he'd pick us up and take us to Griffith Park, or to the studio or somewhere else. It was daddy's day. I attended a small Christian Science school up through third grade, and then went to Immaculate Heart, which I loved. The beauty of the campus, the grottos and shrines, the Stations of the Cross in the Chapel, the tangible yet mysterious faith really appealed to me, and I think that dad thought that I might want to become a nun. He always remained accessible to the sisters there, though, just as he was to the sisters of St Joseph's across the street from the studio.*

*"I do know that he had great respect for all faiths. Rabbi Edgar Magnin (Rabbi and Spiritual leader of Congregation B'nai B'rith/Wilshire Boulevard Temple, and was considered the "Rabbi to the Stars") refers to him as 'my friend Walt Disney' in his book titled 365 Vitamins For the Mind, or something like that. He was the B'nai B'rith Man of the Year for the Beverly Hills Chapter in 1955. My sister dated a*

*Jewish boy for awhile with no objections from either of my
parents. One time, Dad said innocently but proudly, 'Sharon,
I think it's wonderful how these Jewish families have accepted
you.'...and it was a very sincere comment. And she was
accepted. She knew about lox and bagels way before I was
aware of them, went to several bar mitzvahs, etc.*

*"Jules and Doris Styne were good friends. Dad had so many
very good Jewish friends, going back to his childhood. When
I was asked by a young girl, one of my first friends when I
entered Los Feliz Elementary School in the fifth grade if I
was Jewish, I replied 'I don't know. I don't think so.' I asked
my parents that evening. Many of dad's strongest supporters
in his career in Hollywood were Jewish, weren't they? I
have to conclude that dad was not guilty of any kind of anti-
Semitism."*

"As far as I'm concerned, there was no evidence of anti-
Semitism," said storyman and concept artist Joe Grant who
was Jewish and saw Walt's interaction with staff who were of
the Jewish faith. "I think the whole idea should be put to rest
and buried deep."

In January 1943, Walt wrote a letter to his sister Ruth about
his daughter Diane who was then about ten years old: "Little
Diane is going to a Catholic school now, which she seems
to enjoy very much. She is quite taken with the rituals and is
studying catechism. She hasn't quite made up her mind yet
whether she wants to be a Catholic or Protestant. I think she is
intelligent enough to know what she wants to do, and I feel that
whatever her decision may be is her privilege. I have explained
to her that Catholics are people just like us and basically there
is no difference. In giving her this broad view I believe it will
tend to create a spirit of tolerance within her."

Throughout his career, Walt purposely avoided any film material dealing with religion, reasoning that portions of the audience would be displeased by the depiction of a particular sect. For instance the original ending for the *Night on Bald Mountain/Ave Maria* sequence in *Fantasia* (1940) was originally going to take place inside a gothic chapel with multiple statues of the Virgin Mary but Walt reasoned it would be more effective outdoors in a setting that merely suggested a church.

Walt's daughter Diane Disney Miller told one minister that there are no churches on Main Street at Disneyland (even though there were plans for one in the original concept drawings and the then-Governor of California, Goodwin Knight, mentioned to a nationwide television audience on Disneyland's Opening Day that there was a church on Main Street) because her father did not want to favor any particular denomination.

The Reverend Glenn Puder, Walt's nephew-in-law, delivered the invocation at Disneyland's grand opening on July 17, 1955. He stood alongside representatives of the major American religions at that time: Catholic, Jewish and Protestant. Individual invitees to the Opening Day ceremonies included Cardinal James McIntyre (Catholic), Bishop Francis Eric Bloy (Episcopalian), Bishop Gerald Kennedy (Methodist), Dr. Carroll Shuster (Presbyterian) and Rabbi Edgar Magnin. In addition, Walt had invitations sent to editors from eight different religious newspapers (Catholic, Jewish and Protestant) as well as invitees from nearby churches including ten Baptist, nine Methodist, eight Catholic, eight Lutheran, seven Christian, six Church of Christ, six Episcopalian, six Presbyterian, five Free Methodist, two Congregational, one Nazarene and one Jewish Synagogue.

Over the years, Walt received many awards from various religious groups including in 1965 being the recipient of the Amicus Juvenum (Friend of Youth) Award from the Catholic Youth Organization Federation of Single Adults Club presented by Father William G. Hutson.

In 1955, writer Samuel Duff McCoy contacted several celebrities including Lillian Gish, Herbert Hoover, Conrad Hilton, Burl Ives, Harry Truman and Walt Disney to write about in what manner prayer had benefited them. He included those responses in his book *How Prayer Helps Me* (Dial Press). Walt wrote a three paragraph essay entitled "My Faith":

> *I have a strong personal belief and reliance on the power of prayer for divine inspiration.*
>
> *Every person has his own ideas of the act of praying for God's guidance, tolerance and mercy to fulfill his duties and responsibilities. My own concept of prayer is not as a plea for special favors or as a quick palliation for wrongs knowingly committed. A prayer, it seems to me, implies a promise as well as a request.*
>
> *All prayer, by the humble or the highly placed has one thing in common, as I see it: a supplication for strength and inspiration to carry on the best human impulses which should bind us all together for a better world. Without such inspiration, we would rapidly deteriorate and finally perish.*

Walt's brother, Roy, was so moved by these words that he had the studio print shop print a version entitled "Prayer in My Life" to give to selected visitors to the Disney Studio. It was apparently also reprinted as an insert for a 1978 record anthology entitled *Magical Music of Walt Disney*.

In 1963, religious writer Roland Gammon contacted fifty-five Americans including J. Edgar Hoover, Steve Allen, Billy Graham, Eleanor Roosevelt, Roy Rogers, Bud Collyer and of course, Walt Disney. He asked each of them the same question: "What is your faith and what part has it played in your life achievement?"

Gammon spent three years gathering the responses and included them in his book entitled *Faith is a Star* (New York E. P. Dutton and Company).

Walt's contribution includes almost word for word what he had written for the previous book but in addition, he greatly expands on the importance of his faith, mentioning his "study of the Scripture" and "my lifelong habit of prayer." Here is an excerpt from that essay entitled "Deeds Rather Than Words by Walt Disney":

> *In these days of world tensions, when the faith of men is being tested as never before, I am personally thankful that my parents taught me at a very early age to have a strong personal belief and reliance in the power of prayer for Divine inspiration. My people were members of the Congregational Church in our home town of Marceline, Missouri. It was there where I was first taught the efficacy of religion ... how it helps us immeasurably to meet the trial and stress of life and keeps us attuned to the Divine inspiration.*
>
> *A prayer implies a promise as well as a request; at the highest level, prayer not only is a supplication for strength and guidance, but also becomes an affirmation of life and thus a reverent praise of God. Deeds rather than words express my concept of the part religion should play in everyday life.*

Walt continued to write at length about how his commitment to his faith helped in the decisions that he and his brother, Roy, made about not only the films they made but how they handled their business. Walt ended his essay with the following words:

> *"Both my study of Scripture and my career in entertaining children have taught me to cherish them. Most things are good, and they are the strongest things; but there are evil things too, and you are not doing a child a favor by trying to shield him from reality. The important thing is to teach a child that good can always triumph over evil, and that is what our pictures attempt to do.*
>
> *"Thus, whatever success I have had in bringing clean, informative entertainment to people of all ages, I attribute in great part to my Congregational upbringing and my lifelong habit of prayer. To me, today, at age sixty-one, all prayer, by the humble or highly placed, has one thing in common: supplication for strength and inspiration to carry on the best human impulses which should bind us together for a better world."*

Diane Disney Miller reflected about this essay by her father that "It always seemed to me that dad wouldn't have been so pretentious about his attitudes toward prayer, and that he would have had more Lincolnesque views of religion and prayer, not just because of his reverence for Lincoln, but because they would have been his naturally. But there are things in this piece like his mention of DeMolay that wouldn't have come from a publicity person at the studio if someone else had written it and maybe dad was just trying to be more deliberate because of the forum where it would appear."

"Every Sunday he took our daughters to Sunday school," emphasized his wife Lillian. "Walt was very religious but he never went to church himself. He loved every religion and respected them, although he got upset with overly pious ministers. I never knew of his going to church but he was very religious."

## WALT AND DEMOLAY

*In 1963, Walt Disney wrote, "Later in DeMolay, I learned to believe in the basic principle of the right of man to exercise his faith and thoughts as he chooses. In DeMolay, we believe in a supreme being, in the fellowship of man, and the sanctity of the home. DeMolay stands for all that is good for the family and for our country."*

"I've never been quite sure just what dad's connection with DeMolay was all about, but I do know that it meant a lot to dad, when he was younger, to be a member of it. He and mother were very impressed with 'Dad' Land, who, I assume, was the head of the Kansas City chapter. Dad wore a DeMolay ring, but in later years it was replaced with the Claddagh ring that we all bought for each other when we visited Galway Bay, Eire, in the summer of 1947 or 1948," wrote Diane Disney Miller, Walt's daughter.

Walt's involvement with DeMolay meant a great deal to him and he did indeed proudly wear a DeMolay ring on his right hand until around 1948. DeMolay began in Kansas City, Missouri in 1919 with just nine young men. Frank S. Land ("Dad" Land) was the founder.

Near the end of World War I, Land became concerned with the problems of boys who had lost their fathers during the war. He decided there was a need for an organization where boys would have the opportunity to associate with other boys, a place they could share common interests, learn responsibility and other skills that would benefit them throughout their lives.

His ideal model for this organization included having business or professional men, Masons, taking interest in the young people, being a friend to them, advising them, and perhaps even providing them with employment opportunities.

The name of the group came from a story Land told the original boys: "This year I am serving as the head of one of the Masonic Groups. I am the Commander for the DeMolai Council of Kadosh. There are many names and stories directly connected with Masonry, but I think I should tell you about the last leader of the Knights Templar. His name was Jacques DeMolay or as they say in history books, James of Molay."

According to its official Web site: "DeMolay is an organization dedicated to preparing young men to lead successful, happy, and productive lives. DeMolay alumni include Walt Disney, John Wayne, Walter Cronkite, Mel Blanc, football Hall-of-Famer Fran Tarkenton, legendary Nebraska football coach Tom Osborne, news anchor David Goodnow and many others."

Walt joined in 1920 as the 107th member of the original Mother Chapter of DeMolay in Kansas City. He was nineteen years old and his fellow members remembered him as hardworking and extremely imaginative.

Belief in one Supreme Being was a fundamental requirement. In the beginning, at least, the secret stuff was primarily passwords and handshakes, which probably appealed to young boys as well as building a feeling of fraternity. Only boys could join and they had to be between the ages of twelve and twenty-one.

The emphasis was on developing young leaders through personal and civic responsibility. DeMolay emphasized the seven cardinal virtues: Love of parents, reverence for sacred things, courtesy, comradeship (friendship), fidelity (faithfulness), cleanliness and patriotism. It is easy to see how those qualities would appeal to Walt and how those qualities are reflected in his work.

Walt received the DeMolay Legion of Honor in October 1931. Legion of Honor recipients must have actively demonstrated outstanding leadership in some field of endeavor, whether it be a civic, professional, fraternal or spiritual arena. This award should not be confused with France's Legion of Honor medal that Walt received January 1936.

Walt journeyed to Kansas City to receive the honor, a degree corresponding to that of a 33rd degree in Masonry, the highest attainable. Both Walt and his wife, Lillian, were a little overwhelmed by the reception they received.

"This reception rather bewilders me," claimed Walt. "Although I know the DeMolays always do everything in fine shape. I am proud to receive the Legion of Honor, but I feel as though I haven't done anything to merit it."

There's an interesting Disney oddity published by DeMolay that is worthy of being reprinted. In the Thirties, another DeMolay member, Disney animator Fred Spencer at the request of Walt Disney began sending an original Mickey Mouse comic strip entitled "Mickey Mouse Chapter" to be published in the International DeMolay Cordon newsletter. It was signed by Walt Disney and was different than the Mickey Mouse comic strip that was appearing in the newspapers.

Fred Spencer joined the Disney Studio in 1931 and worked on the early Mickey Mouse cartoons. He is perhaps best known for his work on the early Donald Duck, and he met a tragic end in a car accident in 1938. He had no connection with the comic strip department and the artwork has some resemblance to the work of artist Floyd Gottfredson, who was drawing the Mickey Mouse comic strip at the time.

It was a two-tier black and white comic strip and the first installment from December 1932 has Mickey Mouse creating a poster to get all his animal friends to join him in the barn so they can vote on establishing their own barnyard chapter of DeMolay, a Mickey Mouse Chapter. They all enthusiastically vote "aye" including Horace Horsecollar, who apparently is also a member. Another installment had Pluto chasing a cat and disrupting a DeMolay meeting where Mickey is speaking at the podium with a DeMolay emblem on it. So not only was Walt a member of DeMolay but Mickey Mouse was also a member.

The Disney Archives had no knowledge of this unique comic strip until two years ago. The DeMolay Archivist found three strips and a publicity announcement that the strip would appear but nothing else. There is no way of telling how long the strip ran although it probably didn't last beyond Spencer's death and may have ended much earlier. For now, it is just another "lost" Disney treasure waiting to be unearthed and shared.

In 1936, Walt appeared as an honored guest at the first DeMolay Founder's Conference in Kansas City and to participate in the installation of one hundred new members in the Legion of Honor of the Order of DeMolay, the same honor Walt had received in 1931.

"I feel a great sense of obligation and gratitude toward the Order of DeMolay for the important part it played in my life. Its precepts have been invaluable in making decisions, facing dilemmas and crises, holding on the face and ideals, and meeting those tests which are borne when shared with others in a bond of confidence. DeMolay stands for all that is good for the family and for our country. I feel privileged to have enjoyed membership in DeMolay," said Walt.

Disney was a member of the first class to be inducted (posthumously) into the DeMolay Hall of Fame on November 13, 1986. The Masonic Stamp Club of New York had a special First Day Cover commemorative (499,505 were produced) with DeMolay and Walt images and the Walt Disney stamp cancelled in Marceline, Missouri on September 11, 1968. Currently, there is a Walt Disney Chapter of DeMolay in Cumming, Georgia and also in Anaheim, California.

While Walt never hid his connection with DeMolay, he did not actively promote his involvement either or else Disney biographies might be filled with assumptions of how it influenced his work. Walt Disney was never a Mason although some authors have misinterpreted his involvement with DeMolay as being proof that he was. Obviously, "Dad" Land and his original objectives appealed to Walt and this story becomes just another obscure footnote to an amazing life and helps reveal a little more about what values motivated Walt and his choices.

## EXTRA! EXTRA! READ ALL ABOUT IT!

Walt had a tendency to sentimentalize some of his childhood memories. The famous Kansas City paper route that Walt would talk about with such joy also resulted in re-occurring nightmares for him that lasted for the rest of his life. Yet, Walt never felt sorry for himself nor did any of the hardships he faced as a child ever discourage him or make him angry and rebellious.

After selling their farm in Marceline, the Disney family moved to Kansas City, Missouri, where Elias Disney managed a paper route. The local papers, the *Star* and the *Times* were reluctant to give the route to Elias Disney because he was fifty-one years old, so the owner of record for the route was his son, Roy Oliver Disney, who was eighteen at the time. It was probably one of the reasons that Elias tried so hard to make the business a success and exceed his subscribers' expectations to prove that he could handle the responsibility at his age.

Elias was firm that the newspapers were not to be tossed into the yards or even on the porches from boys riding bicycles, but carried up the walk to the house. The papers couldn't be rolled or folded and had to be anchored down with a rock or a heavy object if there was a chance a wind would blow the paper away.

"He insisted that it be delivered fresh and clean, without wrinkles. He was meticulous about it," stated Walt in a 1966 interview.

Route No. 145 was between 27th and 31st streets and Prospect and Indiana Avenues. The Disney family assumed control of the route on July 1, 1911. There were over 600 subscribers for the morning *Times*, 600 for the evening *Star* and 600 for the Sunday *Star* and by the time the Disneys gave up the route the numbers had increased over 200 more subscribers in each category.

Walt remembered there were tough kids along the route including the Pendergast and Costello gangs who in snowball fights would pack their snowballs with rocks. One time, they even threw a brick at Walt and opened a nasty cut on his scalp.

Elias hired boys to deliver the papers, paying them roughly $2.50 a week. His sons, Walt and Roy, also delivered those papers but were paid nothing. Elias felt that since he provided clothing and food and shelter for his sons that doing so was compensation enough for the cash strapped family.

Walt earned money by selling extra newspapers on street corners without his father knowing about it. During the noon recess at school, he swept out the candy store across from the school in return for a hot meal. Some days after school, he wasn't even able to steal a few minutes to play sports with his school friends because he had to deliver the afternoon edition of the newspaper.

For six years, Walt delivered the newspapers (missing only four weeks during all that time because of illness). He delivered in pouring rainstorms and icy blizzards. He got up around 3:30 in the morning in order to get the papers from the delivery truck by 4:30 a.m.

Sometimes Walt never made it home in time for breakfast after the skinny nine year old had hauled over thirty pounds of newsprint through the neighborhood. There was barely time to hustle off to school where he struggled to stay awake during classes. The Sunday edition with all the inserts was three or four times the size of a regular daily edition.

In the morning, as soon as Walt got up to get dressed, he'd fall back asleep sitting on the edge of his bed while trying to tie his shoelaces. His dad would yell 'Walter!' and he'd wake up with his heart racing and finish tying his shoes.

He delivered the papers to the apartments first. He'd go up three floors and deliver to all the doors and come down. Years later, he could remember with clarity those chilly cold days when he was just a kid. One time the snow drifts were higher than he was. The weather records for Kansas City at the time confirm that fact. On those freezing days he'd sometimes have to slowly crawl up those icy, slippery steps.   Walt once told his daughter Diane that he would sometimes slip down the steps and just cry because he was all alone and so cold.

In the winter, Elias would insist that every paper had to go behind the storm door. On those days when Walt finally got home, people had looked out on their porch but wouldn't open the front door. They'd look on the porch and see no paper and they'd go and phone Elias to complain and Walt's dad would say sternly, "Walter, did you forget to deliver to so and so?" And his dad wouldn't believe him when Walt told his father that he had.

Elias would say, "Well, they say they didn't find it. Now here, here's a paper." Walt would have to go all the way back up there. Young Walt would struggle back through the cold and go up and ring the bell. When they'd come to answer, they'd open the storm door and the paper would fall at their feet and Walt would be standing holding another one outside. They'd say something like "Oh, I'm sorry I didn't look there". No matter how often it happened, they'd still forget to look there, claimed Walt.

Walt had re-occurring nightmares throughout his life and one of them was that he had missed customers on his section of the paper route. He'd wake up in a kind of a cold sweat and think, "Gosh, I've got to hurry and get back. My dad will be waiting up at that corner." His dad really wanted to make that business a success after so many of his other business failures and Walt could sense that great anxiety.

The kids who lived along Walt's route were certainly much better off financially than the Disney family at the time. The kids would leave their toys out on the porch after playing with them the previous evening.

Walt didn't have any toys. If he got a top or marbles or something, it was a big deal. Everything his parents gave him was something practical like underwear or a winter jacket. His older brother Roy was the one who set aside some extra money from his job so that Walt and his younger sister Ruth would sometimes get some small toy.

At 5:00 in the morning in the dark, Walt would put his sack of papers down and go up and play with these wind-up trains and things. He'd sit there and play all alone with them. One time he came to a porch and there were some toys as well as a box of half eaten candy. So he sat there and ate some of the half-eaten candy and played with the toys.

When Walt told about this time in his life, he always insisted on saying that he left the toys in good shape and always carefully put them back in the same place so the families wouldn't know he'd played with them. Then he'd have to hurry and finish his route before school started.

Walt liked to recall how he, along with other Kansas City newsboys, had been invited over the weekend of July 27-28, 1917 to see the silent movie live action version of *Snow White* starring Marguerite Clark at the Kansas City Convention Hall for a special event that was sponsored by the *Kansas City Star*. The movie was projected on four different screens in the huge auditorium, and from where he was sitting, Walt could watch two of the screens at the same time that weren't quite in synchronization. It remained his most vivid early memory of attending the movies.

In 1963, Walt wrote: "I'm genuinely glad that I had all this experience when I was a boy. In fact, sometimes I feel sorry for the boys who never have had the chance to carry papers or sell magazines or haven't had some way to earn their own money, because I think you'll all agree that it's a pretty swell feeling to know that the money in your pocket is there by your own efforts, and that you're getting experience in business that can't help but stand you in good stead later on."

Walt had addressed some of those same thoughts a decade earlier. The following excerpt from Walt is from *The Newspaper Boys' Hall of Fame* by Sid Marks and Alban Emley (House-Warven Publishers 1953). Among other things, this book contains testimonies from former newspaper boys like Bob Hope, Al Jolson, Jack Dempsey, and Art Linkletter but here is Walt's contribution:

"I have yet to meet a man who once was a newspaper boy who isn't proud of the experience. I myself look back upon the time when my brother Roy and I delivered papers in Kansas

City, Missouri, with great appreciation for what this daily chore meant then and what it has meant in all my grown-up life.

"At the time, the sense of responsibility which goes with the job may seem like an onerous thing to a boy. Doing his work regularly every day, in all kinds of weather, often against his inclinations to loaf and postpone his accepted duties, gives a youngster a good foundation for his responsibilities as a man and a citizen later on. It helps greatly to equip him for the tasks and the satisfactions of business or professional life."

Walt wrote about how his father instilled in him and his brother the importance of customer satisfaction that served Walt so well in his future projects including an innovative method of guest service at Disneyland that became the model for so many other businesses. Walt concluded by writing:

"Delivering papers to many homes and offices gives a boy an added feeling of being respected by his neighbors and of belonging to his town or community, as well as being an important and reliable member of his own family. In all this he builds a proper pride and confidence in his own abilities—a good self-reliance and competence which comes from earning his own money.

"I believe that the benefits to a boy who carries newspapers on the neighborhood routes of his town or section, if he is not too young and the task is not too burdensome, are as generally sound and valuable today as they were in the days of my youth."

# RETURN TO MARCELINE 1956

*"To tell the truth, more things of importance happened to me in Marceline than have happened since—or are likely to in the future," Walt Disney.*

"Marceline was the most important part of Walt's life. I remember when we used to take the train across country, he would drag people out in the middle of the night when we passed through Marceline. He had to show them where he grew up. He didn't live there very long, but there was something about the farm that was very important to him. He always said apples never tasted so good as when they were picked off of the trees on the farm." Lillian Disney, Walt's wife, recalled in later years.

While he was born in Chicago, Walt Disney truly considered Marceline, Missouri his hometown. His family moved there when he was roughly four years old. He stayed there about five years and experienced his first film, his first theatrical stage production, his first circus, his first interaction with live farm animals and his first artistic attempts. It is clear that all of this and more made a lasting impression on him.

Marceline is about a hundred and twenty miles northeast of Kansas City and was incorporated on March 6, 1888. The Atchison, Topeka and Santa Fe Railway built a line from Chicago to Kansas City in 1887, and Marceline was developed along the route as a stop for refueling, water and crew changes. Marceline received its name from one of the directors of the railroad, whose wife was named "Marcelina." With a change of the last vowel, this became the name of the new railroad city. The train no longer stops there and hasn't for quite a few decades.

In the Spring of 1906, Flora and Elias Disney were living in Chicago with their five children: Herbert, 17; Raymond, 15; Roy, 12; Walt, 4; and 2-year-old Ruth. Chicago was rapidly growing and as part of that growth, the violent crime rate was also increasing and this worried Elias.

The final straw was when two neighborhood boys were arrested for killing a policeman in a car barn robbery. One was sentenced to Joliet Prison for twenty years and the other to life imprisonment. The boys were about the same age of Herbert and Raymond.

Elias' brother Robert already owned a 500-acre farm in Marceline, and so Elias decided that Marceline would be a good place to raise his sons in a healthier environment. Elias purchased a one-story house and forty-five acres of land just north of the city limits for $125 an acre.

Walt had fond memories of his childhood in Marceline, often corresponded with people in the town after he became a Hollywood success, and always made time for visitors from Marceline if they happened to drop by the Disney Studios.

For the September 23, 1938 Golden Jubilee edition of the *Marceline News*, Walt Disney wrote a short letter essay titled "The Marceline I Knew" that included the following memory: "Everything connected with Marceline was a thrill to us, coming as we did from a city the size of Chicago. I'm glad I'm a small town boy and I'm glad Marceline was my town."

Walt spent roughly five formative years in Marceline and its influence on him is easily seen in Disney films and Disneyland, especially in a nostalgic approach to rural America at the turn of the century.

With the popularity of Walt's weekly television program and the opening of Disneyland, Walt was quite well-known so it was no surprise that Marceline decided to honor its favorite son. The city fathers wrote to the Disney Studio asking if they could have permission to name their new swimming pool and park after Walt.

At first, the powers that be at the Studio were suspicious that the Marceline city fathers were looking for a sizable financial contribution, but once they were assured that everything had already been paid for at a cost of approximately $78,500, the Disney Studio quickly agreed. Walt wrote back that he was thrilled and inquired whether there was to be an official dedication and if he could attend.

Walt, being the visionary that he was, had a cameraman document his return to Marceline in silent black and white footage that could later be adapted for *The Mickey Mouse Club* Newsreels. That was his intention because of the shot at the beginning and end of the footage of a *Mickey Mouse Club* newsreel camera. The existing footage runs roughly twenty minutes and includes title cards describing what is being seen to aid in the writing of future narration. The film was never used on the show or anywhere else.

The Walt Disney Municipal Park and Swimming Pool was to be dedicated July 4, 1956 in Marceline. Posters and banners welcomed back the two Disney brothers. At the time, the population of the little town was 3,172.

Walt, Lillian, Roy and Edna Disney flew in to the Municipal Air Terminal (now known as the Downtown Kansas City Airport) on July 3rd. They were met by reporters and Walt gave a short interview where he emphasized that he tried not to condescend to children and how he hated it being done to him as a child.

The Disneys drove three hours in a Cadillac Sedan and arrived in Marceline that afternoon. Event organizers had avoided giving the Disneys a room in Marceline's Hotel Allen because it lacked air conditioning and they didn't want the families to stay in a hotel in nearby Brookfield.

Rush and Inez Johnson had a brand new house on Kansas Avenue and the Disneys stayed there while the Johnson family stayed with neighbors. Walt and Lillian slept in the room of the Johnsons' seven year old daughter Kaye.

The Disneys freshened up and then drove to the Santa Fe Country Club around ten p.m. on July 3rd where they were greeted by hundreds of residents. Walt spent a good part of the evening signing autographs.

Walt recalled that in the early Disney cartoons, they sometimes used outhouses and that he got the idea of using outhouses for gags from Marceline.

"The only other place we lived was Kansas City and everything was up to date in Kansas City. We didn't have those outhouses. But in the early days, we got a lot of laughs with that outhouse. Of course, after we got a little more money, we got a little more refined about it," Walt said with a laugh.

The next day, Walt and Roy visited locations of some of their childhood adventures. Walt and Roy walked down Main Street. While it is apparent that Walt's memory of this street that had changed little since he had lived there is represented at Disneyland, most Disney fans know that Harper Goff's hometown, Fort Collins, Colorado, was also a major influence on the design of Disneyland's Main Street.

First, Walt and Roy stopped by the railroad depot. In 1898, the Santa Fe Railroad donated land to the City of Marceline for a park that was named after the president of the railroad, E.P. Ripley. It soon became the pride of the community and a favorite meeting spot including band concerts that Walt's sister, Ruth fondly remembered the Disney family attending.

The Santa Fe Railroad had helped with the opening of Disneyland. A Santa Fe locomotive and caboose in Ripley Park bear the name "Santa Fe and Disneyland Railway". This was at Walt's suggestion and Walt and Roy climbed aboard the cab of the engine to reminisce and as a photo opportunity.

Walt's first train ride into Marceline was at the depot that preceded the present day one, which was built in 1913. The Santa Fe railroad tracks ran through the countryside, a short distance from the Disney farm. Walt's Uncle Martin was a conductor on the Marceline-Fort Madison route, and would often stay with the Disneys overnight when in town. The depot is currently being restored into a Disney museum run by Kaye Malins who first met Walt when she was seven years old and he slept in her room during his 1956 visit.

Another photo opportunity was at Park School, a two-story red-brick building that had two hundred students in grade school and high school when Walt attended. He was once again surrounded by children wanting autographs. Walt said he loved that school and remembered his first teacher Miss Brown being very strict and she remembered him as being "pretty ornery".

The school had its last term in 1959. In 1960, it was torn down and it was replaced by the new Walt Disney Elementary School.

Walt squeezed into his old first-grade desk at the back of the room and pointed out that the initials "W.D." were carved in the top.

"I remember carving 'WD' once but I forgot I carved it twice," said Walt at the time.

There is some question whether it was actually Walt's carved initials or some other student with the same initials. Walt said he couldn't recall having done it but admitted it certainly was a possibility. In any case, it was a great story and Walt loved a great story.

Then Walt talked with a few townspeople about the fire he remembered at Grandpa Taylor's farm. Walt remembered the time when the old house burned down several months after Grandpa Taylor died in 1909. It went up in a tremendous blaze and made a distinct impression on the young boy who thought the whole world was going up in flames.

The Disney brothers visited their old family farm. The two men crossed a barbed wire fence, a relatively easy task for men from farm country, but more difficult for two city men who were wearing suits and ties. Townsfolk were impressed that the Disney brothers didn't get hung up on the fence. It was obvious that Walt and Roy were real country boys at heart and knew what they were doing.

They walked to a large cottonwood tree, now referred to as Walt's "Dreaming Tree," where Walt and Ruth played and waded in the spring that runs at its base. It is about a quarter mile from the Disney family barn.

Walt and Roy climbed aboard a Peter-Schuttler wagon, made in 1903, at the Frank VanTiger farm. In this wagon in 1908, VanTiger hauled white oak posts to the Disney farm where Elias had paid about sixteen cents per post delivered according to the title card in the film. On this visit, Walt made an attempt to handle the reins on two stubborn Missouri mules, but they would not hold still for him much to everyone's amusement including his own.

Walt and Roy walked to the bridge over Yellow Creek. Yellow Creek was young Walt's favorite fishing spot. On hot summer days, Walt and Roy walked the few miles to Yellow Creek and cooled themselves in the slow-moving water.

"Sometimes, if Mrs. Disney would let him, we'd go fishing in the creek," recalled Walt's boyhood friend, Clem Flickinger, who lived in the farmhouse across the road from Disney's farm. "We'd catch catfish and bowheads. There was a place where the water was four or five feet deep, and me and Walt would take off our clothes and swim. In the winter, a whole bunch of us would go sledding and skating with a big bonfire to keep warm."

On his 1956 return to Marceline, Walt and Roy reminisced about past picnics, swimming, and fishing using sticks for fishing poles and safety pins for hooks. A young boy was standing on the bridge holding a homemade fishing pole with a very small fish dangling at the end of its line.

This was obviously a staged photo opportunity and the fish was long dead but it didn't stop Walt from trying to manipulate the fish with his finger to give the illusion that it was still wiggling on the line. However, there was nothing fake about Walt's wide grin from ear to ear.

That afternoon citizens gathered at the Uptown Theater for the Midwest premiere of *The Great Locomotive Chase*. Walt spoke briefly to the capacity audience, telling the children, "My best memories are the years I spent here. You are lucky children to live here."

Walt and Roy personally greeted each child at the door. When Walt and Roy took the stage before the movie started, the children of Marceline sang *The Mickey Mouse Club Song* to them. Because the afternoon Disney television program was not broadcast in Marceline, the children learned this song especially for this occasion.

---

Officially released June 8, 1956 (roughly a month earlier), *The Great Locomotive Chase* starred Fess Parker and Jeff Hunter. The film recounts the true story of twenty-two Union spies who stole a train from four thousand Confederate troops near Atlanta, Georgia, on April 22, 1862, and began a race that might have brought an early end to the Civil War if it had succeeded.

Some children showed up in Davy Crockett T-shirts, at least one was wearing a *Mickey Mouse Club* T-shirt and another wore *Mickey Mouse Club* ears.

Walt then led the excited, admiring group of youngsters in singing *Davy Crockett*. He told the audience, "I read this book when I was a boy and remembered it. The picture *The Great Locomotive Chase* was a result of remembering what I read."

The movie ran from 1:30 p.m. in the afternoon until very late in the evening so that everyone wanting to see the movie could do so. In 1998, the world premiere of *The Spirit of Mickey* was held in the same theater.

Walt also stopped by St. Francis Hospital. The Sisters of St. Francis (twelve of them) came from Austria to establish missions in America. The group grew and served in many venues including Father Flanagan's Boys Town in Nebraska.

In 1946, the sisters purchased a sixteen bed hospital in Marceline that they named the St. Francis Hospital. In 1952, the building was expanded and the capacity rose to thirty beds. In 1964, a new hospital was built (with an increase to fifty-four beds) and the hospital that Walt visited became St. Joseph's Home for the Elderly.

Watching the film, it is inspiring to see how gentle Walt is with the children in the hospital, often gentling cupping their hands with both of his hands and leaning down to be eye level with them.

Later that day, more than six thousand people turned out for the dedication of the swimming pool.

According to the *Kansas City Times*: "The crowd was drawn up around the pool, standing in lines that were in some instances twelve and thirteen persons deep. Above the men's dressing room a temporary platform was erected and made into an outdoor garden with decorations of potted palm trees, baskets of gladiolas and bunting."

Walt and Roy were seated together on an elevated platform. U.S. Senator Thomas C. Hennings Jr. of Missouri was one of the speakers and he sang the praises of Walt as a native son.

After a bathing beauty contest (won by seventeen year old Deanne Kelly) with both Walt and Roy as judges, the mayor cut the ribbon to the pool (the clock in the background says it is 9:10 pm) and about fifty local boys christened the new pool by jumping in simultaneously creating a "resounding crash" according to the newspaper report.

"It's particularly thrilling for me to see this fine swimming pool here, because when I was a kid here in Marceline, we swam in a cow pasture pond, after we chased the cows out. So it is wonderful to have a pool like this. I feel very humble to think that you all wish to name this the Walt Disney Municipal Pool," said Walt at the dedication.

The day finished with a small fireworks display in the sky. This return visit to Marceline inspired Walt to consider a new project tentatively known as "Walt Disney's Boyhood Farm" that would have been based in Marceline. It was to have been a working farm from the turn of the century for people to visit with their children. It would have had pigs, chickens, horses, cows, a swimming hole, orchards and fields of grain. With Walt's death, Roy cancelled the project to devote all the Disney resources to the Florida project.

In 1950, when designing a barn for his workshop on his property in California, Walt insisted it be a replica of the one on his family farm in Marceline. Watching the film of his return to Marceline in 1956 shows Walt relaxed and happy and apparently, for Walt it was possible to go home again…at least for a few days.

## WALT'S 30ᵀᴴ WEDDING ANNIVERSARY

Walt and Lillian Disney's 30th Wedding Anniversary was an out of the ordinary celebration. Guests sipped mint juleps on the Mark Twain riverboat, followed by a lavish dinner at the Golden Horseshoe Saloon, complete with cancan dancers. Diane, their shy twenty-one year old daughter, wore a "sort of bare" red linen dress that her mother had bought for the occasion. "I never saw my Dad happier, ever, ever, ever," Diane Disney Miller now says.

During the early Summer of 1955, approximately three hundred people including celebrities like Spencer Tracy, Cary Grant, Gary Cooper, Louis B. Mayer and Joe Rosenberg received the following invitation:

*"Tempus Fugit Celebration*

*Where:  Disneyland...where's there's plenty of room...*

*When: ...Wednesday, July 13, 1955, at six o'clock in the afternoon...*

*Why: ...because we've been married Thirty Years...*

*How: ...by cruising down the Mississippi on the Mark Twain's maiden voyage, followed by dinner at Slue-Foot Sue's Golden Horseshoe!*

*Hope you can make it—we especially want you and, by the way, no gifts, please—we have everything, including a grandson!*

*Lilly and Walt"*

Although he was physically and mentally exhausted from the preparation for the opening of Disneyland (just four days after this party), Walt Disney decided to celebrate his 30th wedding anniversary at that very special location that had long been his dream.

It was a warm July evening. After a long day of inspecting the park with his small flip notepad where Walt dutifully made notations of things to be changed or addressed, he ended his day by waiting cheerfully at the front gate to greet his guests to his new magic kingdom.

An unexpected traffic snarl had delayed some of the guests and Walt nervously smoked a cigarette or two as he impatiently waited for them to arrive. Horse drawn surreys transported the guests down the glittering lights of the almost completed Main Street and through the open gates of the wooden fort entrance into Frontierland. The guests were directed across the Frontierland Square to the mighty steamboat, the Mark Twain.

Admiral Joe Fowler who was in charge of construction at Disneyland had arrived over an hour early to make a final inspection of the Mark Twain paddle wheeler to make sure the evening would run smoothly. The boat had never been fully tested on the river and Fowler later confessed to friends that he had had a nightmare the previous night that the artificial river bed had once again sprung a leak and gone dry.

He was taken aback to encounter a woman on deck who was frantically sweeping away at the sawdust and dirt with a broom. She handed him a broom as well and said, "This ship is filthy. Let's get busy and sweep it up." That woman was Walt's wife, Lillian, and the boat was swept clean by the time the first guests got there.

"I'll have to admit there were a lot of shavings and things around. That was Lilly. That's the first time I met Lilly," revealed Fowler. "All of Walt's friends showed up. It was a great party! The Mark Twain never went around the track completely until the night of Walt's party."

By the time the guests arrived, the Mark Twain was all shiny and white and new with twinkling old fashioned light bulbs outlining the decks. A Dixieland band played lively New Orleans style tunes. Appropriately attired waiters wandered the decks with trays full of mint juleps.

A blast from the ship's whistle and it gently pulled away from the dock and began its journey in the approaching dusk around the Rivers of America. There was no distraction from anything on the darkened Tom Sawyer's island since it would be another year before the location came to life. It was a festive mood as the boat glided effortlessly through the man made waterway transporting guests to another time and place and providing a brief preview of what people would experience in a few short days.

After the leisurely cruise, the guests were ushered into the interior of the nearby Golden Horseshoe Saloon designed by Imagineer Harper Goff. It was styled more as a typical turn of the century Opera House than a rip-roaring Old West saloon. With its gilded wallpaper, ornate light fixtures and carved wooden accents it was a luxurious setting for the wedding anniversary celebration. The event included dinner and the cutting of a four-tiered cake as Walt and Lillian's two daughters, Diane and Sharon, smiled broadly near their parents.

"Mother and dad were not seated up in the balcony box, but down with their guests," Diane wrote to me recently. "Dad was so happy, and roamed around the room, which the photos indicate. All the invited guests were people he and mother liked. Everyone enjoyed him, and vice versa. I had come down from Monterrey for the event, with our infant son, Chris. Ron was in the Army stationed at Fort Ord. Mother had bought my dress. As I told you, everyone, my parents and their guests, were sitting at tables awaiting dinner and the show. I forget which came first. Dad was circulating throughout the room, greeting and schmoozing with his guests, which were all people he liked, longtime friends and family."

The stage show changed little over the decades, becoming the longest running musical stage show in history with tens of thousands of performances according to the Guinness Book of World Records. Hostess Slue Foot Sue sang and introduced her dancing can-can girls. There was even a traditional Irish tenor. However, the heart and spirit of the show was the talented comic Wally Boag, who performed a hilariously corny vaudeville routine as a traveling salesman, and then re-appeared in the finale as the wild cowboy boyfriend of Sue, the famous Pecos Bill. With blazing six-guns (later supplemented with water pistols to squirt the audience), Boag and the entire cast filled the stage and brought the show to a raucous memorable ending.

In the Summer of 1956, Diane recalled her memories of the event:

> *"The guests would come and they would ride around in their*
> *surreys which would bring them around to the steamboat dock.*
> *Then, they would ride around the river on the Mark Twain*
> *drinking mint juleps, or whatever they wanted to drink, and*

then we would all have dinner at the Golden Horseshoe. Dad had been out in the park all day prior to this. It had been a dream for so long and here it was. Everything was almost done. The planting was not quite in yet or anything and it was still a little dusty, but it was there. It was very concrete at that point.

"So when he got on the boat, I was with him most of the time and I don't think he'd had much to drink. I really don't. I think he had maybe two or three mint juleps at most on the boat. But he was completely relaxing mentally, physically, everything. He was so stimulated by this thing and by the hundreds of people that were there saying what a wonderful thing it all was. Everyone was surrounding him telling him what a wonderful thing he had. That stimulating response from everyone who was there plus what he was feeling himself, that just combined to have a very bad effect. Well, I don't know if it was good or bad. It was just very entertaining in retrospect.

"It was very entertaining for everyone there but disastrous for the family, I think. The finale of the floor show is Pecos Bill shooting off his guns and all the chorus girls are kicking up their heels and everything. So it is loud and chaotic and for a minute neither I nor my mother knew where daddy was. And all of a sudden, we see him hanging over the balcony trying to get down to the stage.

"You see, by this point Pecos Bill was shooting his guns and daddy was using his fingers to form a gun and he was shooting back. 'Bang! Bang!' like that. And people noticed him and they shouted, 'There's Walt!' There was a little applause and general recognition from the audience and that just spurred

*daddy on. I thought he was going to fall off the balcony but
he made it to stage. He was just standing there and sort of
beamed. Everybody started saying 'Speech! Speech!' or there
was the clear expectation that he should say something. I just
remember him standing there looking happy and pleased.*

*"Then everyone applauded and shouted, 'Lilly! Lilly! We
want Lilly!" So mother got up and walked up the stairs to the
stage thinking 'If I get up there, maybe I can get Walt down'.
Well, that wasn't the case. Mother dragged Sharon and I up
there on stage as well and nothing was happening. My dad
was firmly planted there just basking in the moment, loving
every minute of it. I guess someone must have sensed our
plight because the band started to play and Edgar Bergen
came up on stage and started dancing with me. Someone
came up and danced with mother and Sharon. Everybody
started dancing on the stage and my father was gently elbowed
off into the wings. He was quite content to just stay right up
there. He loved every minute of it. He was just going to stand
there and grin at the people, I think.*

*"Everyone was so worried about him. They were worried
about him driving himself home. Some people had chartered
a bus to get to the park and they wanted Walt to go back with
them on the bus. Somebody else volunteered to drive him back
home. But I was going to drive him. It was fine with me. I
didn't think daddy was that bad off but everybody was asking
as if he was being belligerent and everything. 'We've got to
sneak the car keys out of his pocket' sort of thing. They were
really, sincerely worried.*

*"But I just went up to him and I said, 'Daddy, can I drive you
home?' 'Well, sure, honey!' he said. No problem at all. He*

*was just as meek and mild and willing. So he went out to the*
*car and some people were still worried that he would try to*
*abscond with the car himself. But he just climbed into the*
*back seat of the car. He rolled up these plans, I guess it was a*
*map of Disneyland, and he was tooting through it and into my*
*ear like a little boy with a toy trumpet. Then he was singing*
*a song or something. Before I knew it, all was silent. So I*
*looked around in the back seat and there he was like a little*
*boy with his makeshift trumpet sort of folded in his arms and*
*sound asleep. It was really sweet. But I know he hadn't had*
*too much to drink because the next morning, he didn't have*
*a hangover. He bounced out of the house at seven-thirty and*
*down to Disneyland again."*

---

The following evening was a salute at the Hollywood Bowl honoring Walt Disney. Performers included Fess Parker and Buddy Ebsen, Sterling Holloway and Cliff Edwards. At the end of the night's selection of Disney music, Goodwin Knight, the governor of California who would be an important guest speaker at Disneyland's opening in just a few days, declared Walt to be California's honorary governor and presented him with a Davy Crockett coonskin cap that had been dipped in silver.

Performer Wally Boag remembered clearly that wedding anniversary performance. "Folks saw him (Walt) up there (in the upper stage left balcony box) and they started calling for him to come down to the stage. So he climbed out of the box and down onto the stage during the finale. I shot my final two rounds, and with his hand in the shape of a pistol, he 'shot' back at me. Lilly joined him. Lilly loved to dance and Walt didn't. However, when the band began playing, he took her hand and danced around the stage. She didn't know it but he had taken some dancing lessons because he knew how happy that would make her. I don't remember exactly what he said once he got on the stage, but it was along the lines of finally realizing his long-held dream of an amusement park for the whole family. All of us there that night knew we were going to be part of something that was very special and wonderful, and that the adventure was just beginning."

Diane recently added, "It was a humorous, comic situation, not really an embarrassing one. The story was just as I told it. I thought it was sweet the way he just handed me the car keys. It was a 'silly old dad' kind of thing.

"It was during the show, when Wally Boag made his entrance, guns blazing, that we noticed dad up in the balcony. He exchanged fire with Wally.. thumb and forefinger "bang bang bang" ...do you know what I mean? And then decided, apparently, that he'd like to be down there sharing the stage with Wally, and began his descent which, I found, was well documented by the photographer. It was good theater, actually. One must remember that dad began his career that way, on the vaudeville stages of Kansas City, with his pal Walt Pfeiffer."

July 13, 2010 would have marked the 85th wedding anniversary of Walt and Lillian. While there have been many special parties and celebrations in Disneyland over the decades, there were none as magical and heart-warming as that very first Disneyland party.

PART TWO: DISNEY FILM STORIES

Every Disney film is somebody's favorite Disney film.

I learned this truth the hard way. I have always disliked the animated feature *The Aristocats* for a variety of reasons. I don't hate the film but I am certainly upset by the many plot holes, the use of weak animation and the general feeling that everything including the kitchen sink was tossed in and it's still not soup.

However, once upon a time, I dated for several years a wonderful young lady who I loved deeply and *The Aristocats* was her favorite Disney animated film. As a result, I saw the film over and over and over and while I never grew to love it, I did learn to accept it for what it was and not compare it with what might have been. Surprisingly, after some research, I discovered it was originally intended to be a much different film.

Having worked as a professional actor and director, I know that every performance, stage production, television show or movie has many colorful behind-the-scenes anecdotes of the trials and tribulations of trying to bring the show to the audience.

Some of the Disney films that have been released on DVD have neither a commentary track nor a "Making of" featurette to give some insight into the movie. These unassuming, often formulaic, productions are justly overshadowed by the critically lauded and financial blockbusters that immediately come to mind when thinking of Disney films. However, these smaller films brought delight to audiences for generations and often were closely connected with Walt himself.

Just because *Lt. Robin Crusoe U.S.N.* originated from an idea by Walt Disney (who received story credit for the first and only time on any Disney film as "Retlaw Yensid"-- Walter Disney spelled backwards) unfortunately does not make the film a lost comic gem. However, it does provide an interesting perspective into what Walt thought would be funny for audiences at the time.

*Blackbeard's Ghost* was the last live action film made while Walt was alive. *So Dear To My Heart* brought back nostalgic memories of Walt's growing up in Marceline. *Toby Tyler* captured Walt's boyhood love of the circus.

The success of *The Three Little Pigs* was unparalleled in animation history at the time. *Destino* and *Alice in Wonderland* are examples of how Walt brought in prominent outside artists and writers to inspire Disney animation to greater heights.

Once again, for the most part, the stories in this collection do not appear in any other book about Disney films and hopefully, they will provide some greater enjoyment and insight when you watch these movies again.

Let's Roll 'Em! Lights! Camera! Forgotten Stories!

## DISNEY'S HAM ACTORS: THE THREE LITTLE PIGS

Today, it is hard to imagine the impact of the Disney Silly Symphony, *The Three Little Pigs*. It not only won the 1933 Academy Award for best animated film (the year after *Flowers and Trees* won the very first Oscar given to a cartoon) but it was the most successful cartoon that had ever been released up to that time.

It was the 36th Silly Symphony (the seventh in Technicolor) and cost $22,000 (not counting prints and publicity) but earned over $150,000 in its first fifteen months of release. The average Silly Symphony generally grossed around $50,000 in its first year of release at this time.

*The Three Little Pigs* premiered on May 25,1933. It was so popular that it ran for weeks. Variety stated: "*Three Little Pigs* is proving the most unique picture property in history. It's particularly unique because it's a cartoon running less than ten minutes, yet providing box office draft comparable to a feature, as demonstrated by the numerous repeats."

United Artists could not supply enough prints to meet the demand and some exhibitors had to share a print, running it back and forth between two or more theaters.

The song *Who's Afraid of the Big Bad Wolf?* replaced *Brother, Can You Spare A Dime* as the working man's anthem during the Depression. It was played constantly on the radio and major record companies issued competing records of the song. This was the first time that a cartoon had ever spawned a hit song that captured the fancy of the entire nation. The catchy tune even appeared in MGM's *Babes in Toyland* and Paramount's *Duck Soup* as well as other non-Disney productions.

The song was composed by Frank Churchill with the help of Pinto Colvig, the voice of the Practical Pig, on the ocarina, and storyman Ted Sears providing some of the couplets. A publicity release of the time told the story of how, as a child, Churchill had been given three piglets by his mother to look after and he played them tunes on his harmonica. A real life big bad wolf came down from the hills one day and eliminated one of the pigs. An interesting fun fact is the song is never heard complete and uninterrupted in the actual cartoon.

There was a flood of merchandising for the characters from stationery to playing cards, to toothbrush holders, tea sets, radios, books and even Christmas tree lights. References and images of the pigs and the wolf appeared in editorial cartoons, essays and more.

Walt felt trapped with his popular Mickey Mouse cartoon series because audiences had certain expectations for those cartoons and Mickey Mouse as well. Walt used the Silly Symphonies for the experimentation he couldn't risk in the Mickey Mouse cartoons and that experimentation eventually resulted in *Snow White and the Seven Dwarfs*.

The three pigs were physically the same but could be easily identified by the audience because of their different personalities. In fact, notice how during the film each of the pigs' tails coil and uncoil during the cartoon depending upon their exhaustion or elation.

This type of animated acting was a turning point in the history of animation, where previous characters were often defined by what they looked like rather than how they acted. This lesson was later applied to the dwarfs.

In the original folk tale, the wolf eats the first two pigs after he blows down their houses, and then he drops down the chimney of the pig with the brick house and ends up in a pot of boiling water—and gets eaten himself. It was Walt Disney himself who revised the story so that neither the pigs nor the wolf are eaten. It was also Walt who came up with the idea to give the pigs musical instruments and have them sing and dance.

When Walt first presented the idea of doing a cartoon based on the children's story, he met with no enthusiasm from his staff. "I think the reason they didn't like the idea was that at that time the thing wasn't very clear in my own mind," confessed Disney frankly. "I withdrew it and tried to forget it, but the pigs and the wolf and the little house kept haunting me. I thought about them until I saw the story clearly, and then I proposed it again. This time they liked it. I don't mean they threw up their hats, or that even I thought it would be a tremendous hit. We considered it a typical Silly Symphony."

A memo from Walt circulated to his staff in 1932 states: "These little pig characters look as if they would work up very cute and we should be able to develop quite a bit of personality in them.... Might try to stress the angle of the little pig who worked the hardest, received the reward, or some little story that would teach a moral... These little pigs will be dressed in clothes. They will also have household implements, props, etc. to work with, and not be kept in the natural state. They will be more like human characters."

Animator Fred Moore was the primary animator on the pigs, although Dick Lundy did the sequences where they danced. Moore received coaching from Walt Disney who regaled the young animator with tales of his riding a favorite sow into a mud puddle when he was a small farm boy in Marceline.

Another animation legend, Norm "Fergie" Ferguson, brought the memorable Big Bad Wolf to life, along with the voice work of Billy Bletcher who was also the voice of Peg Leg Pete. Mary Moder was the voice of he Fiddler Pig and Dorothy Compton was the voice of the Fifer Pig. Interestingly, despite all the attention and merchandising, the pigs were not officially given individual names until the short *Practical Pig* (1939).

United Artists, who was distributing the Disney cartoons, was unimpressed with *The Three Little Pigs*. They let Walt know they felt it was a "cheater" since there were only four characters while the previous Silly Symphony, *Father Noah's Ark*, had dozens of animals.

*The Three Little Pigs* premiered at Radio City Music Hall on May 25, 1933 and ran for one week. However, it did very well at local neighborhood theaters as well as runs at other New York theaters, including the Roxy and the Translux. One New York theater played it so long that the manager added beards on the pigs in the lobby poster, and as the cartoon kept playing week after week, the beards grew longer and longer.

Walt said, "It was just another story to us and we were in there gagging it just like any other picture. After we heard all the shouting, we sat back and tried to analyze what made it good."

There were requests from theaters for more cartoons featuring the pigs, and these requests were supported by Roy O. Disney who convinced Walt it would be good for the business. Walt later regretted bowing to pressure and producing three more cartoons featuring the characters: *The Big Bad Wolf* (1934), *Three Little Wolves* (1936) and *The Practical Pig* (1939). These cartoons while somewhat technically superior were not as memorable as the original.

During his speech for the *Showman of the Year Award* in 1966, Walt said:

> *"By nature, I'm an experimenter. To this day, I don't believe in sequels. I can't follow popular cycles. I have to move on to new things. So with the success of Mickey I was determined to diversify. We kept fooling around with the Silly Symphonies until we came up with **The Three Little Pigs**. I could not possibly see how we could top pigs with pigs. But we tried, and I doubt whether one member of this audience can name the other cartoons in which the pigs appeared."*

Walt truly felt that he couldn't top the success of pigs with just more pigs. It meant that instead of sequels and repeats, that the Disney Studio would devote itself to always finding something new. When theaters demanded Disney shorts featuring Dopey from *Snow White*, Walt didn't even consider those requests, remembering what happened with the pigs.

The film itself has been parodied many times over the years from Tex Avery's *The Blitz Wolf* for MGM to Friz Freleng's *Three Little Bops* for Warner Brothers, to name just two of the most popular cartoons. The Disney pigs did pop up in cameos in other Disney cartoons, including *Mickey's Polo Team* (1936), *Toby Tortoise Returns* (1936), *Mickey's Christmas Carol* (1983) and *Who Framed Roger Rabbit* (1988) as well as three World War II commercial shorts including *Thrifty Pig* (1941).

However, there was one Disney Three Little Pigs cartoon that has been generally unknown to United States audiences for decades. In the Fall of 1962, Walt Disney called Bill Justice and X. Atencio to his office to introduce them to Carlos Amador and his movie star wife, Marga. Disney fans may know Justice as the primary animator of Chip'n'Dale in their classic cartoons, and Atencio as the lyricist for both the *Pirates of the Caribbean* and *Haunted Mansion* theme park attractions. However, their many different projects for the Disney Company could literally fill books.

Amador was preparing a live action movie about the life of a famous south-of-the-border writer. Since one of the stories was about the three little pigs, Amador wanted to use Disney's three little pigs in a four-minute animated segment.

The reason Walt agreed and assigned Justice and Atencio to the project was that half of the profits would go to help provide poor Mexican children a free lunch each school day. Walt had decided to donate the animation, especially since the charity was the favorite of the Republic of Mexico's First Lady and it was, in fact, the only way many children could be persuaded to attend school.

Amador wrote the adaptation with Justice and Atencio doing the production work.

In the film, a live action young boy and girl on their bed look at a framed picture of three sleeping pigs. As they gaze at the picture, it comes to cartoon life. The three little pigs are tucked into bed and given a kiss by their mother.

One dreams of being a king and having lots of tasty treats brought for him to gorge on. Another pig dreams of having his own rowboat but with disastrous results when he ends up in the water and then back in bed where a tear trickles down his face.

The Practical Pig dreams of the Big Bad Wolf threatening his mother that she must pay the rent by tomorrow. La Fiesta Las Flores (that features re-used animation from *The Three Caballeros*) offers the pigs an opportunity to win some money to pay the rent as the three pigs perform a musical number.

Of course, they win and return home late at night whistling *Who's Afraid of the Big Bad Wolf*. However, they are attacked by the wolf, but escape as the wolf shakes his fist. The wolf is standing by a palm tree and a coconut drops from its palms to bonk him on the head. The pigs give the money to their mother, who hugs all three of them at one time. The film then shifts back to the live action children.

A few months later the finished product was shown to Walt for his approval, and it was followed by an invitation from Amador for Justice and Atencio, along with Gene Armstrong of the Disney Studio's Foreign Department and their wives to visit for ten days. The Disney staff was treated like royalty. At the Mexico City airport, they were greeted by a mariachi band and their wives were given bouquets of roses. One evening at a special dinner as the guests of honor of the First Lady of Mexico, Justice and Atencio were given gold medals for their work.

A Disney press release from Fall of 1963 announced:

> *"**The Three Sleepy Pigs**, a new four minute segment of animation in Spanish, has been produced by Walt for incorporation in a live action Mexican feature called **Cri-Cri**,*

*El Grillito Cantor or in English, Cri-Cri, the Little Singing Cricket. The feature itself is based on the life of Gabilondo Solar, a famous south of the border song writer, while Walt's contribution to it is based on Solar's popular ballad, Los Cochinitos Dormilones.*

*"Proceeds of the feature, which is set for widespread theatrical release throughout Mexico beginning in October, will go to the Institute for the Protection of Mexican Children, an organization that maintains thirty-two plants engaged in the packaging and shipping of food to millions of school-age youngsters all over the country."*

Justice and Atencio were invited back to Mexico again in November 1963 to attend an international film festival, where the completed film was to be given an award. Tragically, the screening was during the same time that President Kennedy was assassinated. Justice and Atencio attended and the film festival continued, but Bill told me he still remembers how deeply the people at the festival expressed their sympathy when they discovered he was a citizen of the United States.

In December 1933, Walt told an interviewer: "These cartoon comedies last for a long time. They are still showing the first Mickey Mouse comedy after nine years. Maybe ten years from now the big bad wolf will still be huffing and puffing before the door to the house of bricks."

Although they have been eclipsed by other Disney animated stars, at one time the Three Little Pigs were cartoon superstars whose huge success allowed the Disney Studio to briefly live high on the hog and create even greater triumphs.

# SNOW WHITE CHRISTMAS PREMIERE

*"Who says there is no Santy Claus? It seems to me that Walt Disney tonight in giving this feature to the children of the world is indeed the modern Santa Claus." –Jesse Lasky, film pioneer responsible for **The Covered Wagon** and the original film version of **The Ten Commandments** on December 21, 1937*

*"One thing I do know is that this picture is the best Christmas present the children of Hollywood could possibly have." –Louella Parsons, Hollywood columnist on December 21, 1937*

*"Walt Disney ... brings to motion pictures a new medium for a greater art. It looks like a Snow White Christmas for all." –Narrator of RKO Pathe News newsreel released December 1937*

*Snow White and the Seven Dwarfs* premiered at the Carthay Circle Theater in Hollywood on the night of December 21, 1937. There have been countless articles and several good books written about this innovative film but not a detailed look at the memorable premiere at the Carthay Circle Theater.

The first cleaned up animation drawings for *Snow White* were taken to Ink and Paint on January 4, 1937 and were put under the camera nine weeks later to be filmed. The last cels were painted on November 27, 1937 and final photography took place on December 1, 1937. There was a sneak preview at a Pomona theater on December 6, 1937.

"The preview was unsettling," said Wilfred Jackson, who was one of the sequence directors. "The audience seemed to be enjoying the film, laughing, applauding. But about three quarters of the way through, one-third of them got up and walked out. Everybody else kept responding enthusiastically to *Snow White* right to the end, but we were concerned about that third. Later we found out they were local college students who had to get back for their ten p.m. dormitory curfew."

The Carthay Circle Theater was a movie palace designed in a Spanish Mission Revival style by architect Dwight Gibbs. The 1,500 seat theater opened in 1926 at 6316 San Vicente Boulevard in the mid-Wilshire district. Along with Grauman's Chinese Theater, the Carthay Circle hosted more big West Coast movie premieres than any other Hollywood theater (*Gone With the Wind* premiered there in 1939).

A glimpse of what the theater looked like at the time of *Snow White* can be seen in the "Our Gang" film *The Big Premiere*, released in 1940. The first five minutes of this film was shot on location at the Carthay Circle where the gang of children tried to crash a film premiere.

In 1929, Walt decided to produce a new animated series, the Silly Symphonies, and the first installment was *Skeleton Dance*. However, Walt's distributor didn't want to release the cartoon but wanted more Mickey Mouse cartoons instead.

Walt found a salesman he knew at a local pool hall, gave him a copy of *Skeleton Dance* and convinced him to contact Fred Miller, the owner of the Carthay Circle Theater. Miller liked the cartoon and booked it into his theater in August 1929 where it was a huge hit and gave Walt plenty of positive reviews to convince his distributor to book the film in other theaters.

It was this success that convinced Miller to take a chance on the first feature length animated cartoon, *Snow White and the Seven Dwarfs*. It premiered at his Carthay Circle Theater in December 1937. The film had already been booked, sight unseen, as the Christmas attraction at Radio City Music Hall but Walt wanted a Hollywood premiere for his peers to help demonstrate that his work in animation was comparable to the work done in live action films.

"All the Hollywood brass turned out for my cartoon!" remembered Walt years later, "That was the thing. And it went way back to when I first came out here and I went to my first premiere. I'd never seen one in my life. I saw all these Hollywood celebrities coming in and I just had a funny feeling. I just hoped that some day they'd be going in to a premiere of a cartoon. Because people would depreciate the cartoon. You know, they'd kind of look down."

Ken Anderson, talking to Disney historian Paul Anderson, remembered that night when the Disney's animators in tuxedos were completely unprepared for the reaction of the celebrities: "So then there came the premiere of the film. It was a big deal. We all had monkey suits the first night. We were wearing these; we were really dressed up in clothes that weren't ours. We were standing around trying to listen to what the big shots were saying. And these stars were all coming. We were looking at these stars. And they were coming to this thing to see it and they were pretty off-hand about it. They came, 'Oh, what the hell. It's a damn cartoon. We wouldn't waste any time on this damn thing or not if it was up to us to do it.' And so they were kind of put upon to do this thing.

"And they came, they walked in the theater, did this kind of down their nose thing. And they filled the theater. When they left, they were all talking about the story. In fact, you can't really begin to convey what they felt. Because they were astounded. They stood and they clapped and they had a terrific time at the end of the thing. And they were all kids again. These people were just moved by this thing, this cartoon. They could not understand it. We were never prepared for this type of reception. And, boy, they were crowding around Walt. And each of us. They crowded all around, 'What did you do?' And such and such. We're standing out there in the foyer and these people just went on and on and on and on about this marvelous picture. And I, for one, and I know everybody must have felt the same way, was thrilled."

That bright starlit night was fairly cold. Animator Marc Davis, who was not invited to the premiere nor could afford a ticket, remembered trying to dress up warmly to stand with over thirty thousand other people to see the celebrities and top Disney staff enter the theater and then quickly left once the film started. There were approximately one hundred and fifty policemen there to maintain order.

There was a long canopy stretching from the theater to the edge of the sidewalk. It covered a deep blue carpet for the many film executives and glamorous celebrities who had come out for a premiere that was unusual even for Hollywood. A small elevated platform was there for celebrities like Charlie Chaplin, Ed Sullivan, Joe Penner and the actors who portrayed Amos'n'Andy to be briefly interviewed on radio. The glare of floodlights surrounded the theater as searchlight beams waved across the sky.

RKO Pathe News newsreel claimed that "Blasé Hollywood accustomed to gala openings turns out for the most spectacular of them all, the world premiere of the million and a half dollar fantasy *Snow White and the Seven Dwarfs*."

Those celebrities included Marlene Dietrich, Preston Foster, Shirley Temple, Bob "Bazooka" Burns, Charles Correll and Freeman Gosden (Amos and Andy), Joe Penner, Helen Vincent, Fred Perry, George McCall, Charlie Chaplin with Paulette Goddard, Gail Patrick, Ed Sullivan, Clark Gable and Carol Lombard, Norma Shearer, Judy Garland, Charles Laughton and Elsa Lanchester, Jack Benny and Mary Livingstone, George Burns and Gracie Allen, Cary Grant and many more.

Roy O. Disney had cleverly included invitations for Joseph Rosenberg (who had arranged for the Bank of America to loan money to the Disney brothers for the film) and the board of directors of Bank of America.

The distributor, RKO, teamed with the Disney Studios to do promotion for the film. In the weeks before the premiere, more than a thousand posters decorated billboards around the Los Angeles area. There were promotional visits by Walt and his characters to radio shows from the Lux Radio Theater to Charlie McCarthy to make audiences aware of the film.

Bleachers were erected to accommodate four thousand fans, although almost ten times that number actually showed up that night. Hundreds of people waited for long hours in the brisk night air to catch a glimpse of the stars. The show had been sold out for many, many days, but a long line of people were at the ticket box office buying tickets for future shows thirty minutes before the premiere.

There was a full orchestra including the singers who had recorded the movie's songs who performed under the direction of Manny Harman. Usherettes wore Snow White costumes. NBC radio was there for a coast-to-coast half-hour broadcast with announcer Don Wilson.

There was a special display on the street, and here is the radio description of that unique addition: "Believe it or not, ladies and gentlemen, Dwarf Land was moved to Hollywood. Down at the corner of Wilshire Boulevard just outside the Carthay Circle, Walt Disney built a replica of the dwarf cottage that appeared in the film. The cottage is only ten feet high and not quite so wide but every kid in this town has been through it. Outside are mushrooms three feet tall painted yellow and blue and pink. Weird looking trees with eyes that light up and long arms that reach out and grab at you just like the way they grab at Snow White.

"There's a little Dwarfs' mill wheel and a diamond mine sparkling in the spotlights that illuminate the entire scene. The Dwarfs garden stretches for about two blocks. It's filled with all sorts of strange looking statuary and stumps and toadstools and flowers by the hundred and hundreds. A stream flows through the garden that turns the mill wheel. The crowds stand around watching the antics of the seven little dwarfs. Actual dwarfs dressed in quaint medieval costumes who work the diamond mine, rake the garden, run in and out of the house, putting on a great show."

This was probably the first time that the Disney Studio attempted to do costumed characters for such a star-studded event. Mickey Mouse, Minnie Mouse and Donald Duck were there looking as if the famous three-dimensional Charlotte Clark dolls had been blown up to life size.

Mickey and Minnie had the famous "pie-eyes" but the missing "slice" was used by animators to indicate a highlight to show where the round eye was looking. Both slices should be pointing in the same direction. On these faces, the slices were facing each other so Mickey and Minnie looked cross-eyed.

The costumes were typical "pajama" costumes, meaning that the costume followed the shape of the person's body. The costumes for the dwarfs were even worse, so that they looked like blow-up dolls from a mail-order company with mouths frozen open in an oval shape and dead eyes not anchored but staring straight out.

Animator Bill Justice, who attended the premiere and who would decades later be in charge of designing Disneyland character costumes remembered that "When *Snow White* was finally completed, all employees were invited to the premiere at the Carthay Circle Theater. Everybody went, and as it turned out, enjoyed a success beyond anyone's dreams. My most vivid memory of the evening, however, was the dwarf costumes. To help generate some atmosphere the Company made one of its first attempts at costumed characters. They must have been an after thought because they sure weren't close to the model sheets. It's a wonder those dwarfs didn't scare people away."

To explain the process involved in making *Snow White*, a large display of original art was set-up in a gallery-type setting around the corner of the Carthay entrance. The outdoor display included black and white photos as well as cels, backgrounds and layout drawings. Above the protective lattice work were huge three-dimensional heads of the dwarfs.

Clarence Nash, the voice of Donald Duck, was there, as well, with one of his early Donald Duck ventriloquist dummies.

Looking at stills from the premiere it is amusing to see that everyone's eyes are focused on the small dummy and not on Clarence who was happily quacking away.

Mickey Mouse, Minnie Mouse and Donald Duck were interviewed by Wilson on the radio. Mickey was nervous and Donald was upset that someone seemed to have stolen his ticket. Donald Duck starts singing for the radio audience and Mickey, Minnie and Pluto try to shut him up and take him away.

Donald wasn't the only one who didn't have a ticket, neither did Adrianna Caselotti who voiced Snow White nor Harry Stockwell, the father of actor Dean Stockwell, who voiced the Prince.

Caselotti loved telling the following story: "When we got to the door, the girl said, 'May I have your tickets, please?' I said, 'Tickets? We don't have any tickets—I'm Snow White and this is Prince Charming!' She said, "I don't care who you are, you don't get in unless you've got tickets!' So, we sneaked in when she wasn't looking and we went upstairs to one side of the balcony and I stood there watching myself on the screen and all those movie stars clapping for me. Boy! Did I get a thrill out of that!"

Walt was also interviewed for the radio: "Well, I'm very happy about everything. It's been a lot of fun making it and we're very happy that it's been given this big premiere here tonight and all these people turning out to take a look at it and I hope they aren't too disappointed. Well, our favorites are the little dwarfs. There's seven of them. We got names for them all that sort of fit their personality such as Doc whose the pompous leader and then there's old Happy, the smiling little fellow and Grumpy, the old sourpuss, the woman hater and ... I can't remember them all here tonight. (Laughs). And little Dopey. He's sort of our pet, you know. He hasn't any lines. He doesn't talk. Well, I don't know. I guess he just never tried."

Announcer: "Are you going in to watch the premiere?"

Walt: "Yes, and have my wife hold my hand."

Amazingly, since all the publicity emphasized only Walt's name, another Disney staffer was also interviewed. Dave Hand, who was introduced as the supervising director of *Snow White and the Seven Dwarfs*, the general manager of Disney Studios and "Walt Disney's right-hand man" told the radio audience the following among other comments: "At times it appeared to be an almost impossible task. The fact that we did it is a tribute to the guiding genius of Walt and the whole-hearted efforts and perfect cooperation of the seven hundred artists and technicians of the studio staff. We found we have only scratched the surface of the wonderful possibilities of the full length animated feature. We have recently started work on two new feature length features. Our staff thrives on tough assignments. We are hoping to produce things far above anything imaginable."

Animator Ward Kimball who had worked for many months on a scene of the dwarfs eating soup that was cut from the final film before it went to ink and paint attended the premiere with his wife, Betty, and shared the following memories:

*"I was at the premiere in 1937. We were worried. It was being shown at the Carthay Circle Hollywood. We didn't know how it would go over. Walt was on pins and needles. We sat down. Movie stars were sitting in seats. Betty and I*

*sat behind Clark Gable and Carol Lombard and he got upset
when Snow White was poisoned. He started to sniffle and
borrowed a handkerchief. That type of reaction is hard to get
with a cartoon because after all you are exaggerating and
caricaturing and the tendency is to do a put on. Not Walt! I
think that was the key to his secret.*

*"In the beginning the audience warmed up to the first little
gags. Gradually, there was this buzz that arose with the whole
theater. They laughed at the gags, especially that dancing
thing with Dopey on Sneezy's shoulders. It just tore up the
place. You knew what was going to happen. Sneezy lets go and
off goes Dopey. That was Walt's timing. He criticized the first
version. He said, 'Blow Dopey out of the screen and then you
don't go and see what happened to him. You cut to Snow White
and she's laughing and all the dwarves are laughing. And then
go to Dopey and he's up there swinging and wiggling his ears.'
On the night of the premiere, that scene got the biggest laugh.
That was Walt's timing.*

*"Anyway, when Snow White is laid out on the marble bier and
in comes the prince and everybody in the audience is sniffing
and I heard people blowing their noses. It was weird. It really
got to them. I knew the picture was a winner because they
laughed at the gags and cried at a silly thing of a cartoon of a
girl who comes to at the prince's first kiss.*

*"It's hard to believe but the people in the audience were really
blowing their noses. I heard all this noise and I said, 'Betty,
let's run out and watch them come out in the lobby.' They
came out and they were rummaging around putting on dark
glasses so no one would know they had been crying and their*

*eyes were all red. They were wiping their eyes. It was a very moving experience. We knew it was a winner then."*

Layout artist Ken O'Connor shared with Steve Hulett the following memory: "The audience was wildly enthusiastic. They even applauded the background and layouts when no animation was on the screen. I was sitting near John Barrymore when the shot of the Queen's castle above the mist came on with the Queen poling across the marsh in a little boat. He was bouncing up and down in his seat he was so excited. Barrymore was an artist as well as an actor, and he knew the kind of work that went into something like that."

Animator Wolfgang Reitherman recalled that, "The audience was so taken by the magic of what they had seen that they applauded after individual sequences, just as though they were watching a stage play. I've never seen anything quite like it since."

As the house lights came up, the audience who was already applauding rose to its feet. "It was the most receptive, enthusiastic audience I have ever seen," animator Shamus Culhane recalled.

Walt, who appeared on stage with his wife, said "I always dreamed that one day I would attend a gala premiere in Hollywood of one of my cartoons. Tonight you've made it come true. You make me feel like one of you."

*Snow White* played at the Carthay Circle for four months. The Spanish-language edition of the feature, *Blanca Nieves y los Siete Enanos,* was unveiled at the Carthay Circle on Sunday, February 27, 1938, and became a regular Sunday-afternoon feature during the remainder of *Snow White's* run there.

Animator Woolie Reitherman recalled, "I ran into Walt the next morning after the premiere. Instead of talking about how he could now take a little rest, he began talking about the next animated feature, and how he wanted to get started right away. There was only one Walt Disney."

However, the Disney connection with the Carthay Circle doesn't end with *Snow White*. The Carthay Circle was one of only fourteen theaters to be fitted with the full Fantasound equipment for the presentation of *Fantasia* just a few years later in 1940.

At the Academy Award ceremony on February 23, 1939, Walt received a special Oscar for *Snow White and the Seven Dwarfs*. It was one large statue and seven small Oscars. The inscription read: "To Walt Disney for *Snow White and the Seven Dwarfs* recognized as a significant screen innovation which has charmed millions and pioneered a great new entertainment field for the motion picture cartoon." It was presented by nine year old Shirley Temple who had been at the premiere and posed for pictures with the costumed dwarfs that were almost exactly her size.

The final box office gross for the first release of *Snow White* was close to $8.5 million dollars, making it the highest-grossing Hollywood film of all time. This was when adults in general paid a quarter and children a dime to see a movie. That record breaking gross would be broken two years later with the release of *Gone With the Wind* but at that moment in time, it really was a Snow White Christmas.

## DESTINO

According to a 2008 Disney press release: "*Destino* began in 1946 as a collaboration between Walt Disney and the famed surrealist painter Salvador Dali. A first-hand example of Disney's interest in avant garde and experimental work in animation, *Destino* was to be awash with Dali's iconic melting clocks, marching ants and floating eyeballs. However, *Destino* was not completed at that time. In 2003, it was rediscovered by Walt's nephew, Roy E. Disney, who took on the challenge of bringing the creation of these two great artists to fruition."

Apparently, Dali contacted Walt Disney briefly as early as 1937 on a trip to Hollywood. During that era, Walt was always bringing high-profile artists, writers and more to the Disney Studios to share ideas with his artists.

However it was a dinner party, nearly a decade later, in 1945 that resulted in an official collaboration between the two high profile celebrities. Dali was staying with Jack Warner and his wife to paint their portraits. Dali had been in Hollywood to design sets for a dream sequence in the Alfred Hitchcock film *Spellbound* (1945). Walt attended the dinner party at the Warner home in 1945, and Disney and Dali immediately bonded, resulting in a friendship that would last until Walt's passing two decades later.

Besides the similar artistic recognition the two men had each received for their innovative work, Dali and Disney were also both workaholics, loved controlling their work, were terrific self-promoters, and filled with a seemingly endless supply of ideas, optimism, and humor. So, this unusual friendship began with a good many strong connections already in place commented some of Disney's staff.

Dali officially moved into a room on the third floor of the Animation building at the Disney Studios in 1946. Originally, the project was top secret because they had not settled on exactly what that project would be. At the time, because of financial and labor restrictions, Walt was producing what was known as "package films"—a feature comprised of several short self-contained segments. Walt had purchased a romantic Mexican ballad by Armando Dominquez titled *Destino* that Walt thought might be a good vehicle for South American singer and dancer Dora Luz, who had recently appeared in *The Three Caballeros* (1945). It was intended to be a segment in another upcoming package film and Walt felt that Dali might provide some interesting backgrounds for the piece.

Dali disliked the song but loved the word "*destino*" (meaning "destiny") and his imagination began to run wild as he created an entire elaborate scenario. Dali visualized two lovers in an ever changing dreamlike landscape and the effect that time and other obstacles had on that relationship. It would be a combination of animation, live action (live ballet dancers in a Daliesque landscape) and special effects and would run six-to-eight minutes long. As work progressed on the story, Dali continued to add new ideas and symbolism so that the story became ever more complicated and unwieldy.

"It is a magical exposition of the problem of life in the labyrinth of time," proclaimed Dali. (Walt added that it was really "just a simple story about a young girl in search of her real love.")

"We have to keep breaking new trails," Walt announced in 1946 at Dali's arrival. "Ordinarily, good story ideas don't come easily and have to be fought for. Dali is communicative. He bubbles with new ideas."

At the time, Dali declared, "I have been given absolute freedom! That is paradise for the artist!"

Dali in his own publication, *Dali News*, declared, "Dali and Disney will produce the first motion picture of the 'Never Seen Before,' and the most rigorous secrecy on this subject will prevail."

Walt assigned artists John Hench and Bob Cormack to assist Dali so that his visions could be adapted to the necessities of animation. Dali painted the key scenes while Hench and Cormack made continuity sketches to help segue from one image to another. Dali painted some key scenes working in watercolors, a medium he never used for his exhibition paintings.

As Hench remembered, "Walt came in and looked at the work from time to time. He saw the storyboards in progress and decided to let Dali go ahead and see what would happen. Dali was given complete freedom."

That didn't prevent Walt from contributing ideas. "Well, they had a Roman god and it represented a blockage to a labyrinth, but the hummingbird opened it and it became a passageway. I don't know if people got that or not but that was Walt's suggestion," Hench recalled. Perhaps that might explain why Dali's painting of the head of Jupiter from the film was framed and hung in Walt's office until he passed away. Dali said that Jupiter determined the course of all human affairs which is why a giant sundial emerged from that great stone face in the film.

"Now the metamorphosis! We see the face of Jupiter, which becomes a big stone sun dial. His hair is a magical arch.

Time stops the way into the labyrinth of life, and true love is not possible until time is destructed," stated the cryptic and flamboyant Dali.

The film is filled with Dali symbolism. The ravaging ants signify humanity's desolation. The crutches suggest that mankind cannot live without support. The famous melting watches denote the death of time. The whole idea of a sculpture coming to life was something Dali originally proposed for Hitchcock's *Spellbound*. However, actress Ingrid Bergman vetoed the idea in the dream sequence because Dali wanted to cover her with live ants when she came to life. Dali was not adverse to borrowing ideas from his previous work. The heroine in *Destino* seems similar to the woman from his painting *Suburbs of the Paranoiac-Critical Town* done nearly a decade earlier.

There were scenes of the girl running up a cliff, pursued by a horde of figures whose heads were eyeballs, representing the eyes of public opinion trying to prevent her from achieving happiness. There are drawings of these eyeballs flaring like giant flashbulbs on contemporary cameras just like today's paparazzi. To emphasize that theme even more, there are drawings of newspapers with scorpion legs who are also chasing the helpless girl.

For more than two months, Dali arrived no later than nine a.m. each day at the Disney Studios to diligently work at his easel. He was often accompanied by his wife Gala who not only helped inspire him but interpreted for him since he often chatted away in an odd mixture of French, Spanish, broken English and his own unique language. Dali sometimes had lunch with Walt and Hench in the Disney Studios' Coral Room restaurant. Disney Legend Ward Kimball remembered that Gala would sometimes pin directions to Dali's house on Salvador's jacket if he came to studio by himself so if he got on a bus someone would be able to help him find his way home.

For several months, Dali worked out of his Monterrey, California, studio, near the old Del Monte Lodge Hotel and Hench would commute there on weekends.

As interest in the project was starting to wane at the studio, Hench put together what might be considered a fifteen second "animatic" of a scene to help everyone visualize what the finished film might look like.

"I thought I'd shoot this one scene because I thought it was so astonishing," said Hench. "It was an appearance of the female character, the ballerina, and it was an empty field with just a white ball floating on a field and then two turtles, one approaching from the left and then the right, and I used sliding fills because I didn't have an animator that I could use. But we pulled these slides across and then when they met, the negative space turned into the ballerina and the ball was her head. And I thought, yeah, I can show that to Walt. He may just go ahead with the thing anyway. But it was very surprising and I thought it would interest him. And it did interest him too but he put it aside, though. Years afterward, whenever Walt and I talked about Dali, he always said we should have made that thing anyway."

"Salvador was back in Monterrey, so once I finished filming the test, I drove up to show it to him," Hench revealed.  "I tipped the manager of this little theater that was showing some B Western to show it after the film was over and the audience had left. The lights went out, and Salvador saw his artwork in full motion. He loved it. Just then the projectionist came out and practically roared, 'What was THAT?' Dali and I looked at each other, and we both knew that it was a unique moment in art."

There were two completely different storyboards and five different written treatments and none of them give any clue to what Dali intended the narrative to be.

Officially, Walt told Dali that the *Destino* project was unfortunately canceled because he felt, supposedly urged by his film distributor RKO, that the market for package films was gone. This didn't prevent Walt from releasing *Melody Time* two years later, considered the last of the package films.

Actually, the little-known final package film, *Music Land*, was released October 5, 1955. Disney had by that time created its own company to release its films to theaters but still owed its current distributor, RKO, one more film under the existing contract. In order to fulfill that final film commitment, Disney took a combination of four sequences from *Make Mine Music* and five from *Melody Time* to create a new compilation film titled *Music Land*. The poster boldly declared it was "The Big Parade of Mirth and Melody!" The film was never shown again except once at a retrospective "Tribute to Walt Disney" at the National Film Theater in 1970.

Walt said, "It was certainly no fault of Dali's that the project we were working on was not completed. It was simply a case of policy changes in our distribution plan."

Diane Disney Miller, recalled, "Salvador Dali came to our home and rode Dad's train, and although it was the middle of summer, he was dressed in a black overcoat, with a collar and cravat. He sat on a little boxcar with his cane upright in front of him."

Dali remained convinced that he and Disney would collaborate on something eventually, perhaps even reviving *Destino*. Walt did, in fact, visit the artist at his home in Spain several times during the Fifties. They talked about a possible animated sequence from *Dante's Divine Comedy* (that Dali had illustrated for the Italian government), an animated feature version of *Don Quixote* and even *El Cid* (Dali supposedly developed a story concept) that might have included a live-action Errol Flynn. Walt told people he thought that Dali was "a friend, a very swell guy, and a person whom I thoroughly enjoyed working with."

Walt prepared an *Art of Animation* museum exhibit in 1958 that would tour the United States (eventually ending up as a display attraction in Tomorrowland at Disneyland), Europe and Japan. This exhibit was to promote the upcoming release of *Sleeping Beauty* in 1959. To put the exhibit together, Walt sent people to the animation "morgue" where the animation art was kept. Walt wanted some specific pieces and it wasn't just cel setups but backgrounds, concept art, story sketches, and more. There were three versions of this exhibit and each featured different original art.

Walt felt the inclusion of art done by Dali would add another dimension (and additional publicity) to the exhibit. Walt was shocked to discover that practically all of the major Dali art had disappeared from the morgue. Walt never had the heart to tell Dali what had happened.

When Dave Smith started the Disney Archives in 1970, he began making an appeal to Disney employees to donate any Disneyana they had. Five Dali paintings mysteriously reappeared and they were cleaned and put safely away. Also in the Seventies, Albert Field who was a New York-based appraiser, approached Dali and showed him some unsigned, newly discovered artwork from *Destino*. Dali couldn't distinguish the drawings by Hench from his own work so he signed them all.

Roy E. Disney stated, "They [Hench and Dali] worked closely together to the point where they couldn't tell each other's drawings apart... John was the only one in the world, until he died, who could sit down with us and say: 'That's mine; that's his.'"

There is some dispute about how much of the *Destino* artwork was recovered by the Disney Studios, although at least one reliable source indicated that 55 sketches by Dali and 75 by Hench were preserved at the studio in the early 1990s. Supposedly, the original portfolio for the project had almost 375 sketches and 22 completed paintings.

Robert Descharnes, recognized as one of the foremost experts on Dali artwork, has pointed out that some *enterprising* seller has faked Dali signatures on some of the unsigned *Destino* originals and even painted some phony *Destino* artwork that has been sold over the years.

In 1997, John Hench said, "Walt abandoned *Destino* very regretfully. He hoped to pick it up later. He had gotten a great kick out of the project and besides admiring Dali's talent, he liked him personally."

While working on *Fantasia 2000* on the interstitial with actress Bette Midler that made reference to Dali's work, executive producer Roy E. Disney thought about using Dali artwork to promote the film.

"During the filming, I learned from one of the attorneys that we actually didn't have legal possession of the Dali art, because the contract signed in 1945 stated that it wouldn't become the company's until the film was made," Roy Disney said. "When I've told this story, some people think my motivation was to make a lot of money by acquiring the valuable artwork. The fun of it was the idea of finishing something that had grown to almost mythic proportions, and getting it out to the public."

Roy Disney decided to complete the film with input from Hench. Approximately twenty percent of the finished film had computer generated art work to help move the virtual camera around objects. It was directed by Dominique Monfery and produced by Baker Bloodworth.

"Some of it was incomprehensible." Bloodworth explained. "Dali had always said, 'If you understand this, then I've failed'. We pulled together the love story and compressed. And yet there is a long baseball sequence that no one could make sense of that we only touched on. We were true to the look that Dali painted. Dali would start with an image, which would become another one, and just when you thought it would hold on that image, it would become something else. Monfrey took the best of the drawings and then went back to the Dali works to find patterns."

Regarding the infamous extended baseball sequence, Dali stated, "Baseball, it is fascinating. About the game, I know nothing. But as an artist, I am obsessed!"

*Destino* has played at several film festivals in 2003, including the Telluride Film Festival, the New York Film Festival and the Chicago Film Festival and was nominated for an Academy Award but did not win.  Some people love the film while others find it completely incomprehensible and boring but there is no denying that it is a unique achievement of two distinct artistic innovators.

## SONG OF THE SOUTH PREMIERE

*"It wasn't yesterday nor the day before, but it was a long time*
*ago... back when the critters, they were closer to the folks and*
*the folks, they was closer to the critters—and if you'll excuse*
*me for saying so, it was better all around." –Uncle Remus in*
**Song of the South**

Walt Disney bought the rights to the Uncle Remus stories
from the Harris family in 1939. In the late 1870s, newspaper
man Joel Chandler Harris had written the original folk stories
as a popular newspaper column. Disney got the rights to all
the Remus characters for $10,000 and that was a sizeable sum
in those days.

Walt stopped in Atlanta, Georgia, in November 1939 to
meet with the Harris family and as he told the entertainment
press "to get an authentic feeling of Uncle Remus country so
we can do as faithful a job as possible to these stories."

According to the program for the world premiere, the
Harris family had hoped for many years that Disney would
dramatize the Uncle Remus stories, perhaps as two-reel
animated shorts, but "during the years of discussion leading up
to final negotiation [in 1939], the idea of full-length animated
cartoon pictures interested the Disney studios and later gripped
the public." Pre-production news items indicated that Disney
originally intended to produce the film as an all-animation
feature, but by the time production began, it was decided to
have the picture feature live action. Walt was interested in
getting into live action and it was less time consuming and less
expensive than a full animated feature.

"I was familiar with the Uncle Remus tales since boyhood. From the time I began making animated features, I have had them definitely in my production plans," Walt said in 1946.

Walt had two research reports done by the studio, *Background on the Uncle Remus Tales* (April 8, 1938) and *The Uncle Remus Stories* (April 11, 1938), to determine the feasibility of transferring these stories to the screen. Through 1938 and into the early 1940s when the film was still being considered as a full-length animated feature, many individual animated segments were being developed from the Remus stories including "Brer Rabbit Rides the Fox" and "The Wuller de Wust" (where Brer Rabbit pretends to be a ghost to scare Brer Bear).

One of the early story treatments from 1939 was more connected to the African-American spirituals. Uncle Remus gathered the critters together for a prayer meeting to help them build a church so that peace could finally exist between the prey animals and the predators. Another storyline showed Brer Rabbit doing battle with the temptation of gambling. Versions of some of these tales being developed later appeared in Disney's children books and comics.

"Three generations of readers have learned to love the laughter and the wisdom in the tales of Uncle Remus. During the preparation of material for *Song of the South* a great quantity of the early Remus tales were studied and adapted by the Disney staff. Unfortunately, only a few of them could be included in the short space of one film," stated Walt Disney.

The closure of foreign markets for its animated films during the war years had choked off a vital source of income for the Disney Studios. In addition, while a handful of animated shorts had been produced during the war years, the majority of the labor and creative energy at the studio had been funneled to the production of military training films that were made only covering the actual production expenses with no profit.

Fortunately, re-releases of *Snow White* and *Pinocchio* helped prevent the Disney Studio from showing losses in 1945 and 1946 but that did not prevent the studio from laying off almost half its total work force in 1946. So, time and talent were major considerations for any new production.

Walt had wanted to diversify into live action films but his contract with RKO specified that he produce animated features or features that combined animation and live action like *Saludos Amigos* and *The Three Caballeros*.

Over the years, Walt had considered several projects combining animation and live action including a feature film that would have showcased a live-action girl interacting with an animated world in *Alice in Wonderland*. In fact, when *Song of the South* was in production, Walt announced Alice might be his next feature with Luana Patten from *Song of the South* playing Alice.

Walt decided to take a risk and experiment by combining live action and animation in *Song of the South*. He assumed that the live action would be less expensive to film than animation and filmed more quickly as well. The animation would only appear in less than one-third of the film and thus take less time and labor. Supposedly, Walt himself chose the final three animated sequences to include in the film.

Walt's brother, Roy, was doubtful about the project from the beginning but not because of any fears of racial sensitivities. He just felt the project was not "big enough in caliber" to warrant the time and budget for a full-length film. Despite his reported dislike for sequels, if *Song of the South* had proven financially and critically successful, Walt considered it as just the first of a series of Uncle Remus pictures that would combine live action and animation.

*Song of the South* cost approximately $2,125,000 to make and made over $60 million dollars worldwide by the time of its last theatrical re-release in 1986. However, that first year release only netted the Disney Studio a modest profit of $226,000.

Plans for the world premiere began long in advance of the scheduled date of November 12, 1946. The Disney Studio contacted prominent movie critics and arranged for them to travel to Atlanta, Georgia.

Four reporters from *Atlanta Constitution* and *Atlanta Journal* visited the studio in early October 1946 to begin a series of stories that would run daily in Atlanta newspapers until the premiere. Many recording artists released versions of the film's music in advance of the premiere, including Dinah Shore, the Merry Macs, Woody Herman and the Modernaires, according to a September 25, 1946 *Hollywood Reporter* news item.

The State of Georgia agreed to have a joint holiday, celebrating Armistice Day and a tribute to Joel Chandler Harris since it was in Georgia that his stories had first gained recognition.

Arrangements were made for Walt to dedicate an Uncle Remus cabin at Wren's Nest, author Harris' former home. About two weeks before the premiere on November 1, 1946, artists Fred Moore and Dick Mitchell, along with "production expert" Frank Bresson and Clarence Nash (the vocal artist who was the voice of Donald Duck) opened a "miniature studio" at the Belle Isle Building Arcade in Atlanta.

The exhibit included Moore and Mitchell drawing sketches for visitors, demonstrations of the animation process and showings of a preview of the picture and scenes from the 1941 Disney film *The Reluctant Dragon*, because it contained a live action tour of the actual Walt Disney Studios. They were later joined by Pinto Colvig (the voice of Goofy) and Adriana Caselotti (the voice of Snow White).

On November 11th (Armistice Day), a gigantic parade moved down Atlanta's Peachtree Street. There were bands and slow moving floats, some of which featured characters from the film. Children were cheering since they had been given a school holiday. Flags adorned the buildings. There was a luncheon at the Capital Club and a tea at the Wren's Nest, where a crowd of autograph-seekers got out of hand and knocked Walt Disney to his knees. Full sized dummies of the characters of Uncle Remus and Johnny were placed in the parlor reportedly as a gift from the Disney Studio and were recently re-discovered and put out for display again.

The world premiere was set for 8:30 p.m. on November 12, 1946. The premiere itself was sponsored jointly by the Atlanta Junior League and the Uncle Remus Memorial Association. Celestine Sibley, who covered the event for the *Atlanta Constitution*, called it "D Day" in honor of Disney.

Prior to the screening of the film, radio shows participated in the film's premiere including *Queen for a Day*, *Bride and Groom*, Art Linkletter's *GE Houseparty* and *Vox Pop*, a show that conducted live interviews on the Fox Theater stage the night of the premiere. More than five thousand people attended the premiere, which benefited charities overseen by Atlanta's Junior League and the Uncle Remus Memorial Society's renovation of Wren's Nest.

Bobby Driscoll, Luana Patten and Ruth Warrick represented the cast. Walt and Lillian Disney were there accompanied by Disney Studio staff including Perce Pearce, Milt Kahl, Bill Peet, Ken Anderson, Claude Coats and Wilfred Jackson. Other celebrities included Bill Williams and Barbara Hale and Cliff "Jiminy Cricket" Edwards.

The film was shown at the majestic Fox Theater, the South's largest theater which seated more than five thousand people. Not since *Gone With the Wind* had all of Atlanta turned out for a Hollywood movie. On the night of the gala, Disney took the stage at the Fox and welcomed the sellout audience in the voice of Mickey Mouse with a Southern accent: "How are y'all?" As soon as the film began, Walt ducked out of the theater and waited across the street at the Georgian Terrace Hotel, chain-smoking and biting his fingernails.

There was some dissension in the Atlanta papers because "Uncle Remus" wasn't in the title. The *Atlanta Journal* movie editor saw a preview and wrote that people shouldn't worry because it was Uncle Remus' picture from start to finish and that he was faithfully portrayed. According to the paper, it "was a film that is certain to take its place alongside *Gone With the Wind* as a celluloid piece of Americana."

However, the celebration and good feelings were overshadowed by a dark secret. *Song of the South*'s African-American cast members were not able to join Walt Disney and the white cast members at the movie's premiere in Atlanta because Atlanta was a segregated city. African-Americans could not enter the movie theater or any other public buildings downtown.

In describing the premiere, local newspapers recounted the actions of Atlanta's mayor, William B. Hartsfield, who urged Disney to wire actor James Baskett with news of the city's appreciation for his portrayal of Uncle Remus. Although some Southern newspapers stated that Baskett could not be present due to his commitment to the *Amos 'n' Andy* radio show where he performed as fast-talking Gabby Gibson, none of the African-American cast members attended the premiere.

In an October 15, 1946 article in the *Atlanta Constitution* newspaper, columnist Harold Martin noted that to bring Baskett to Atlanta, where he would not have been allowed to participate in any of the festivities because of the highly strict segregation laws, "would cause him many embarrassments, for his feelings are the same as any man's."

There is an urban legend that no Atlanta hotel would give Baskett accommodation because white-owned hotels denied rooms to blacks. That assumption is not entirely correct since there were several black-owned hotels in the Sweet Auburn area of downtown Atlanta at the time, including the Savoy and the McKay. However, even if the African-American cast stayed at those hotels, they would have still been denied access to other areas that would be frequented by the white cast members, including restaurants and the theater itself. Even the women running the Wren's Nest had a firm rule that no African-Americans could visit the location.

The reviews for the film were decidedly mixed although in general there was high praise for the animation. Many reviewers, despite liking James Baskett's Uncle Remus, found the rest of the live-action performances underwhelming.

Local reviews in Georgia, including a notice in the African-American newspaper, the *Atlanta Daily World*, were largely positive, but nationally the film was not well received.

*Time* magazine called Uncle Remus "a character bound to enrage all educated Negroes, and a number of damn Yankees" while still referring to the film as "topnotch Disney." It added that: "it could have used a much heavier helping of cartooning" claiming that except for the two youngsters "the live actors are bores." Others found the film "mawkish," "slipshod," and "inconsequential."

*Variety* said: "Story of misunderstood Johnny gets away to an ambling start and only picks up when the live Uncle Remus segues into the first cartoon sequence... the rest of the story, including the confused and insufficiently explained estrangement of the parents, overbalances the three cartoon sequences and could be cut...these cartoon sequences are great stuff."

*New York Times*: "The ratio of live to cartoon action is approximately two to one, and that is approximately the ratio of its mediocrity to its charm.... The Disney wonder workers here just a lot of conventional hacks when it comes to telling a story with live action instead of cartoons."

*PM Magazine*: Disney "was not trying to put across any message but was making a sincere effort to depict American folklore, to put Uncle Remus stories into pictures." *Time* magazine: "Artistically, *Song of the South* could have used a much heavier helping of cartooning. Technically, the blending of two movie mediums is pure Disney wizardry. Ideologically, the picture is certain to land its maker in hot water." *The Afro-American*, an African-American newspaper, declared that the reviewer was "thoroughly disgusted" by the film.

Herman Hill's review in the black newspaper *The Pittsburgh Courier*: "The truly sympathetic handling of the entire production from a racial standpoint is calculated... to prove of estimable good in the furthering of interracial relations."

The review discussed the negative statements made by *Ebony* magazine and found the comments to be "unadulterated hogwash symptomatic of the unfortunate racial neurosis that seems to be gripping so many of our humorless brethren these days."

In 1956 during the film's first re-release, actress Luana Patten, who played the part of "Ginny" in the film, was a high school student working after school in the box office at The Lakewood Theatre in Long Beach, California, when the theater was robbed. The film playing at the time was the first theatrical re-release of *Song of the South*.

The re-release in 1972 was two years after the Disney Company claimed in a statement in the February 25, 1970 issue of *Variety* that the Disney Studio had put the film "permanently on the shelf as offensive to Negroes and present concepts of race." During its 1972 reissue, the picture became the highest grossing Disney re-release up to that time.

The film was re-released two more times theatrically in 1980 and 1986. The 1986 reissue included a November 15, 1986 "re-premiere" held in Atlanta to celebrate the film's 40th anniversary. By gubernatorial proclamation, the day of the premiere was declared *Song of the South* Day in Georgia. Proceeds from the 1986 premiere, which was attended by actress Ruth Warrick, benefited the preservation of Wren's Nest.

Segments from *Song of the South* were showcased on the first two Disney Christmas television specials for NBC and CBS. There were books of the Disney version with covers by Mary Blair and interior illustrations by Bill Justice adapting the stories from the Disney film, as well as stories that would have been in a sequel. The characters frequently popped up in the Disney comic books over the years. Popular Disney "Sing-A-Long" videos have featured animated segments from the film.

There was a long running Disney Sunday newspaper comic strip, *Uncle Remus and His Tales of Brer Rabbit*. Written by Bill Walsh and drawn by Paul Murry and later Dick Moores, the strip began on October 14, 1945 and ended on December 31, 1972, more than twenty-seven years later.

Currently, the Disney Company has announced it will not re-release the film because it is "antiquated" and can be construed as fairly "offensive" and that it will remain in the Disney vault where it has been safely hidden for a quarter of a century.

## THE ALICE IN WONDERLAND THAT NEVER WAS

There were three silent film versions of *Alice's Adventures in Wonderland* (1903, 1910 and 1915) and while Walt Disney never mentioned seeing any of them, it is certainly possible that he might have seen at least one of them either when they were released or in preparation for his film version. However, Walt had read the famous book.

"It fascinated me the first time I read it as a schoolboy and after I started making animated cartoons, I acquired the film rights to it. Carroll with his nonsense and fantasy furnished a balance between seriousness and enjoyment which everybody needed then and still needs today." — Walt Disney, quoted in *American Weekly* (August 11, 1946)

It is well documented that Walt not only read but studied and recommended a 1920 book titled *Animated Cartoons* by E.G. Lutz.

In the final chapter, discussing the future of animation, author Lutz states: "Lewis Carroll's *Alice in Wonderland* is a good example of the type of fanciful tale on the order of which animated cartoons could be made for children. The Mad Hatter would make an admirable figure to pace across the screen. An artist desiring to be the author of an animated story built on the model of Carroll's classics would need a gleeful imagination and a turn for the fantastic. And he would require, besides, if he hoped to draw characters of a par with Tenniel's depictions, more than the ordinary qualifications of a screen draftsman."

This suggestion might have inspired Walt's decision to title his successful animated series, about a live-action little girl interacting with a fantastical world of cartoon characters, the Alice Comedies and call the first installment *Alice's Wonderland*.

The year 1932 marked the centennial of the birth of Lewis Carroll (the pseudonym for the Reverend Charles Dodgson) who authored the adventures of Alice, inspired by the child Alice Liddell. That year, Liddell, who grew up to be Mrs. Alice Hargreaves, visited the United States to receive an honorary degree and make personal appearances. In June 1932, she got to view three Mickey Mouse cartoons on a theatrical screen and was quite pleased and felt that Carroll would have enjoyed the new medium to tell stories.

At the time, silent screen star Mary Pickford, who was one of the founding members of United Artists, proposed to Walt Disney filming a feature-length version of *Alice in Wonderland* with little Mary playing the role of Alice in an animated Wonderland supplied by Walt Disney and his artists. Pickford was hugely excited about the project, did costume tests for the character, and issued press announcements. The film was planned for black and white, although some of the costume tests that survive were done in three-strip Technicolor. Walt did not appear to be equally enthusiastic about the project and with the announcement that Paramount Pictures was producing an all-star live-action film to be released December 1933, it ended work on the Pickford-Disney film.

"We have been asked to make *Alice in Wonderland* with Mary Pickford," said Walt in the *New York Times Magazine* (June 3, 1934). "We have discouraged the idea, for we aren't ready for a feature yet."

Prompted by the success of *Snow White and the Seven Dwarfs*, Walt purchased several projects for future animated features, including the rights to *Alice in Wonderland* in 1938—in particular the rights to reproduce the original Tenniel drawings. Again, Walt told the *New York Times Magazine* (March 1938), "*Alice in Wonderland* should never have been done in the realistic medium of motion picture [referring to the 1933 Paramount film] but we regard it as a natural for our medium."

Between December 1938 and April 1941, Walt held at least eleven documented meetings with various members of his staff to discuss the possibilities of making *Alice in Wonderland*.

"I'll tell you what has been wrong with every one of these productions on Carroll," said Walt Disney at a January 4, 1939 story meeting. "They have depended on his dialogue to be funny. But if you can use some of Carroll's phrases that are funny, use them. If they aren't funny, throw them out. There is a spirit behind Carroll's story. It's fantasy, imagination, screwball logic...but it must be funny. I mean funny to an American audience. To hell with the English audiences or the people who love Carroll...I'd like to make it more or less a 1940 or 1945 version—right up to date. I wouldn't put in any modern slang that wouldn't fit, but the stuff can be modernized. I want to put my money into something that will go in Podunk, Iowa, and they will go in and laugh at it because they have experienced it. They wouldn't laugh at a lot of English sayings that they've never heard or that don't mean anything to them. Yet, we can keep it very much Carroll—keep his spirit."

Disney storyman Al Perkins researched Carroll and his work and produced a 161 page analysis of the book *Alice in Wonderland* that broke down the book chapter by chapter, pointing out the possibilities for animation. Some of these suggestions were later used in the final animated feature, including the idea that the White Rabbit should wear glasses because Carroll once commented that he thought the White Rabbit should have spectacles, even though Tenniel never drew the character that way. Perkins also felt that the Cheshire Cat should be expanded and appear in other scenes of the story and that the watch that the Mad Hatter and the March Hare fix should belong to the White Rabbit.

Beginning June 1939, British artist David Hall spent about three months to produce roughly four hundred paintings, drawings and sketches using the Perkins' analysis as a guide. Hall had a background as a production artist in the film industry including DeMille's *The King of Kings* (1927). Story conferences at the time were not helpful to Hall because Walt felt that his story people didn't understand the spirit of the story.

For instance, they had suggested changing the croquet match into a football game. According to the story conference notes, Walt considered this approach at humor as "Donald Duck gags" and that "I think the book is funnier than the way you guys have got it. Get in and study characters and personalities, and that's where the real humor will come from."

In November 1939, the Disney Studio filmed a Leica reel (a film of the concept drawings and story sketches with a soundtrack to get an idea about the continuity and flow of the story) using Hall's artwork. The soundtrack included Cliff "Jiminy Cricket" Edwards doing the voice of the Talking Bottle (later changed in the final film to a talking doorknob).

"There are certain things in there that I like very much and there are other things in there that I think we ought to tear right out. I don't think there would be any harm in letting this thing sit for a while. Everyone is stale now. You'll look at it again and maybe have another idea on it. That's the way it works for me. I still feel that we can stick close to *Alice in Wonderland* and make it look like it and feel like it, you know," said Walt after viewing the reel that over the decades seems to have disappeared. David Hall left the Disney Studio January 1940.

At a meeting in April 8, 1941, Walt brought up the project again, "I've been wondering if we could do this thing with a live action girl. Here's the value in the live girl over trying to animate it—we can animate a girl, make her run around and things—but carrying this story is different. There's a lot of story here with the girl, and trying to carry the story with a cartoon girl puts us in a hell of a spot. We might, in the whole picture, have, say a dozen complicated trick shots, but the rest of them would be close-ups and working around it. We can get some good characters and good music. There's so much stuff in this business, we could work around the girl."

At the meeting, it was suggested that actress Gloria Jean, who was fourteen at the time and had just appeared as W.C. Fields' niece in the film *Never Give a Sucker An Even Break*, should be considered.

The outbreak of World War II prevented further work on that project. In 1944, the Disney Studios provided the cover artwork of a massive mushroom and the famous caterpillar for a record album based on *Alice in Wonderland* read by actress Ginger Rogers, who was thirty-three years old at the time. The album featured original music composed by Frank Luther and conducted by Victor Young. Besides Rogers, voices on the album included Lou Merrill, Bea Benaderet, Arthur Q. Bryan, Joe Kearns, Ferdy Munier and Martha Wentworth.

In the fall of 1945, Walt brought in writer Aldous Huxley to work on the live action/animation script for what was to become *Alice and the Mysterious Mr. Carroll.* The idea was that the film would star actress Luana Patten, who later appeared in Disney films *Song of the South* (1946) and *So Dear To My Heart* (1949). Huxley was a well-known and prolific English writer probably best remembered for his novel *Brave New World,* written in 1932 about the anti-utopian London of 2540 A.D., where the human spirit is subjected to conditioning and control.

Very highly regarded for his ideas as well as his writing, Huxley through his friend novelist Anita Loos, spent some time in Hollywood in the Forties doing some work on screenplays, including MGM's *Madame Curie, Pride and Prejudice* and *Jane Eyre* although his work was not always credited or used in its entirety.

The Disney Studio agreed to pay Huxley $7,500 to write the treatment for the film. They paid him $2,500 on October 18, 1945 with the balance to be paid on the delivery of the final treatment no later than January 15, 1946. Huxley delivered his fourteen page treatment on November 23, 1945. The Disney Studio also took out an option for Huxley to do the final screenplay for $15,000 that would have included "all additions, changes and revisions." The first draft of the script was delivered December 5, 1945.

Walt Disney had been seriously thinking of diversifying into live-action since World War II had shown him how vulnerable his business was when his talented animators were drafted into the service and foreign markets were closed to his films. It became very apparent that the time consuming and costly process of producing animated features would not supply a steady income for the studio. It was thought that live action could be done quicker and with less upfront investment.

One example of this thinking was the film *Song of the South*, which was primarily live-action with animated segments supporting the story. Huxley's script was very much in this same style with the story of Carroll and Alice told in live action with Alice seeking safety from her troubles by imagining an animated Wonderland. Huxley tried to set a premise that Carroll and Alice were very much alike in their love of fantasy, but their personal happiness was thwarted by very stern, no-nonsense people who controlled their lives.

Here is a brief paraphrasing of Huxley's synopsis for *Alice and the Mysterious Mr. Carroll* from November 1945.

The synopsis begins with a letter stating that the Queen of England wants to know and meet the author of *Alice in Wonderland*. She has been told he is an Oxford don and that she wishes the vice chancellor of the University, Langham, to discover his identity.

Langham tosses aside the request since he has other concerns, including the Reverend Charles Dodgson lobbying to become the new librarian. Dodgson loves books and wants to be relieved of his duties lecturing since he stutters badly when nervous. (In real life, the Dodo in Wonderland was named after Dodgson who sometimes because of his stutter would introduce himself as "Do-Do-Dodgson".) Langham is not inclined to endorse Dodgson for the new job because he feels it is inappropriate for the good reverend to be interested in the theater and in photography. Langham's assistant, Grove, who knows Dodgson quite well and just considers him a little eccentric tries to plead Dodgson's case to no avail.

Grove is the weak-willed guardian of a little girl named Alice, whose parents are temporarily off in India. Grove has hired Miss Beale to take care of Alice. Miss Beale is a no-nonsense person who is very strict and dislikes Dodgson because he fills Alice's mind with nonsense. Huxley points out that it is important to establish that Alice is "temporarily an orphan at the mercy of a governess and an old man who do not truly understand her or love her."

Dodgson has invited Alice to join him for a theatrical performance of *Romeo and Juliet* featuring one of his former students now grown up into an attractive and talented young woman, Ellen Terry. Miss Beale is outraged and orders Alice to write a letter to Dodgson informing him she can not attend because of her "religious principles".

Dodgson visits Terry in the theater and she immediately guesses that he is the mysterious author Lewis Carroll because he used to tell her stories of the Cheshire Cat when she was younger. Dodgson begs her to keep his secret since he is up for the job of librarian and that if it were revealed he was the one who wrote the children's book it would go badly for him. He also talks about bringing Alice to the play the following day.

Mrs. Beale discovers that Alice has not posted the letter to Dodgson but hidden it so she could sneak out and attend the theater with him. Enraged, Beale locks Alice in the garden house. When "Grove expresses concern about the severity of Alice's punishment, Miss Beale assures him that this is how it was always done in the best and most pious families. Grove ends by agreeing, as he always does when confronted by a personality stronger than his own."

Miss Beale raises the question of her pension that must be submitted to the Bishop within days (or wait another two years for the next opportunity) and Grove advises her that the

Bishop was good friends with Dodgson's father and perhaps the reverend could write a recommendation. Miss Beale's appears visibly shaken.

Alice is terrified at being locked in the garden house, but Miss Beale informs her that if she does not stop her screaming and pounding she will remain locked in there both day and night. To escape her terrors, Alice starts to imagine that a hanging rope is the caterpillar from the book and that a stuffed tiger's head is the Cheshire Cat. Eventually, by remembering that in Wonderland there "is a garden at the bottom of every rabbit hole," she finds a small shuttered window and is able to escape.

She rushes down the street towards the theater but has some horrendous adventures including being robbed by street urchins and trying to escape from a policeman remembering "Miss Beale's blood curdling accounts of what happens to children who fall into the clutches of the Law."

Alice eventually finds her way to the theater and rushes tearfully to Ellen Terry and the surrounding performers who are taking a break on stage. She incoherently blurts out her tale. Terry sends for Dodgson and is indignant about the way Alice has been treated. Alice confesses her "system of overcoming fear is pretending to be in Wonderland."

Ellen Terry says that is the purpose of theater to "take people out of Dull Land and Worry Land and carry them into Wonderland."

She, eventually joined by the other actors, recounts the story of the Red Queen's croquet game and the film transitions into animation. Dodgson arrives to take Alice home but Terry insists that Alice stay until she's had an opportunity to talk "with that old dragon" who has been persecuting Alice. Dodgson agrees and joins in on the storytelling that transforms into another animated segment.

At the point in the animated story where the Red Queen yells "Off With Her Head!" it returns to live-action and the appearance of Miss Beale followed by Grove and two policemen. Grove is persuaded to dismiss the policemen and Terry eloquently convinces Beale of the need to be kinder to Alice. During the discussion, Alice blurts out that Dodgson is really Lewis Carroll. A disgusted and frustrated Grove proclaims that this is the final straw why Dodgson is unfit for the job of librarian and leaves to confront Langham with the news.

Langham has no time for Grove, because he has been informed that the Queen is arriving that very afternoon to meet the author of *Alice in Wonderland* and he fears what her reaction will be for his inaction in finding the author. Grove announces he can produce the author and returns to the theater. There, without telling them the reason other than Langham needs to see them immediately, he gathers Beale, Alice and Dodgson and takes them in a cab back to the University.

Langham and the other dignitaries are paying their respects to the Queen and, just as Langham is about to admit he does not know who Carroll is, Grove arrives and shoves Dodgson forward. Alice is terrified the Queen will cut off his head, but the Queen is quite pleased. When she leaves, Dodgson finds himself lionized by those who had previously looked at him askance.

Even Miss Beale apologizes and shyly asks for Dodgson's recommendation to the bishop about her pension. Once assured that this means Miss Beale will not teach any more children in the future, Dodgson warmly agrees.

As all the new found flatterers cluster around Dodgson they all appear in Alice's eyes to transform into residents of Wonderland with only Dodgson himself remaining human.

A brief epilogue shows a gothic doorway with the word "Librarian" painted on the door and Dodgson seated comfortably at a table, writing, and surrounded by walls of books. A scout comes in and announces the carriage is ready and Dodgson leaves and goes to a nearby park where children are having a party including a Punch and Judy show. Alice runs up to Dodgson to introduce her new governess who is a "young and charming girl" who seems to be enjoying the party as much as Alice herself.

A stout middle aged woman approaches Dodgson to tell him how much she loves his wonderful book. Dodgson bows, smiles and hands her a printed card from his pocket and walks away. The card states: "The Reverend Charles L. Dodgson takes no responsibility for any publication not issued under his own name". The woman looks back up to see Dodgson walking away with Alice and animated characters from Wonderland.

There was a story meeting on December 7, 1945 with Walt and Huxley as well as Dick Huemer, Joe Grant, D. Koch, Cap Palmer, Bill Cottrell, and Ham Luske. On the infamous day that Pearl Harbor was attacked, Walt was at the Disney Studios having a meeting on Huxley's screenplay derived from this treatment for *Alice in Wonderland* with others who were completely oblivious to the historic impact of the day.

Huxley had made some significant changes in the screenplay. For instance, the transition into Wonderland was shifted from the theater to Dodgson's studio where Alice is looking through proofs of the book for *Alice in Wonderland*. The existing copy of the screenplay has pencil notations that Alice enters Wonderland in dissolves as Dodgson begins to tell her the story. With only the first thirty one pages remaining from the screenplay, regrettably whatever changes were made may never be known.

Joe Grant suggested Harold Lloyd to play the role of Carroll/Dodgson but Walt preferred Cary Grant. Walt also wanted to play up a suggested romantic interest between Carroll and actress Ellen Terry in the script because "we don't want him to look like a 'queer'. I don't want to see us build up any sex story here…We don't bring sex into it all at." Cap Palmer added, "Just a healthy interest in a grown woman."

Walt was insistent that the importance of nonsense be made clear. "We are driving toward another underlying point, which is that, often times, the best sense is non-sense. I'd like to finish the whole thing by coming out with some bit of nonsense that makes very good sense—and the implication would be—'There, that's what we've been trying to tell you.'"

Walt concluded, "I'd like to work it so that there's only one heavy in the picture and that's Beale and we can lay everything on her. Have no other heavy, you see? The thing that makes the whole story pay off is that there is a conflict between Beale and her theory on how children should be handled—there should be no nonsense at all—everything has to drive toward something practical."

There were vast differences of opinion on how Miss Beale's villainy should be shown. It was suggested a jealousy of Ellen Terry, pleasure in the merciless domination of Grove (who it was discussed making Alice's uncle or father rather than just a guardian), inhumane punishment of Alice, or actually discovering Carroll's identity to use as blackmail to prevent him from helping Alice.

Walt stated, "But to strengthen the whole thing, Beale is trying to bring this child up in a certain way. When she comes back from Dodgson's, the child has come back with a certain amount of nonsense and a certain philosophy along those lines. If he has said, for example, 'Going through life with nothing but Sense is like trying to run a race with one foot'. Well, now that's a heck of a philosophy to give a child—in other words, it clashes with what Beale is trying to do."

For the final scene, Walt suggested, "Maybe in the last scene we see Mr. Carroll with all these little characters around him and all of a sudden he turns into the little character we want him to be. We can just make a tag ending. Suddenly, the whole thing changes. We make an overlap right on into this fantasy and don't go into any other scenes. Everybody's happy. Grove is all right and when the Queen comes you can bring Miss Terry and her mother in. Everybody can be happy while this is happening. It's a natural place to bring everybody together."

Earlier, Walt had suggested, "There is this chance to have a scene in the end where they all go on a picnic—there is Dodgson, Grove, Alice, Terry, Mrs. Terry, and the new governess. And the new governess is not so bad to look at, and it is quite a change for Grove, so Grove becomes a sort of comic figure in a way. Or there is another play. There could be a suggestion that Mrs. Terry and Grove become rather friendly. But we could do the same thing through the new governess who is an entirely different character. That could be a very happy setting and you would leave with a very happy thought."

It has been stated that Walt rejected Huxley's script because it was too "literary" and he could only understand every third word. Reading the story meeting notes it is more likely that Walt just felt it didn't capture what he wanted. Apparently, Walt did comment that the approach was "too literary" for his tastes but judging from the story meeting notes, Walt was actively excited about shaping the story into something workable.

Huxley's wife, Maria, later stated, "this was the first movie he [Huxley] liked doing".

Unfortunately, a massive fire in 1961 destroyed more than four thousand of Huxley's annotated books and documents, including his involvement on the *Alice* project. Fortunately, the Disney Archives does have some of the story meeting notes, some memorandums, the fourteen page treatment and thirty-one pages of the script written by Huxley.

At the end of World War II, Walt was eager to get into production of full-length animated features and began work on *Cinderella*, *Alice in Wonderland* and *Peter Pan*. So instead of a live-action/animation mix, Alice became full animation and veered from the original Tenniel illustrations to the more modernistic design work of Mary Blair. When the animated feature was released in 1951, it contained no elements from Huxley's work.

Ward Kimball who animated the Cheshire Cat and the Mad Tea Party scene for the film revealed, "I think perhaps the decision to make *Alice* was based fifty percent on the fact that we sorely needed another feature at the time because a lot of animators had to be kept busy. Disney had many, many artists on the payroll during this period, and he preferred to keep them working on his own projects rather than to let them seek employment elsewhere between features.

"Surely an economic factor here was the combination of *Alice's* good name as a famous property and the fact that many animators were out of work. Also, because of the story's episodic nature, Walt could quickly assign different people to different sequences or characters without worrying too much about hook-ups between the sequences."

Audiences and critics didn't care for the film on its initial release and even Kimball referred to it as a "loud-mouthed vaudeville show. There's no denying that there are many charming bits in our Alice, but it lacks warmth and an overall story glue."

"Walt thought it didn't have any emotional appeal," stated storyman Winston Hibler. "As he said himself, there was no heart in Alice. You really didn't pull for her. She was a mischievous, adventuresome gal and you never really felt sorry for her. I really think that he made Alice almost out of a sense of duty to the public, that he was expected to make it, so he made it. I think he worked extremely hard on it, and probably gave it as much or more of himself in an effort to make it satisfying and rewarding to himself."

What did Huxley think of the final animated film? "He was a real *Alice* fan and he was particularly complimentary about the talking doorknob sequence. After he had said how really 'Carrollesque' it was, Walt said, 'But we invented that. There was no talking doorknob.' Which is true," said Hibler.

## SECRET ORIGIN OF THE ARISTOCATS

*The Aristocats* premiered December 24, 1970, almost forty years ago and is rarely discussed, even though it was really the first animated film made after Walt's death. *Jungle Book* was released a year after Walt's passing, but the perception was that, since it was in production during Walt's lifetime, it still included his spirit and direct input and was a final tribute to his contributions.

"*The Artistocats* reveals how essential Walt Disney was in shaping the studio's animated features—and how significant a gap he left. *Aristocats* was the first film made entirely after his death. The plot does little more than link a string of vaguely related episodes," said animation historian Charles Solomon in his movie review in the *Los Angeles Times* (April 9, 1987).

Certainly, there are major story issues from the inclusion of two giddy English geese and their drunken uncle (basted in white wine and the last voice work of the talented Bill Thompson known as the Little Ranger, White Rabbit and Mr. Smee) and two dim witted Southern American dogs (voiced by well known country performers Pat Buttram and George "Goober" Lindsey) in Belle Epoch France—and what the devil do all these diverse characters contribute to the story or the growth of the characters anyway?

How did a Sixties cat with love beads and indoor sunglasses end up in an all cat jazz band with distasteful stereotypes (remember the Chinese Cat with slanted eyes and buck teeth voiced by Paul Winchell?) when American jazz didn't really become popular in France until after World War I? Remember that this story is supposedly set in 1910 pre-war Paris, France.

There seems to be extensive "borrowing" from moments from other Disney films including the feeling that *Ev'rybody Wants To Be A Cat* is desperately trying to ape the song hit *I Wanna Be Like You* from *The Jungle Book*. Also, the defeat of one of Disney's weakest villains ever, Edgar the Butler (and why does he feel the desperate need to kill the cats when the Duchess is still in fine health? Is he planning on killing the Duchess now, as well?) by the animals is strongly reminiscent of Horace and Jasper's downfall in *101 Dalmatians*.

The film was released in December 1970 and was a box-office success, although critics were more than a little under-whelmed, especially after the charms of the previous release, *The Jungle Book*. Today, the little white kitten named Marie is a huge favorite of the Japanese Disney fans and there is a ton of merchandise featuring her. In fact, the Disney Channel considered making Marie and her brothers into teenagers and using them in a syndicated television series in 2003. In 2005, Disney announced it was going to do a direct-to-video sequel of the film, but that project was canceled in 2006 along with several other proposed sequels.

However, *The Aristocats* proves that every Disney movie is somebody's favorite and the film has many ardent fans. Perhaps the most fascinating thing about the film is its genesis.

Originally, it was to be a two-part live-action story for *Wonderful World of Color* and Walt was deeply involved and was also the one who decided the story would be better in animation.

It all begins with a gentleman named Harry Tytle. Tytle spent forty years at the Disney Studio, eventually becoming a producer on live-action films. He was well-liked and was close to Walt.

On December 9, 1961, Tytle was in London where Tom McGowan, who had directed some of the animal films for *Wonderful World of Disney* like *The Hound Who Thought He Was a Raccoon* (1963), lived with his family. Walt Disney was also in London at the time and suggested that Tytle make a deal with McGowan to find some animal stories for the Disney Studio. McGowan also developed *Born Free*, which he offered to the Disney Studio and Disney passed on the project.

By the New Year, McGowan had found several stories. One was a children's book about a mother cat and her kittens set in New York City. Tytle felt that a London location had added a significant element to the story of *101 Dalmatians* and suggested setting the story of the cats in Paris.

McGowan and Tytle worked out a rough storyline, assuming it would be done in live-action and run as a two-part television show that could later be combined into a theatrical release just as previous two part episodes had been done.

Originally, the story revolved around two servants (a butler and a maid) who were in line to inherit a fortune of an eccentric mistress after the pet cats died and focused on their feeble and foolish attempts to eliminate the felines. Then there was an extended section of the mother cat hiding the kittens to keep them out of danger in a variety of different homes and locales around Paris, France.

The concept was that the live-action cats talked to each other, much in the manner of the popular talking horse *Mr. Ed* television program. Walt was all in favor of the animals talking as long as it was not in the presence of humans. He felt it helped develop the animals' personalities and moved along the story line.

About two months later, when Tytle was in Rome supervising the shooting of *Escapade in Florence* (1962 starring Annette), McGowan brought him the story that had been written by Tom Rowe, an American writer then living in Paris. McGowan had paid for all of Rowe's expenses out of his own pocket. Rowe had an interesting career as a writer from starting as a film reviewer for *Variety* and moving on to writing scripts for television shows like *Fantasy Island* to films like *The Green Slime* (1968) and *Tarzan the Ape Man* (1981). He was also a painter with several exhibitions in Paris.

Tytle and McGowan spent a few days making revisions to Rowe's version. By August, they sent the completed script to Burbank, where it was returned as "rejected" by the Disney Studio.

However, this rejection did not come from Walt who had not seen the treatment but by underlings. Tytle was hesitant to contact Walt directly but that didn't stop McGowan who tracked Walt down in London and slipped the treatment into an envelope and delivered it to the front desk of the Conaught, the hotel where Walt was staying.

Walt liked the story and called McGowan at his home before McGowan had even returned from dropping off the envelope. Walt told McGowan that he would be seeing Tytle in Lisbon and they would go over the treatment. Tytle did meet with Walt in Lisbon and on the plane trip back to London, Walt told Tytle to buy the story, prepare it as a live-action feature that McGowan would direct and Tytle would produce.

Walt felt there was too much material in the script and suggested eliminating the musical kitten, as well as other cuts and revisions.

Beginning August 30, 1962, Tytle and McGowan worked for six straight days on working out a contract. The London Disney office actually amended the contract to cut McGowan in on any possible merchandising royalties. (This wasn't a problem when it was a live-action project. When it became an animation project, those rights were purchased back from McGowan.)

In January 1963, Tytle was in a London hospital for some surgery and during his recovery, he worked in his hospital room with McGowan and Rowe on revisions. The script was finally finished February 1st, and Tytle returned to Burbank to begin preparations for shooting in Paris.

In June, Walt showed Tytle a letter from Rowe. Apparently the writer was unhappy with the revisions to the script and in particular with Tytle who he felt was a "minion" of Walt's sent to corrupt the work. Walt, however, was happy with Tytle's work and allowed Tytle to respond to the letter himself. Tytle informed Rowe that it was just a difference of opinion and was sorry about his feelings on the matter but that Walt liked the changes and they would remain.

For a variety of reasons, the Disney Studio shelved the story for awhile and McGowan attempted to buy back the rights from Disney but was refused.

Since stories for animated films were becoming more difficult to come by, Tytle, in a discussion with Walt, suggested *The Aristocats* might make a good Disney animated feature.

The idea was run past Woolie Reitherman (who was then the supervising director on the animated features) and some of the key animators and they all agreed.

In August 1963, Walt asked for a copy of *The Aristocats* script and, two days later, Card Walker announced it would be the next animated feature. However work on the project didn't continue until May 1964.

In Tytle's diary for November 25, 1964, is the following entry of a discussion with Walt:

> *We spent some time discussing the idea. I told him of various gags and bits of business that were not in this script because when we were planning live-action, we had felt they were too 'cartoony,' but now could be used. For instance, where the mother cat uses her whiskers as radar, protecting her from the two servants. The other one I told him about was when the servants were in the cellar. They get locked in (the mother cat pushes the door shut) when digging a hole to bury the cats, they hit the water main, flooding the wine cellar. The butler grabs for a floating wine bottle, can't pour the contents into the already rising water, so drinks it, puts in a note (for help), then floats it out the cellar window. After doing this a couple of times, he gets 'high' and doesn't care about help coming. Walt felt the **Aristocats** should follow the same tack as **Dalmatians**. He said it would be good if the cats could talk amongst themselves, but never in front of humans. He seemed to especially like the various artists in the story, and the characters. He says when we get started, he would like the Sherman boys to come in and write songs. We discussed Waterloo (one of the kittens) and some of the earlier business that Walt had cut out. We have to stay to (just) three kittens, as there is too much business in the original treatment. Walt*

> *seemed to agree that the (family) history of the cats that was*
> *written by Tom Rowe was good, but extraneous.*

Studio nurse Hazel George asked for a copy of the script (apparently at Walt's suggestion), read it and returned it a few days later saying that she liked it very much and told Walt so. Walt valued George's opinion. Grace Bailey, head of the Ink and Paint department and another Disney employee whose opinion Walt respected, also read the script and liked it.

This leisurely process of delays on the film while work focused on other projects caused some problems after Walt's passing. Tytle was told he was to centralize his efforts on live-action and that Winston Hibler would take over *The Aristocats* project. Hibler ran into production troubles and Woolie Reitherman took over and Hibler was never again involved on animation projects. Major changes in the story were made.

"The part of the story that most intrigued Walt, that is, adoption into homes befitting the kittens' talents, was cut," Tytle remembered. "In my opinion, the resulting film lost the very element we tried to build, the Parisian atmosphere and characters, all the French charm. I honestly think the original story that Walt bought was much better. We didn't have a mouse in the original story; I, for one, felt it was a cliché and not vital to a cat story. For once, I wanted to do a cat story without a mouse."

Elsa Lanchester (who had been in *Mary Poppins* among many other credits) had been cast as the voice and live-action reference for the part of Elvira the maid who wanted to eliminate the kittens. However, after Walt's passing, the voice cast was recast and Elsa's role was eliminated. Much of the original business was thrown out and replaced with other things, including the geese.

After Walt's death, Rowe sued the studio claiming that, because he had written his sections, he was entitled, under French law, the rights to those characters, even though he acknowledged the original idea was not his own. Obviously, that claim wasn't supported by the Disney Studio and Rowe did not win his suit.

"It would have meant much more if the story that McGowan, Walt and I wrote had reached the screen, and had been left for the audience to judge. Thus ended my working on any cartoon product," Tytle said with a sigh.

In the final film, Tom McGowan and Tom Rowe are given credit for the story along with Disney storymen Larry Clemmons, Vance Gerry, Ken Anderson, Frank Thomas, Eric Cleworth, Julius Svendsen and Ralph Wright.

Walt did do some work on the story for *The Aristocats*, but his work was tossed aside in the final version. The publicity for the film claimed it was in production for over four years and cost over four million dollars. Perhaps if it had included some of the earlier work done on the story, it could indeed have been the cat's pajamas, an old fashioned term meaning incredible, rather than what some people consider kitty litter.

## SO DEAR TO MY HEART

*"Come One! Come All! To the Walt Disney County Fair!*
*Filled with music, laughter and heartwarming drama!"*
*proclaimed the theatrical poster for the Disney feature film* **So**
**Dear To My Heart***.*

It was the film that directly inspired the creation of Disneylandia and eventually Disneyland. There were plans for it to be the first all live action Disney film. A part of the film ended up in the backyard of animator Ward Kimball but it resulted in some unusual problems. A significant part of Walt Disney's personal childhood in Marceline is physically represented in the film including a classic structure that provided Walt with countless hours of private pleasure at his own home until his death. The film featured an Academy Award nominated song sung by "America's favorite balladeer" and gave him his first hit single. The book adaptation of the film was the first children's book illustrations by the legendary storyman Bill Peet who would later find a successful career as a children's book writer and illustrator.

Yet, this simple story of a boy and his black lamb is largely forgotten today even though it won the *Parent's Magazine* Box Office Award. *So Dear to My Heart* released nationwide on January 19, 1949 by RKO Radio Pictures is a sentimental snapshot of a bygone period close to the heart of Walt Disney. It was meant to be an affectionate and respectful look at country life at the turn of the century rather than to snicker at the antics of country yokels.

There is no huge melodramatic conflict. No villain is trying to foreclose on the farm. No natural disaster or illness threatens the family. There is no trauma over the fact that the young boy's parents have apparently been dead for quite some time. While the grandmother is practical and God-fearing, it never prevents the young boy from pretty much getting whatever he wants and overcoming obstacles like bees, bogs, a lost pet and poverty with relative ease.

Despite being pivotal in many ways, this Disney live action film has been largely ignored and undocumented in comparison with other Disney films. Surprisingly, the film influenced many other areas of the Disney history.

Sterling North was an acclaimed American author of books including 1963's bestselling autobiographical *Rascal*, the story of raising a baby raccoon that was eventually made into a Disney feature film. North's 1943 book *Midnight and Jeremiah* was the source material for *So Dear To My Heart*.

Set in1903, in the fictional Fulton Corners, Indiana, *So Dear to My Heart* tells the tale of a young boy named Jeremiah Kincaid (Bobby Driscoll fresh from his appearance in *Song of the South*) who adopts a rejected and mischievous black lamb named Danny (named after the famed champion race horse, Dan Patch, who was also black). Jeremiah's dream of entering Danny at the Pike County Fair is almost crushed by the objections of his loving but strict grandmother, Granny Kincaid (twice nominated Academy Award actress Beulah Bondi). Jeremiah's only adult ally seems to be the blacksmith, Uncle Hiram Douglas (Burl Ives in one of his very first film roles) although Jeremiah also gets encouragement from his animated daydreams, featuring the Wise Old Owl, that magically spring to life from his scrapbook. He is also supported by his best friend Tildy (Luana Patten also from *Song of the South*) although we never see her parents even at the Fair. Of course, there are tough challenges along the way, especially when the grown Danny in typical Disney film fashion becomes comically destructive and wrecks havoc on the farm and the local store. Eventually, Jeremiah does earn enough money to enter Danny at the Fair and there is a clever and satisfying ending.

"I knew I had found the perfect story for a new kind of motion picture when I read the book," claimed Walt in publicity for the film.

Walt had begun meeting about adapting the story with screenwriter Edwin Justus Mayer in 1945. The final credits list the screenplay by John Tucker Battle (the same screenwriter responsible for 1953's still frightening *Invaders from Mars*) with adaptation work by Maurice Rapf and Ted Sears (both of whom had done some preliminary story work on *Song of the South*). That same year, producer Perce Pearce had gone to Indiana in the summer of 1945 to get a sense of the atmosphere for *So Dear To My Heart*. Pearce would later do some second unit directing on the film.

The early scripts, including one from December 1945 did not feature any animation. However scripts from 1946 include sections for animated inserts as does the official budget for the film. An article in the June 30, 1946 *Los Angeles Times* stated the film would be "about 90 per cent live action. In that one, Walt will resort to cartoons only when nature can't provide his needs."

RKO salesmen argued that it would be hard to sell a Disney picture without cartoons so some feel that Walt was pushed into adding short animation sequences that sometimes feel intrusive. In actuality, Walt's contract with RKO indicated that the features he would make for RKO distribution "shall be animated cartoon or may be part animated cartoon and part live action". There was no provision for just a wholly live action feature and truthfully, when the public saw the name "Disney" there was the expectation of animation and that may be why the first two minutes of the film are completely animated.

"I saw the cartoon characters as figments of a small boy's imagination, and I think they were justified," said Walt in a later interview.

Disney Legend Hamilton Luske was the supervising director of the animation that according to the pressbook amounted to only fifteen percent of the total footage of the film. Story was credited to Marc Davis, Ken Anderson and Bill Peet. Animation was credited to Eric Larson, John Lounsbery, Hal King, Milt Kahl, Les Clark, Don Lusk, and Marvin Woodward. Art direction was done by Mary Blair, John Hench and Dick Kelsey.

Many of Blair's concept paintings done in a primitive quilt-inspired pattern still exist and there is a strong connection between these drawings and the designs of the completed film like the appearance of the Grundy store.

The animation is surprisingly good and it is interesting that these sequences are never discussed. Besides the standard character animation (featuring everything from a Scottish dancing spider to a threatening sea serpent to a professorial Wise Old Owl), there are some intriguing impressionistically designed scenes that would have stood out in an animated feature. While the film itself is often forgotten, it is puzzling why some of these self contained animated "lessons" didn't get re-used on other projects including the Disney television shows.

Walt Disney was fond of the film *My Friend Flicka* (1943) directed by Harold Schuster who over the years had risen in the ranks from actor to cameraman to finally being a director. In fact, Walt's wife and daughters loved the film so much that they ran it many times in their home theater. Under contract to 20th Century Fox, Schuster was lent to the Disney Studios to do the live action scenes for *So Dear To My Heart*. "The idea of working with Walt Disney appealed to me greatly," stated Schuster as he signed on to the project.

Schuster later claimed that the lamb was the hardest one to direct, even though it was often tempted with food to provide the appropriate actions. The lamb stole so many scenes that actor Burl Ives described the animal as "a ham in sheep's clothing". After he had finished filming a scene at the County Fair sheep judging, little Bobby Driscoll remarked, "Sheep and actors back to their pens!" It greatly amused the crew. Driscoll eventually was awarded a special Oscar as "Outstanding Juvenile Actor" for his work on this film and a non-Disney thriller, *The Window*.

Cinematographer Winton Hoch would go on to film *Darby O'Gill* and *The Little People* (1959) but Walt was quite familiar with his work since Hoch was the director of photography for the live action sequences in *Reluctant Dragon* (1941) and the live action Roy Rogers "Pecos Bill" segment from *Melody Time* (1948).

Filming began on April 30, 1946 and continued until August 23, 1946. Additional shooting was done on February 5, 1947 through March 28, 1947. Some filming was also done in May and August 1947. Initial filming went into late summer so the landscape had started to dry up. Every night twenty-seven greens men watered the soil and plants so they would look fresh and green for the next day's shooting. Temperatures exceeded a hundred degrees and while the cast and extras suffered in their heavily layered period costumes, cool air was pumped into the animal paddocks.

The movie was filmed, according to the official pressbook, around the homes and farms "amidst the grain fields, the orchards and vineyards, the alfalfa pastures, the cattle corral under the great spreading elms near Tulare, Visalia and Porterville" in the San Joaquin Valley about 250 miles north of Hollywood and supposedly some photography done in Sequoia National Park. Director Schuster described the San Joaquin Valley as "one of the loveliest valleys in the world".

Schuster suggested Beluah Bondi for the role of Granny. She was only fifty-six years old at the time but had the reputation of playing care worn mothers including the mom of Jimmy Stewart's characters in four films including *It's A Wonderful Life* (1946) and *Mr. Smith Goes To Washington* (1939). She actually played her first "old lady" part when she was just twenty years old. For the film, she had to learn to take care of sheep, plow a field, spin wool and work a loom. In the final film, she does these activities and more as if she had been doing them all her life.

Schuster also chose beloved character actor Harry Carey for the part of the County Fair judge. Carey was well known for his work in silent Westerns and had the persona of a man of integrity and authority which is why Schuster wanted him. Sadly, Carey died before the film was released but after all principal photography had been done.

Unusually, some interior sets like the Grundy store were actually built on location since the Disney Studio at the time had only one small stage. Schuster told noted film historian Leonard Maltin, "They found an old, and I mean old, hardware store near the town of Porterville. It was closed, and the various wares inside were bought lock, stock and barrel and moved into the Grundy store. Both the barn and Granny's house were built on the location. The railroad station was already there as were the railroad tracks. We rented the old engine and cars from Paramount, who had used them for *Union Pacific* (1939)."

According to Disney publicity, "Old No. 99 of the Evansville and Indianapolis Railroad as it is labeled for the (Technicolor film) was actually one of the Virginia and Truckee Railroad's venerable engines, long since retired." Reportedly, it first saw service in 1875.

Close to five hundred local residents gathered daily at the set to perform as background extras "dressed in the period clothes of their forbears, providing the familiar farm chores and animals and the behavior of farmers at their fairs and picnics half a century ago. Disney personally supervised much of the action." At least Walt supposedly did that according to the publicity releases that also pointed out Walt helped supervise the train scenes.

Shuster told Maltin that "Walt would come up sometimes on weekends. We would have Sunday breakfast, and talk over the rushes. He was a very enthusiastic gentleman, and a joy to be around. His suggestions were always presented as suggestions only. He left the reins firmly in my hands."

"*So Dear* was especially close to me. Why, that's the life my brother and I grew up with as kids out in Missouri. The great racehorse, Dan Patch, was a hero to us. We had Dan Patch's grandson on my father's farm," claimed Walt Disney when the film was released.

To promote the film, Walt, actress Beulah Bondi and the child stars went on a tour that included Nashville and Chicago. While the film itself was not as profitable in its initial release or re-releases as some other Disney films, it inspired many pivotal moments in Disney history. Here are just a few:

*The barn from the film was recreated in Walt's backyard and provided him endless hours of pleasure.*

Working as an architect at the Disney studio was John Cowles Jr., the son of Dr. John Cowles who had been a financial supporter of Walt Disney's first animation studio that produced the Laugh-O-Grams cartoons. In addition to his set designs, Cowles Jr. also helped plan many of the permanent buildings at the Burbank studio as well as the blueprint for the layout of Walt's backyard railroad, the Carolwood Pacific.

Cowles Jr. was responsible for designing the authentic red barn in *So Dear To My Heart* that reminded Walt so strongly of the one from his own childhood on a farm in Marceline, Missouri. Walt had Cowles Jr. adapt that same structure for Walt's backyard workshop. The only variations in that new building was a concrete slab foundation, windows along the east wall and a small room housing the central track control board for Walt's railroad. So a piece of *So Dear To My Heart* remained close to Walt until his death and it was one of his favorite locations to get away from the burdens of work and just have fun.

*The railroad station from the film ended up in the backyard of animator Ward Kimball.*

A long time railroad buff, Kimball designed the railroad depot in *So Dear To My Heart* based upon a Lehigh Valley Railroad flag depot at Pottsville, New York. After the filming, Walt (perhaps in a good mood after accompanying Kimball to the Chicago Railroad Fair) decided that Kimball's backyard Grizzly Flats railroad needed a train station and a Disney studio truck delivered the disassembled train station building from the film to Ward's home in San Gabriel. It was an unexpected and appreciated gift until Kimball tried to re-assemble it.

Kimball claimed it was like a jigsaw puzzle trying to put the unmarked pieces back together on a concrete foundation. However, he was even more frustrated when he had a big crane put the roof on the final structure and the whole thing collapsed. It was only a movie set so it only had three sides and there was not enough framing to support the roof. Kimball had to start over from scratch but was able to salvage the roof, the windows and the doors. Kimball never revealed to Walt at the time how much extra effort and expense it took to rebuild the depot.

Years later, Walt decided that the depot would be perfect for the railroad stop in Frontierland in the new Disneyland theme park he was building and it would save some money to have Kimball simply return the train station. Kimball refused and finally revealed how he had to completely rebuild the building. Walt ordered the station built in Frontierland according to the same blueprints but with the addition of double doors, covered loading platforms on both ends and a separate freight office. Decades later, it was used as one of the sets for the *Two Brothers* short film run at the Disney theme parks including as a segment in the American Adventure pavilion film at Epcot and the *Great Moments With Mr. Lincoln* pre-show film at Disneyland.

*Before there was Disneyland, Walt had toyed with a concept
entitled Disneylandia that would entail several three
dimensional mechanical miniature exhibits in train baggage
cars that would travel the country. Walt imagined people,
especially school children, visiting their local train station to
learn about their history and heritage. The first tableau was
inspired by the film.*

Walt was quite skilled at making miniatures. Working from
plans that Imagineer Ken Anderson adapted from *So Dear To
My Heart*, Walt personally built Granny Kincaid's cabin from
the film. It was a 1/8th scale mockup and is now showcased
at the *One Man's Dream* attraction at Disney Hollywood Studios
in Orlando, Florida. Walt displayed his hand built model at the
Los Angeles Pan Pacific Auditorium in November 1952 as part
of the "Festival of Living" show.

To build the chimney, Walt picked up pebbles at his vacation
home, the Smoke Tree Ranch, in Palm Springs. Inside, a hand-
braided rag rug warmed a floor of planks not much larger than
matchsticks. A china washbowl and pitcher, guitar with strings
thin as cat whiskers and a small family Bible sat on the table.
A tiny flintlock rifle hung on the wall, and a spinning wheel
with flax sat in the corner. The scene looked as if Granny
herself had just stepped away from her small rocking chair to
go outside but viewers heard Granny's voice describing the
cozy scene. Walt had recorded a narration by Beulah Bondi,
the famous character actress who played Granny in *So Dear to
My Heart*.

"This little cabin is part of a project I am working on,
and it was exhibited as a test to obtain the public's reaction
to my plans for a complete village," Walt explained in a 1953
interview. Walt was later convinced that the Disneylandia

project would not be able to generate enough income to maintain the exhibits and only a small handful of people at a time could enjoy the experience. The project evolved into the full sized Disneyland.

*So Dear To My Heart also provided the first opportunity for legendary Disney storyman Bill Peet to illustrate a children's book.*

In 1950, Simon and Schuster released a one hundred and twenty-six page Golden Story Book (GS-12) of the film with text by Helen Palmer and illustrations by Bill Peet. (This was one of a series of twenty books that included two other Disney titles: *Mystery in Disneyville* and *Donald Duck and the Hidden Gold*.) Peet would later find success and acclaim as a children's book writer and artist. His first book is usually considered *Hubert's Hair-Raising Adventure* in 1959 but in actuality, this film adaptation was his first published artwork in any children's book. He provided ink and watercolor drawings for almost every page of the book very much in the same style that would be evident in his own books. It was not unusual for Disney artists to moonlight by doing illustrations especially for Disney related storybooks and comic books. Other Disney artists from John Hench to Mary Blair to Bill Justice to Retta Scott and many more provided outstanding work for Disney related children's storybooks. Unfortunately, the lack of success of the film has resulted in this particular book never being reprinted.

*So Dear To My Heart provided "America's favorite Balladeer" (as the pressbook described singer Burl Ives) with his first hit single.*

Burl Ives was a collector and performer of authentic American folk songs and at the time of the film was perhaps best known for his appearances on radio and various concerts. He had been performing for well over a decade when he recorded songs for the film. *Lavender Blue (Dilly Dilly)* was an English folk song and nursery rhyme that dated from the seventeenth century. Disney song writers Eliot Daniel and Larry Morey did an adaptation of the tune for the film and it was sung by Ives. It was nominated for an Academy Award for Best Song. It was Ives' first hit single.

Daniel and Morey contributed two other songs to the score: *Ol' Dan Patch* and *Stick-To-It-Ivity*. By the way, Daniel was later responsible for the *I Love Lucy* theme song. The title tune *So Dear To My Heart* was from Ticker Freeman and Irving Taylor. Mel Torme provided the lyrics for Robert Wells' music for the song *County Fair*. Bondi and Ives duet on the traditional folk song, *Billy Boy*. While the publicity for the film prominently proclaimed that Ives would also sing the traditional folk song, *Sourwood Mountain*, that song does not appear in the final film. Apparently other folk songs were cut as well.

However, the most important thing about the film is its stated moral: "It's what you do with what you got." Certainly that philosophy was important back then in a kinder, more innocent time but even more so today.

Animation historian John Culhane has claimed it was a phrase that Walt said frequently. It's not hard to imagine that it was a philosophy that Walt would agree with completely. One of the reasons Walt wanted to recapture the nostalgic memories of his youth with this film was to remind himself of what he did with what he had been given.

# TOBY TYLER

*"Strike up the Band! Here Comes the Happiest Show on
Earth! Roaring with Thrills! Ringing with Laughter!"*

Those colorful advertising phrases seem a trifle excessive
to describe one of Walt Disney's unassuming formulaic live-
action films that achieved its modest intentions at the time
quite successfully.

The year 2010 marked the 50th anniversary of the Disney
live-action film, *Toby Tyler*. While it is not considered a classic
film, it is still an enjoyable experience and, like most of the
live-action films made during Walt Disney's lifetime, it has
some delightful little touches and some production stories that
deserve documentation.

*Toby Tyler*, or *Ten Weeks with a Circus*, was the first novel by
James Otis Kaler. It was originally serialized in *Harper's Young
People* in 1877 and then was later collected and published as a
book in 1881. It became a very popular book for young boys
over the years. Writer Carl Sandburg told people that *Toby Tyler*
was one of his favorite books. Writer Harlan Ellison claimed
that it inspired him to run away and join a carnival.

Basically, the film recounts the story of an orphan who,
after being verbally abused by his poor struggling "uncle",
runs away to join the circus. Toby gets a job as a concessionaire
selling lemonade, peanuts and candy apples under the tutelage
of Harry Tupper, a slick con man who takes Toby's tips and
keeps secret the fact that Toby's uncle and aunt need Toby
back at the farm. Toby is befriended by the circus strongman
and one of the clowns and eventually gets a chance to perform
in an equestrian act. Along the way, Toby makes friends with

a mischievous chimp named Mr. Stubbs who is constantly causing trouble for Toby.

The novel is much darker than the Disney film—with a fat and lazy Toby being punished in a brutal orphan home for his dishonesty and Mr. Stubbs a much older less cuter monkey who dies after being shot, among many other significant changes, including Toby giving up his life with the circus to return to the orphanage for what is implied will be a difficult life.

However, the story of a young boy in a small town running away to join a traveling "mud show" type of circus as a refreshment "concessionaire" appealed to Walt Disney. As a child, Walt saw his first circus parade in Marceline, Missouri, and attempted to create his own circus in his family barn with cats dressed up in his little sister's doll clothes. When he was fifteen years old, Walt worked one summer as a news butcher for the Van Noyes Interstate News Company on trains that went to a half-dozen different states. Selling newspapers, popcorn, peanuts, fruit, cold drinks, and other snacks to the passengers from the box strapped over his shoulders was supposedly one of the happiest periods of his life.

"Everyone loves a circus and I'm no exception. I've been fascinated by the clowns and the animals, the music and the excitement ever since I worked in one of these wonderful shows for a few days as a youngster," wrote Walt in the introduction to the program of *The Mickey Mouse Club* Circus at Disneyland in 1955.

The publicity material for the film quotes Walt as saying, "What a spectacle! A treat for the youngsters who have never seen a circus and for their elders who remember it."

Kevin Corcoran was discovered at the age of six by Walt Disney who dubbed him "the typical American kid" and cast him in the role of "Moochie" in several productions including *The Further Adventures of Spin and Marty*, *Moochie of the Little League* and *Moochie of Pop Warner Football*. *Toby Tyler* was his third theatrical Disney film—he was roughly eleven years old. Kevin had previously appeared in *Old Yeller* (1957) and *The Shaggy Dog* (1959).

During the production of the picture, Corcoran's father had just died, but the crew on the film remember little Kevin being the professional trouper and finishing the film without incident with his mother at his side. He performed his own stunts on the horse, although he was connected to piano wires as a safety precaution. His co-star, Mr. Stubbs, received much more publicity and attention than he did.

Mr. Stubbs was born in 1956 in the Belgian Congo jungle. When only a few months old, he was captured and shipped to Portland, Maine, with fifteen other young chimpanzees. In 1957, he was bought by Gene Detroy, the trainer and creator of the famous "Marquis Family" of four performing chimps. Mr. Stubbs was actually officially known as "Marquis Jr." and Walt was intrigued when he saw the chimp perform on a 1959 episode of the Jack Benny television show. Publicity for the film claimed that Mr. Stubbs had the intelligence of a three year old child, had been purchased for $1,000, but was insured for $12,000 and often wore $75 suits. He lived at a spacious ranch in Las Vegas with Detroy and his family.

"He puts on the most convincing act since Cheetah talked to Tarzan," claimed director Charles Barton, "After a rehearsal or two, he knows the scene backward. Then we get around to doing it forward. When I first met him in Las Vegas, he was watching television with Detroy's three children. We shook hands. After the kids went to bed, he looked in on them from time to time to be sure they were all right. It was a very pleasant evening. I haven't gotten over it yet. He has looks, talent and real humility. And when he rolls those big brown eyes, wow! He even works for peanuts."

Previously for Disney, Charles Barton had directed the *New Adventures of Spin and Marty*, several episodes of *Zorro* and the film *The Shaggy Dog*. Barton had a long history of being a competent professional when it came to directing B movies on shoestring budgets, including several Abbott and Costello comedies, but was not known for his innovation or anything that would identify a distinctive directorial style. He finished his career directing a number of television shows, including being the principal director for *Family Affair*. Barton had worked with Corcoran in both *New Adventures of Spin and Marty* and *The Shaggy Dog*.

*Toby Tyler* not only reunited Barton and Corcoran from *The Shaggy Dog*, but also writers Lillie Hayward and Bill Walsh (Walsh was also producer on both films.)

A lively seventy-two year old Ollie Wallace who composed many memorable melodies for Disney cartoons (beginning in the late 1930s) and live-action films (but not *Toby Tyler*) made his on-screen film introduction as the enthusiastic bandleader. He would pass away in 1963. That is Jimmy Macdonald, the voice of Mickey Mouse and member of the musical group, the Firehouse Five Plus Two, as the drummer.

Several actual circus acts were featured in the film: The Flying Viennas was a famous aerialist act (including Del and Babs Graham) that was performing with Ringling Brothers at the time; The Jungleland Elephants came from Jungleland in Thousand Oaks, California that supplied animals for television and the movies and were probably handled by Eugene "Arky" Scott who also trained Bimbo for the *Circus Boy* television series.

The clowns were identified as from Ringling Brothers and included Eddie "Spaghetti" Emerson who was 75, "Duke" Johnson who was 63, and his son Harry who was about twenty years younger.

Abe "Korkey" Goldstein was 64 at the time. Known as "Korkey the Komic Kop," Goldstein had appeared most frequently before circus audiences as the keeper of several mutt dogs who would fall dead as Goldstein emptied a toy gun at them and then miraculously arose to bite him on his rear end. He died in 1990 at age 94, spending his last years performing free at hospitals and children's clubs while still awaiting another professional job offer.

On July 2, 1959, Disney filed a lawsuit against ABC. The network has stated that it would not be renewing the *Zorro* series because it cost so much to produce, but that Disney was contractually bound not to offer the program to another television network because ABC had exclusive rights.

Henry Calvin played the buffoonish Sergeant Garcia and Gene Sheldon portrayed Bernardo, the "deaf-mute" servant of Don Diego, in that popular series. Because Walt assumed that the lawsuit would get resolved quickly and filming would resume on the series, he wanted to keep the two actors around, so they were cast in *Toby Tyler*. Calvin was the strongman with the soft heart, Ben Cotter. Sheldon was the gentle and articulate clown with a dog act, Sam Treat. They were also cast in *Babes in Toyland* (1961). Guy Williams, Zorro himself, was making a lucrative living doing personal appearances as the character and was still on full salary from the Disney Studio, as well.

Eventually four new hour-long episodes were shown on the weekly *Walt Disney Presents* series in 1961 and the contract dispute with ABC was resolved. However, with the move of the weekly Disney television series to NBC in full color, and the assumed declining interest in *Zorro*, the series was never revived and none of the three actors appeared in another Disney production after 1962.

The circus parade at the beginning of the film was staged by assistant director Arthur Vitarelli on the Western street on the Disney Studios backlot. Amazingly, Vitarelli was able to have it done in one continuous shot (using multiple cameras) that completed filming by noon. Lining up all the wagons and people meant the procession snaked through the backlot's Residential Street and out the studio gate onto Buena Vista Street in front of the studio.

In the days before computer-generated imagery, special segments had to be created live, including the few seconds of "auguste" clown Gene Sheldon leading his line of mixed-breed dogs, who were dressed in elephant heads, down the dusty main street.

Animal trainer William Koehler, who worked with many animals on Disney films like *The Shaggy Dog*, *Swiss Family Robinson*, *The Incredible Journey*, *That Darn Cat* and others, remembered that brief gag almost led to disaster in his book The *Wonderful World of Disney Animals* (Howell Book House Inc. 1979):

"Where else would a trainer be asked to teach dogs to wear elephant costumes and parade single file, trunk to tail?" Koehler said. "First of all came lots of careful measuring by our Special Effects department. In between fittings, we worked the dogs in harnesses that were linked together with wood shafts so that they would become accustomed to the positions and speed of the parade order."

However all the training in the world, did not prepare Koehler for what happened next after he took all five dogs to Stage Four and fitted them into their costumes.

"Except for size, the latex costumes appeared real to sight. Each elephant head was molded smoothly into the body shell and tail assembly, regardless of each dog's size and form. A traditional ornamental star was cut in the center of each forehead. A narrow vertical bar of the material was left in the middle of the star to strengthen the forehead. Many fittings had conditioned the dogs to their costumes and they stood, tails wagging and responsive to the attention, while their heads and body skirtings were fastened."

"Ginger" the tallest was at the front of the line of dogs to be led by actor Gene Sheldon. When "Ginger" started forward with the dogs following as they had been trained, a strange thing happened. The procession stopped abruptly. A smaller dog, "Mouse" fell over on his side and laid very quiet and still. Another dog, "Rags" was next to topple. Within seconds the entire parade was lying on its side and scattered on the ground.

The trainers rushed to the dogs and immediately removed the costumes. Slowly, the dazed canines revived and showed no ill effects. It was as if they had been hypnotized. Animals can be placed in a trance by unusual conditions or a "forced focus" as when a chicken is placed with its eyes to a line drawn on a pavement.

"On a hunch," said Koehler, "I picked up a mask and put it to my face. If a dog looked through the eye holes, there was no line. But if he chose to look through the star, there was the bar in the middle. Right in the middle of his focus as he moved along would be an endless line. It only took a few minutes for a workman to snip out the bars. We put the costumes back on the dogs and re-established the line. No dog seemed stressed or even suspicious. Once more we started our parade across the big sound stage. Ten feet. Twenty feet. No stops. No falls. There were mixed sighs of relief and cheers as our 'elephants' paraded across the stage in the best circus tradition."

Just as the parade and the credits are ending, the Dragon Calliope comes in to view and is followed by the eager Toby Tyler as music and steam billow from the colorful wagon.

The Tri-Circle-D Ranch at the Fort Wilderness Resort and Campground at Walt Disney World is now the home for the famous Dragon Calliope. This calliope, discovered in disrepair, was included with the nine wagons Walt Disney purchased from the Bradley and Kaye Amusement Park for possible use at Disneyland. Originally it debuted in the Mugivan and Bowers shows in England circa 1907. It was sold to Ken Maynard's Diamond K Circus in 1936. Disney re-designed it to resemble the others in the collection, at a cost of $50,000 in order to house the refurbished steam-powered musical instrument. The wagon was adorned with decorative pieces from some of the other circus wagons in Disney's possession.

The calliope was part of the short-lived Disneyland *Mickey Mouse Club* Circus Parade in 1955. The calliope went on to appear at Disneyland parades up until Disneyland's 25th Anniversary (where it was repainted silver and blue and pulled by six black Percherons), and then it was relocated to Florida for the Walt Disney World *Tencennial* celebration in 1981, where it was seen in numerous parades, including several Christmas broadcasts.

Walt purchased nine authentic circus wagons from the Bradley & Kaye Amusement Park at the corner of Beverly and La Cienga boulevards in Los Angeles that had been sitting there as a sort of a backdrop for the entertainment venue. Later, Walt purchased an additional five wagons that had been used in the Jimmie Wood Los Angeles based circus that had fallen into disrepair.

In 1962, Walt would donate these wagons to the Circus World Museum in Baraboo, Wisconsin, where they are taken care of and are displayed to this day. However, at the time of filming *Toby Tyler*, many of these classics were called into service to recreate a turn-of-the-century traveling circus.

Ben Cotter and Toby Tyler ride on the Golden Bros. Cage wagon from 1910, which was originally yellow, but painted blue for the film. The wagon houses the impish Mr. Stubbs. This antique was actually tipped over in the film without any movie trickery (other than a stunt double substituting for Kevin Corcoran).

The Beauty Wagon from 1883 has a set of four female harem statues with exposed breasts. The opening parade shows an uncensored version of the wagon, but, later in the film, when Ben Cotter tosses the villainous Harry Tupper into a lake, the Beauty Wagon in the background shows the female figures demurely covered with sack dresses.

The office wagon in the film is actually the Lady and the Lion Tableau wagon from 1917. To use it as the office in the film, the Disney carpenters had to remove the beautiful center carvings and replace them with a door on one side and a window on the other.

Many of the other wagons Disney purchased can be seen briefly in the film including the Carl Hagenback Cage (housing the two tigers) from 1905, J.H. Eschman Bandwagon from 1915, Christy Bros. Canvas Wagon and more.

*Toby Tyler* was the first film to be shot at the Golden Oak Ranch since it was purchased by the Disney Studio. Mr. Stubbs is shot in a glade with the great oak where Francisco Lopez once discovered some gold flakes leading to a minor gold rush on the property.

*Toby Tyler* had its world premiere January 21, 1960 at the Florida Theater in Sarasota, Florida, the winter home of the Ringling Brothers Barnum and Bailey Circus now owned and operated by Feld Entertainment who produce the *Disney on Ice* shows.

The film captures the spirit of a turn of a century rural American circus and provides a much happier ending than its original source material for this story of the happiest little show on earth.

# LT. ROBIN CRUSOE U.S.N.

The story idea for *Lt. Robin Crusoe, U.S.N.* is credited to "Retlaw Yensid" ("Walter Disney" spelled backward.). Walt Disney himself came up with the idea for the story and for the one and only time in the history of the Disney Studio received a story credit on a Disney film.

"It's the only story that Walt ever wrote (for a live action film). He wrote it on the back of an envelope on the plane or the back of a throw-up bag or whatever it is. At the end of it I said, 'Walt, you don't want your name on this, do you?' And he said, 'I do too!' And by gosh he did and he got it," recalled Bill Walsh who was credited as co-writer of the screenplay and co-producer.

Walt gave an interview to reporter Sean O'Neil of the *Honolulu Advertiser* in the summer of 1965 when filming for *Lt. Robin Crusoe, U.S.N.* was taking place on the island of Kauai.

"The Retlaw Yensid is an old joke we've had around the Studio for years. I started using my name backward on the slate to identify the scenes," Walt told the reporter. "This will be the first time it has been used in the credits."

"Dad pitched the concept of *Lt. Robin Crusoe* to Ron and me, wanting to encourage us to become a writing team," wrote Diane Disney Miller, Walt's daughter. "I wasn't taken with the idea at all, and had six children who took up all of my time and a large house and yard. That was my career of choice, and I cherished it. He finally did it himself."

On May 7,1965, the Disney family left for Kauai to visit the location filming for *Lt. Robin Crusoe, U.S.N.*

Lawai-Kai, the estate of Queen Emma, wife of King Kamehameha IV who planted a number of plants that are still there today in the Allerton Garden, was used for additional beach scenes. Its 125-acre botanical gardens doubled for the dense jungle through which Crusoe fled from a group of spear carrying native girls.

"The location was really a wonderful time for us," wrote Diane. "We left the youngest, Ronnie, who wasn't quite two years old, home with the wonderful FouFou (Thelma Howard, the Disney housekeeper) and spent about three weeks at the Waiohai Hotel with mom and dad, Bill and Nolie Walsh, the Van Dykes, Byron Paul and his family. The Van Dykes were a wonderful family. Dick's a superb human being as well as a great talent."

The film does not take place in Hawaii but like in so many other Hollywood productions, Hawaii was substituting for a tropical paradise.

The first unit rolled on a Monday and folded on a Friday, departing for the mainland after a week of shooting in and out of the rain. The second unit put in three weeks, starting before the first and wrapping a week later. While there was some location shooting, most of the picture was filmed on the Disney Studio backlot.

Art directors Carroll Clark and Carl Anderson and set decorators Emile Kuri and Frank R. McKelvy had to match the Wailua Beach locale from Kauai so they transported tons of white sand from nearby Pacific beaches along with palm trees and tropical plants. A tropical lagoon was also created on the backlot in the area known as Berm One for additional exterior shooting but for the actors' comfort and safety the pool had an elaborate filtering and heating system installed. Crusoe's bamboo house was recreated as both an interior and exterior set. The immense stone idol, Kaboona, surrounded by jungle growth that was a key element in the film's climax took over one of the Disney Studio largest sound stages, Stage 2.

The film begins when Lt. Robin Crusoe, played by Dick Van Dyke, flies a routine mission in the Pacific but has to parachute to safety in the sea when the plane has a malfunction.

Adrift for days at sea and menaced by a threatening shark, he finally finds himself on a deserted jungle island. He soon discovers an odd set of footprints and follows them to a beached World War II Japanese submarine that is now the home for Floyd, an astro-chimp who has survived a misadventure in space.

Together, utilizing materials from the submarine, the pair build a bamboo hut and a golf course. One day, in the sand trap, they discover another set of footprints that lead them to a beautiful native girl played by Nancy Kwan. Crusoe names her "Wednesday" and discovers she has been exiled to the island by her father, played by Akim Tamiroff, for refusing to marry his choice for her husband. Soon, Wednesday's sisters and female cousins join her to also escape the tyranny of the chief. The following morning war canoes arrive and there is a confrontation. The two warring factors march off to consult the great stone idol, Kaboona.

However, Crusoe and Floyd have rigged the idol with flashing eyes, fiery breath, and booming voice to scare off the warriors but unfortunately, one of the tricks backfires and, as they say, hilarity ensues.

The chief isn't really as bad as expected and he admits his defeat and joins Crusoe and the girls in a victory celebration. Unfortunately, when Crusoe starts to dance he doesn't realize he is actually performing the marriage dance with Wednesday and then finds he can't talk his way out of it.

In the nick of time, a Navy helicopter rescues Crusoe and Floyd and returns them to the aircraft carrier where one final surprise awaits.

Also in the film is an Audio-Animatronics mynah bird who seems to have escaped from the Enchanted Tiki Room at Disneyland who constantly argues with Crusoe, but then disappears midway through the film.

Like most of the Disney films of the time, a lot of award-winning talent was assigned to make this story come to life.

Believe it or not, Dick Van Dyke's first encouragement to act professionally came while serving in the Army Air Corps, where a fellow airman nabbed him to be an announcer on *Flight Time*, an Air Force radio program. That friendship even led to them working up an act together with Dick as the straight man and his friend as the comedian but the act was terrible.

Eventually, that friend who was named Byron Paul became Van Dyke's personal manager and was the director of *Lt. Robin Crusoe, U.S.N.* After his military stint, Paul pursued a career in television, first as a cameraman and then later as a director. He went on to direct several thousand television shows between 1949 and 1961, including episodes of *Gunsmoke*, *Ben Casey* and *Have Gun, Will Travel*.

He had also directed a number of the Disney television shows including *A Taste of Melon*, *Treasure in the Haunted House*, *The Tenderfoot* and the first three episode series of the *Gallegher* stories.

It was Paul who helped Van Dyke negotiate a four-picture deal with Disney with *Lt. Robin Crusoe, U.S.N.* being the first of the four. However, there must have been some re-negotiation later because Van Dyke only appeared in one other Disney film, *Never a Dull Moment* in 1968.

Bill Walsh who co-wrote the screenplay with Don DaGradi was also the co-producer of the film along with Ron Miller. Walsh had a long and varied career at the Disney Studio from writing the Mickey Mouse comic strip to scripting the first two big Disney Christmas shows for television in 1950 and 1951.

As a writer/co-producer, Walsh was responsible for Disney films like *The Shaggy Dog*, *The Absent-Minded Professor*, *Bon Voyage*, *Son of Flubber* and, most impressively, *Mary Poppins*.

The musical director of the film was Bob Brunner who scored some of the *Wonderful World of Color* programs and films like *That Darn Cat*. For this film, he found his inspiration in the traditional songs and chants and various dialects of the Polynesian people.

According to a press release: "Brunner conducted an extensive preliminary research program which then resulted in one of the most exciting musical scores to emanate from a Disney film. Largely Polynesian in mood and tempo, the background accompaniment varies from lilting island themes, broken, occasionally by a haunting oriental strain to the pulsating rhythms of a ceremonial dance and the frantic staccato beat of an exciting chase.

"Brunner was so inspired by the melody and fluidity of the Tahitian dialect that he gave each of his original musical themes an appropriate title, borrowing words and phrases from the language. Among these are colorful titles like 'Mahana Toru' (Wednesday), 'Mataro Vahine' (Girl Sailors), 'Tamahine Ata Ata' (Giggling Daughters), 'Hora Rahi Mahi' (Clock Bird) and 'Tama'I Nui' (Big Fight)."

While working on the film, Van Dyke was quoted as saying, "People enjoy laughing, and movie makers are gradually waking up to that fact. Disney has always been aware of this."

Van Dyke's wife, Marjorie, makes an unbilled cameo appearance in the film. She is seen in the photo that the Crusoe character has of his girlfriend, Jane, whom he missed marrying when his plane went down. In the film, Crusoe writes to Jane of his misadventures on the island. The Wednesday character gets jealous when she sees the photo. Marjorie was "disguised" in the photo with a long blonde wig.

"I knew I'd be working with a chimp, so the first morning he was on the set I went over to have a look at him," recalled Van Dyke. "He was good-sized, about 130 pounds, and he was sitting in a director's chair. I stood there drinking coffee out of a Styrofoam cup and smoking a cigarette, when he crooked his finger to beckon me closer. He reached out, took the cigarette and coffee and he smoked the cigarette and drank the coffee. So every morning for the next three months I brought that monkey a cigarette and a cup of coffee and the two of us would sit and have our coffee and cigarette together. Walt always gave us a funny look when he visited the set."

All that smoking didn't slow the actor down at all from doing physical stunts. "I never ran so much in all my life. Up and down beaches, through jungles, over hills and even mountains," Van Dyke said. "It was like being on a treadmill… always on the move but never getting anywhere."

Walt wasn't always right as Van Dyke found out. "We needed about a dozen Hawaiian war canoes. Walt didn't want to use any that were at hand, so he had some built at the Studio. They arrived—big, heavy war canoes, made of fiberglass, with the big figureheads on the front. We got them out about a half mile off shore with the actors in place and the cameras ready to roll and they all sank. They all went down. I thought Walt was going to have a fit!"

"We brought our own palm trees with us. And our own catamarans and they sunk, within five minutes… our whole fleet. They were selling tickets down on the shore. 'Everybody come down and watch the funny people from Hollywood sink their catamarans'," remembered Walsh.

Unfortunately, the film was not a critical success. It was nearly a half-hour longer than any other Disney comedy released at this time and rather than a satisfying story, it seemed more like just a series of amusing sketches one after another.

"It was not one of your great bits of literature but it made dough. It made a lot of money. I think aesthetically Walt would have liked something a little better but he was a reasonable man. It made a lot of money. And it was a fair job. I got a couple of laughs out of it, personally," said Walsh.

## BLACKBEARD'S GHOST

Avast, matey! It be time to hoist anchor for ghostly adventure with a bumbling phantom pirate. Released theatrically February 1968, *Blackbeard's Ghost* is the last live-action film to have been touched by Walt Disney before his untimely passing. He watched it being filmed before he checked into St. Joseph's Hospital for the final time.

The film recounts the story of a young track coach named Steve Walker (played by Dean Jones) who has been hired to help the hopeless team at Godolphin College before an upcoming track meet.

Walker accidentally conjures up the ghost of the notorious pirate captain, Blackbeard (played by Peter Ustinov) who must perform a good deed to break the curse of his tenth wife that condemned him to limbo. To make matters more challenging, only Walker can see and hear Blackbeard and the ghost is full of mischief.

There are additional complications, including Walker trying to woo another Godolphin professor (Suzanne Pleshette) and a local crime boss named Silky Seymour who is trying to take over the hotel where Walker is staying from some little old ladies. Blackbeard provides some of his special help at the track meet and helps the little old ladies save their hotel—and is allowed to join his former crew in the hereafter.

As might be suspected, the film emphasizes physical humor and relies heavily on the charm of Jones and Ustinov to sustain interest in the predictable family film formula.

It is not a bad film but it is definitely not a memorable one. The gangster slapstick section seems very dated and surprisingly, after the excellence of the special effects in *Mary Poppins*, a wire is clearly visible when Blackbeard takes a bottle of rum from a motorcycle policeman and also when Blackbeard helps the Godolphin pole-vaulter.

The special effects for the film were handled by a legendary crew: Eustace Lycett, head of special photographic effects; Peter Ellenshaw, supervising matte painter; Art Vitarelli, second unit director; and Bob Mattey, head of special visual effects.

Under the direction of Vitarelli, the second unit shot background footage on location at San Luis Obispo and Trancas that was later combined with shots from the sound stage. Additional location shooting was done at Disney's Golden Oak Ranch. With the use of several fog machines, the small lake on the ranch doubled for the Atlantic coastline in the scene where the ghost of Blackbeard rows to shore. Simple effects like floating rum bottles were done in real time on the set itself. More complicated effects were done on a special effects stage.

One effect went very wrong. Hank Jones, playing the part of Gudger, was rigged up in the same wire harness that was used in *Mary Poppins* but without the padding of that bulky Victorian dress. The sharp wires cut into his skimpy track suit and he started trickling blood into Ustinov's face down below. Suddenly, the wires unraveled and Jones fell more than ten feet right on top of Ustinov. Jones remembers that Ustinov's only concern was whether Jones was hurt.

Producer Bill Walsh offered to stop shooting for the whole day but Jones decided to try it again. Unfortunately, it took ten more takes to get it right. It was Hank Jones's first Disney film and he played a nerd character in several other Disney films.

The real Blackbeard was born Edward Drummond (although he later changed his name to Edward Teach). When he sailed from his homeport of Bristol, England, he was apparently an honest, hardworking seaman. There are conflicting stories about his transformation into one of the most notorious pirates with flaming wicks tied into his long black beard to frighten his foes.

He was known as North Carolina's most infamous pirate citizen. Many people still believe that Blackbeard's treasure will one day be found somewhere between Smith and Tangier Islands in the middle of Chesapeake Bay and today, tales abound of Blackbeard's ghost roaming the area.

Ben Stahl was a well-known and prolific artist who won many prestigious awards. He later taught at the Art Institute, as well as at the American Academy of Art, the Art Students League of New York, Brooklyn's Pratt Institute and at various universities. His work appeared in many magazines including approximately seven hundred and fifty stories in the *Saturday Evening Post*.

Stahl was one of the founding faculty members for the Famous Artists School. In addition, he produced advertising artwork for various companies, and posters for several movies, including *Ben-Hur*. He illustrated a number of books, including the twenty-fifth anniversary edition of *Gone With the Wind*.

Stahl wrote two novels. *Blackbeard's Ghost* was published in 1965 by Houghton Mifflin. *The Secret of Red Skull*, a sequel to *Blackbeard's Ghost*, was also published by Houghton Mifflin.

Stahl lived in Sarasota, Florida, and according to Disney publicity at the time: "With an illustrator's eye, he visualized every scene in *Blackbeard's Ghost* in great detail and then translated that vision into words on paper."

Commissioned by Warner Brothers to paint a portrait, Ben took along a copy of his nearly completed book manuscript to Hollywood and showed it to Walt over lunch. Three days later Walt called to say he was interested in the film rights. The same day Austin Olney, editor of Houghton Mifflin, wired that his company would publish it.

Why Blackbeard instead of Captain Kidd or other villainous pirates?

"Because Edward Teach, alias Blackbeard, was the craftiest rogue who ever buckled a swash and yet he had a streak of fun and humor in him that made many of his victims almost forgive his outrages," Stahl said. That description of Blackbeard isn't quite accurate but for an artist, the pirate was certainly a visually striking character.

Filmed in Technicolor, Robert Stevenson directed from a screenplay by Bill Walsh and Don DaGradi from the book by Ben Stahl. Walsh also served as co-producer.

At the time, Bill Walsh had spent twenty-two years at Disney working on films like *The Shaggy Dog*, *The Absent Minded Professor*, *That Darn Cat*, *Mary Poppins* and many more. In fact by the time of this film, Walsh had co-scripted thirteen of the sixteen films he had done for Disney and was preparing a new script called *Boy-Car-Girl* that became *The Love Bug* and a film titled *Khrushchev in Disneyland*. It was a comedy about what would have happened if Russian leader Nitka Khrushchev (to be played by Peter Ustinov) had been allowed to visit Disneyland.

Walsh explained how he approached the script for *Blackbeard's Ghost*: "The first portion of each film takes time to establish characters and to delineate situation. Although this initial part may move more slowly than the rest of the film, it is a necessary and deliberate movement. Walt used to call this part of the picture, 'winding the clock'. Once the stage is set, the action picks up momentum as the picture unfolds. Too often comedies begin at a nervous clip, moving at a fast pace until they run out of gas, without having told a good story. The most important single consideration of any picture is the script.

"The second most important consideration is the cast. Comedy-fantasy requires actors who can play unbelievable situations for real. The success of Dean Jones lies in his sincerity. The nuttier the situation gets, the more he believes in it. Actors often go wrong in fantasy. They become cute with the material and lose audience contact."

However, Walsh also had a little secret to his successful Disney film scripts. "I always stuck a little bit of Walt in the main character. So he could recognize himself. He would say, 'Now this kid's got it here. It's true, real, the character is real.' If I'm doing *Blackbeard's Ghost* or anything, I made Blackbeard like Walt. Or if I'd make the father in *the Shaggy Dog* or the professor in *Absent-Minded Professor*, I'd give him some of Walt's own personal characteristics," laughed Walsh.

Director Robert Stevenson also directed Disney classics like *Mary Poppins*, *That Darn Cat*, *Old Yeller*, *The Absent Minded Professor*, and *The Monkey's Uncle* besides several other top Disney credits. He was a direct descendent of Robert Louis Stevenson who authored the famous pirate novel, *Treasure Island*. His first Disney directing assignment came in 1956 when he filmed *Johnny Tremain*.

Actor Dean Jones remembered talking with Walt about the script before filming began:

> *"I had an interesting lunch with Walt once. There were five things I felt were kind of corny and old-fashioned in **Blackbeard's Ghost**, which I thought should be taken out. On two of them, Walt said, 'OK, but you're pushing your luck.' On the fourth and fifth point he got upset and said, 'If there are so many things about this picture you don't like, you don't have to do it. I'll get another actor!'*

> *"Look, Walt," I said, "I'm not asking for more close-ups. I'm not asking for more money. I'm trying to make the picture better and I'm just pointing out that we've seen this joke a hundred times on screen and I don't think it's funny anymore."*

> *"Walt countered, 'That joke was funny in 1923 and it'll be funny today!' (The joke stayed in the picture and I laughed at it along with the rest of the audience at the premiere. Walt was right!)*

> *"On another one of my objections, Walt dug in his heels. Later, we were walking back toward his office and he started up the steps of the Animation Building. We said goodbye and I was walking on when he stopped me. 'Oh, that scene with the phony gun—we'll do it your way.' Then he pointed his finger at me and added, 'but you better be right!' And I knew I'd better be."*

Why was Walt so adamant about the script? According to director Stevenson, "He (Walt) worked closer on the script of *Blackbeard's Ghost* than on any other. He seemed to have an enormous energy when he worked on it."

In his autobiography, Dean remembered the following:

> *"Walt had said once that I was perfect for his pictures because I was such a good family man. What he didn't know, and what I hoped he hadn't found out, was that half the nights I came home smelling of perfume my wife didn't wear. The one thing about Walt Disney that never failed to impress me was his genius for remaining himself. Walt would spend the rest of that sunny afternoon in the northeast corner of the third floor, in the room with the baby grand piano and the walls filled with mementos of past triumphs. And in less than two months, he would be dead."*

"I really wasn't sure what to expect from Peter," said director Stevenson, "He is, after all, a director, too. I didn't know how he would like taking orders rather than giving them. Many actor-directors become boorish in the way they try to influence the direction of every picture they're in. On the first day of shooting, I was prepared to fight him back should he attempt a takeover. But he disarmed me with his simple wholehearted co-operation. Not a word from him all day about how we should do a scene.

"My curiosity gnawed at me until I had to ask him if he had a suggestion about a particular shot. 'It's kind of you to ask. I do have one little idea,' he said. But he wasn't pushy. He earnestly wanted to help. And he figured that the best way he could help was to leave the directing to me unless I asked for his opinion. I should think that, being a director, he understood full well the problems of direction and gave his full support as he would have liked me to give mine had our positions been reversed."

At the time, Ustinov, besides being an actor in countless movies, plays and television shows, had written eighteen plays, seven movie scripts and seven books. He had directed six movies. He also dabbled as an artist. From those who worked with him on this film, there was nothing but terrific stories of Ustinov being very playful and doing imitations, speaking in foreign languages and telling marvelous stories.

What was his approach to Blackbeard? He told a Disney publicist: "Nothing to it if you get the right camera angles. Everyone has a certain amount of spirit. It's simply a matter, then, of getting it on film. Right?"

"To make the sequence come across as an authentic college meet, we needed some cheerleaders to complete the picture," said Bill Walsh, "We were watching a UCLA football game and it seemed that the cameraman was enamored with the UCLA cheerleaders, and we saw more of them than we did the game. We practically had to call the paper to get the results of the game. UCLA won. But the point is that we did see a lot of the girls in action. And they were very attractive. When the time came to select cheerleaders for the track meet, there was no question in our minds. They did an excellent job. Just like on TV."

The UCLA cheerleaders in the film were Linda Lockwood, Elaine Larkins, Holly Borowiak, Donna Laughlin, Lynn Switzer and Renee Stuber.

"Peter, who is probably one of the most brilliant figures in our industry today, even learned their routine for one of the scenes," Walsh said.

Disney Costume Department Head Chuck Keane said, "(We) fitted (Ustinov) with off-white canvas pants, a beige raw silk shirt, brown velveteen vest, navy blue wool full-length coat, and auburn velour hat. All of which were tailored to design specifications of our chief designer, Bill Thomas. His boots were specially designed cavalier boots, coming knee high with an extra-wide cuff. Constructed of black kangaroo leather, the boots had to be sturdy enough to support his massive bulk, yet still be comfortable to his wide foot and high instep. At the cost of $175, they were made by a craftsman who does nothing but make footwear for stars in specific roles. To age these boots two centuries, we sandpapered the leather and bruised it without breaking the support features down. Then we sprayed them with a brown aging solution, waxed and powdered them. It's not really a complicated process, but it certainly gets results.

"We use the same process to age clothing. But in addition to sanding the material, we sometimes sandblast it, and that ages it in a hurry. His blue coat became an antique in a matter of seconds, buttons and all. A light brown spray of the aging solution was followed by a generous dusting with 'rottenstone', a grey and brown powder, which discolored the navy fabric to a non-descript blue. Blackbeard's other garments were made old in a similar fashion."

Ustinov said, "I felt like a walking antique wearing these relics from the costume department where they became museum collector's items overnight."

There was merchandise and promotional giveaways including a VariVue (flicker) badge that would change the image when you tipped it. On one view it had a pirate hat and crossbones and said "Only YOU can see" and when tipped there was a cartoon caricature of Ustinov as Blackbeard's Ghost and the phrase "Walt Disney's *Blackbeard's Ghost.*"

The Walt Disney Treasury of Classic Tales Sunday comic strip featured an adaptation of the film. There was also a coloring book, a Gold Key comic book adaptation, a Whitman storybook and a Story Teller LP with twelve color pages of artwork and story where Peter Ustinov himself narrated the "Story of *Blackbeard's Ghost.*"

Director Stevenson remembered Walt visiting the set: "Suddenly I came onto the set and saw him sitting on one of those stools and he was drinking coffee. I said, 'Walt, I thought you were in the hospital.' He said, 'Yeah, well, they cut away my ribs to get to something. It's just some damn thing they're fooling around with.'"

Both Stevenson and Ustinov were upset by Walt's sickly appearance but both tried not show it. Walt even joked with Ustinov about an upcoming film he wanted to make titled *Khrushchev in Disneyland* that was to star the actor.

Walt Disney saw Suzanne Pleshette in a television guest appearance and after inquiring about her credits held a special screening of the film *40 Pounds of Trouble*, the only non-Disney live action film that included nearly twenty minutes of footage shot at Disneyland. Producer Winston Hibler agreed with Walt that she would be ideal for *The Ugly Dachshund* and co-starred her with Dean Jones. She again played Jones' love interest in *Blackbeard's Ghost*.

Pleshette recalled: "The morning he (Walt) came out of the hospital, he came onto our set. We were filming *Blackbeard's Ghost*. He looked so gray and yellow, yet still had a sparkle in his eyes. He must have been in terrible pain. I knew it was coming. If you've ever seen anybody with cancer, you know that color. He said, 'Come out from behind that desk. I wanna see if you're wearing a mini-skirt.'

"I said, 'You just want to see my thighs, you devil you.' Those were the last words we spoke. I gave him a big hug and went home that night and cried and cried."

Actor Dean Jones wrote extensively about that final meeting on the set in his autobiography, *Under Running Laughter* (1982, Chosen Books):

"One day, after the director yelled 'cut,' I glanced up and right behind the camera stood Walt. He looked terrible. His cheeks were sunken and his face looked thin and extremely tired. I looked at him in shock.

"'We're ready to roll, Dean,' called the assistant, 'Everybody be quiet!' Then, remembering that Walt was there, he yelled just as loudly, 'Almost everybody be quiet!' Several members of the crew laughed appreciatively. Walt just stood there. His face was haggard and colorless, and there were large circles under his eyes. It was his last visit to his favorite spot on earth."

There is one final tribute to *Blackbeard's Ghost* in the Disneyland *Pirates of the Caribbean* attraction. The original captain on the pirate ship was supposed to be Blackbeard and that was Imagineer Marc Davis's intent but that reference is now gone with the captain transformed into Captain Barbossa from the *Pirates* movie trilogy.

However, as guests exit the attraction, on the left, there were two pirates pushing up a treasure chest and sticking out of that chest, is a replica of the painting from the movie *Blackbeard's Ghost*. It was a fitting tribute because the attraction was preparing to open while the film was in production and the Disney Company has dozens of photos of Ustinov in costume as Blackbeard cavorting in the attraction and mugging with the Audio-Animatronics figures.

The last attraction that Walt personally supervised and the last live action film with Walt's touch together at last as a reminder of a remarkable man.

PART THREE:  DISNEY PARK STORIES

Whenever I visit Walt Disney World with a good friend of mine who is a recognized Disney authority, he is enthralled when I share some of the history behind the various attractions. He is fond of telling the thousands of fans of his podcast that these are the stories that "only Jim Korkis knows".

At first, I was flattered by that compliment and then the more I thought about it, I became increasingly frightened. Over the decades, I have had the opportunity to interview many of the Imagineers who worked on the Disney theme park attractions. I had the chance to work with and talk with Disney cast members who helped open Disneyland and Walt Disney World. They shared many terrific stories and facts that I later discovered were never documented. Thankfully, I tried to take good notes and often recorded those conversations.

Was it true that I might be one of the last people left who knew the stories about these attractions? Was that the reason that some arbitrary changes have been made to the Disney theme parks with no regard to the original story lines? Was there no one left working at the Disney Company who was the "keeper of the stories" or in a position to share those stories with the proper decision makers?

Suddenly, I was filled with the need to share these stories with as many people as I could to keep that history alive. Not relying solely on the oral memories of the people who I had talked with over the years, I tried to find as much confirmation as I could from a vast variety of sources. I was shocked to discover that some documents had been destroyed over the years in order to save on storage costs or when an attraction closed or was never built. Fortunately, some individual cast members often saved this material as a personal souvenir so I could use it to verify information.

Surprisingly, some material had never been recorded at all because in the heat of final deadlines, no one had the time, especially if something had to be changed at the last minute. There was always a tradition of "oral history" at the Disney Studios and the Disney Parks. The belief was that if someone had a question, they would be sent to the person who worked on the project to get the answer. It never occurred to anyone what would happen when that person died or retired and the information was needed. The situation only grew worse year after year after year as talented people left the company.

So, here are some of the stories about the Disney theme parks that I may be one of the few people to know. I definitely do not want these great tales to go to the grave with me. I am grateful that people shared these stories and so many others with me and I am regretful that I was not more aggressive and astute to retrieve even more information. Perhaps these stories will bring new appreciation to these attractions from those who have visited them countless times over the years.

## CINDERELLA'S GOLDEN CARROUSEL

On June 1, 2010, the Disney Company decided that to expand on the stories of Walt Disney World's Fantasyland that the popular *Cinderella's Golden Carrousel* would be renamed *Prince Charming Regal Carrousel*. No physical changes were made except for a new sign.

According to the official press release, this was the new storyline:

> *Following their fairy-tale romance and happily ever after wedding, Cinderella and Prince Charming took up residence in Cinderella's Castle. With peace throughout the kingdom, Prince Charming had time to practice for jousting tournaments. In the countryside near the castle, he built a training device of carved horses, on which he could practice the art of ring-spearing, a tournament event in which a knight rides his horse full speed, lance in hand, toward a small ring hanging from a tree limb, with the object of spearing the ring. This event was known by various names throughout the lands, but generally came to be called 'carrousel'.*

> *The carrousel device drew the attention of the villagers, who wanted to take a turn on this amazing spinning contraption. So Prince Charming had a second carrousel constructed closer to the Castle, where everyone could take a spin on this wondrous invention. Instead of a working knight's training device, however, this new carrousel is more befitting its regal location in the Castle Courtyard—its rustic training horses replaced with ornately decorated prancing steeds adorned with golden helmets and shields, flower garlands, feathers and*

*other festoons. Prince Charming invites one and all to test*
*their horsemanship skills and to enjoy their own happy ending.*

Some Disney fans have debated whether such a re-branding was necessary since for forty years the beloved icon at the entrance to Fantasyland at the Magic Kingdom already had a rich history beginning with Walt Disney's own fondness for carousels.

Walt Disney revealed in a 1963 conversation where he first got the notion for Disneyland, "Well, it came about when my daughters were very young and Saturday was always Daddy's day with the two daughters. So we'd start out and try to go someplace, you know, different things. I'd take them to the merry-go-round and I took them different places and I'd sit while they rode the merry-go-round. Sit on a bench, you know, eating peanuts. I felt that there should be something built where the parents and the children could have fun together. So that's how Disneyland started."

That famous merry-go-round that inspired Walt still operates today in Griffith Park in Los Angeles. Located in Park Center between the Los Angeles Zoo and the Los Feliz park entrance, the Griffith Park Merry-Go-Round has been a family attraction for over five generations. It was built in 1926 by the Spillman Engineering Company and is the only Spillman built carousel still in existence. It has most of its original parts and paint.

Originally purchased by the Spreckles family for use in San Diego's Mission Beach, the pier was a victim of the Depression and the carousel was moved to Balboa Park for the Exposition. At its close, the carousel was purchased by Ross Davis and moved to its home in Griffith Park in 1937 where it has operated since then. Davis helped Walt obtain and refurbish another carousel for Disneyland that became the famous *King Arthur's Carousel.*

The Griffith Park Merry-Go-Round boasts sixty-eight elaborately hand carved horses, every one a jumper. All four rows of horses boast jewel-encrusted bridles, detailed draped blankets and are decorated with sunflowers and lion's heads. In addition there are two chariots supposedly depicting Adam chasing Eve and one of them features a plaque stating: "Restored in memory of Walt Disney through the generosity of the Walt Disney Family Foundation."

A Stinson 165 Military Band Organ, claimed to be the largest band organ accompanying a carousel on the West Coast, plays over 1500 selections of marches and waltz music.

In 1984 the merry-go-round was purchased by Rosemary West and Warren Deasy and they began the enormous and painfully slow task of restoration using the profit from the carousel to pay for the restoration. The ravages of age are very evident on this vintage attraction.

At the Disney Gallery at Disneyland, against the wall in the front entrance of the Main Street Opera House sits a green wooden park bench. A plaque on the bench reads "The actual park bench from the Griffith Park Merry-Go-Round in Los Angeles, where Walt Disney first dreamed of Disneyland." The bench is on loan from Imagineer Tony Baxter's personal collection

The most magnificent carousel at any Disney theme park may be the one at the Magic Kingdom in Walt Disney World. Its rich history and fine detail are unsurpassed.

Every day, unsuspecting guests at Walt Disney World ride a genuine antique by mounting a horse that might be valued at more than $100,000 and decorated with 23 karat gold leaf. For two minutes, they are transported to the joy of their youth or a royal fantasy where they heroically ride round and round through a land of enchantment. Ironically, that experience was originally valued at just an "A" ticket, only ten cents, the lowest price for any Walt Disney World attraction. Today, it is free.

Most historians have stated that the birth of the carousel began in the 1100s when Italian and Spanish crusaders watched Arabian and Turkish horsemen play a very serious game on horseback (actually a cavalry training preparation exercise) that the crusaders dubbed "little battles" or "little war". In Italian, that is "garosello and in Spanish "carosella".

The French adapted this game into an extravagant display of horsemanship replacing jousting called "carrousel" (with two "r"s). Both the riders and the horses performing choreographed routines were elaborated costumed for the entertainment of royalty. One of the activities was a man on horseback using his lance to spear a small ring dangling from a tree limb or pole.

Roughly three hundred years ago, the French built a rotating device that moved up and down featuring carved horses and chariots suspended by chains radiating from a center pole to train young nobleman for the event without tiring their horses.

By the late 1700s, there were numerous carousels (powered by men, mule or horsepower) scattered throughout Europe built solely for amusement at fairs and special venues. In the

1860s, Gustav Dentzel was the man who pioneered the modern carousel in America inspiring other talented craftsmen.

The American carousels were bigger and more elaborate. The horses and chariots were extravagantly decorated in keeping with the tradition that this was an event for the entertainment of royalty. American carousel horses are much more active than their European counterparts with expressives eyes, tossed manes and extreme poses of movement. It truly is an art to bring the illusion of life to a piece of wood.

Technological advances allowed for a stationary circular platform for people to walk on and stationary animals (standers or prancers) to be added, with bevel gears and cranks to give the up and down motion to other animals around a center pole.

During the Great Depression, the decline of amusement parks resulted in many carousels being abandoned or destroyed as the few remaining companies producing them shifted their manufacturing focus or went out of business. Carousels were now considered just a children's ride rather than something to be enjoyed by adults. With a huge interest in collecting the carousel animals as antiques in the Seventies, many of the remaining carousels were dismantled to sell the individual figures for a huge profit of thousands of dollars.

Just over a hundred carousels built during the Golden Age before the Great Depression still exist intact today in the United States. It was estimated that during the Golden Age there were more than four thousand operating carousels.

The sole Disney craftswoman who supervised and maintained the Walt Disney World carousel from its installation for over two decades, was a delightfully talented woman named

Isle Voght.  Roughly ten years ago, she was removed from that responsibility but fortunately, I got to visit her many times in the late Nineties at Central Shops and see her at work.  She was always eager to share information with me about the history of the WDW carousel and about her job.  I watched in awe as she worked her magic.

Isle composed a memorandum dated September 18, 1990 detailing the history of the WDW carousel and sent to multiple recipients including Disney University so that the true story could be saved and documented.  At the time, Isle was involved with the carousel for EuroDisneyland.  For that carousel, the outer ring had new wooden horses carved by an artist in Ohio, while all the inner rings had fiberglass horses that had been cast from molds of the wooden horses on the Walt Disney World carousel.  As she did with Imagineer John Hench for the WDW carousel, Isle was in charge of the color selection for each horse.

Two of the paragraphs from her two page single spaced memo have been excerpted for publicity during the last twenty years with those same small bits repeated over and over while the remainder of the information has seemingly disappeared along with that document.

During the Golden Age of American Carousels, there were three primary styles:  Philadelphia style (inspired by the work of Dentzel and the Philadelphia Toboggan Company), Coney Island style and County Fair style.

Isle told me: "The Walt Disney World Carousel in the Magic Kingdom was produced in 1917 by the Philadelphia Toboggan Company, which created some of the most beautiful horses of the era.  It was carved by German and Italian carvers to express the patriotism that was prevalent in the United States after the First World War. The carousel was named *Liberty*, and was one of the largest carousels ever built, being some sixty feet in diameter.

"The first home of the *Liberty Carousel* was at the Detroit Palace Garden Park where it stayed until it was rehabilitated in Philadelphia in 1928 and set up in Olympic Park in Maplewood, New Jersey for the next 39 years."

The *Liberty Carousel* originally had seventy-two horses and two chariots (not four as is reported in some articles). The distinctly American horses were black, brown, gray, and white. Their saddles included items that celebrated the American frontier including images of buffalo and bison now painted silver or gold, faces of Native Americans, bows and arrows and even holsters with pistols or rifles.

Carved figures of Lady Liberty holding shields that featured a red, white and blue flag emblem decorated the interior top circle. There were eighteen landscape paintings of American scenery. Just below was a running board decorated with golden American eagles. Over the years, less skilled craftsmen slopped coats of paint and lacquer over the horses, eventually obscuring the intricate and uniquely engraved features underneath.

The Philadelphia Toboggan Company only built eighty-nine carousels before 1929 and the Great Depression. The Liberty Carousel is number forty-six and one of only a dozen or so of those classic originals from the Philadelphia Toboggan Company that still exist and operate today.

Olympic Park closed in 1965. By that point, the *Liberty Carousel* had fallen into a state of disrepair and was slated for almost-certain demolition. Antique carousel horses are in such demand that it was planned to sell them and the decorations off individually. Studies have shown that when an entertainment venue sells off or removes its carousel that the venue usually closes permanently within a year. By 1967, Disney had located and acquired the antique masterpiece for the Magic Kingdom.

Isle shared with me: "All of the horses were shipped to Disney Shops where craftsmen were surprised by the detail and artistic grace uncovered when all the years of paint and grime was removed down to the gleaming Maplewood of the horses. Months of Disney artistry went into the rehabilitation. The chariots were removed and the carousel was filled out to the present number of ninety horses when Disney purchased some antique horses that were made by two other well-known producers of carousels, the Dentzel Co. and the Parker Co."

The horses were sanded down carefully to the original wood so that no detail was lost. Sanding down to the actual wood could have resulted in damage and loss of detail so today they are only sanded down to roughly the level of primer and no further. Then the horses were primed and painted white.

The horses are white for two reasons. First, since it is Cinderella's carousel, the white horses reference the white horses that pulled Cinderella's pumpkin carriage. Second, one of the things Disney discovered with the *King Arthur's Carousel* at Disneyland, was that when people rode a carousel, they first tried to get on a white horse because it was considered the "hero" horse. For over a decade or so of operation the Disneyland carousel featured horses of different colors until Imagineer John Hench made the decision to make them all Arctic white. The decision was made that at a Disney theme park, every guest no matter what their size gets a chance to be a hero. Walt also wanted every guest to have a "jumper" rather than a "stander" so some horses on the Disneyland carousel were refitted into running horses.

For the WDW carousel, Imagineer John Hench and Isle selected the unique color palette for each horse. Each horse's tack has a different color scheme and is numbered on its bridle. One time, Isle tried to test my color awareness and asked me to look carefully at the saddle she was painting and tell her what color it was. I immediately responded that it was blue, a dark royal blue. She laughed and pointed out that I was not looking carefully enough because not only was it blue but it had a touch of red in it. Not enough red to turn the color to purple but enough so that it was different from another blue saddle horse she showed me nearby. Once she pointed it out, it was very obvious.

One of my many regrets is that when I knew Isle I was transitioning into a different job and assuming new responsibilities so I wasn't able to spend as much time visiting with her as I would have liked. She told me that she and Hench had determined the sex of each of the horses (no, you do not look underneath) and whether they were a young horse or a more mature horse. She was planning to teach me how to tell the difference between male and female and young and old but I never followed up on that opportunity. Isle might still have that documentation somewhere.

She was also going to teach me how to determine whether the horse was wood or fiberglass. All the horses are wood but Disney made molds of some of the antique wood horses so that about eleven fiberglass horses were created (and painted in the same process as the wooden ones) as "understudies". These understudies replace horses on the carousel when the originals are pulled off for repair and repainted. The horses do suffer wear and tear from the guests. Usually a complete row of five horses at a time are pulled although each might be pulled from different rows. Isle indicated that knocking at the right location on the upper chest near the neck was one of the ways of determining the difference since fiberglass is hollow while the wood is solid.

A "row" of horses on a carousel does not go around the carousel but goes from the outer edge of the carousel toward the center of the carousel. On the WDW carousel, a row is five horses deep with the largest "A" horse being on the outside and the smallest "E" horse being on the inside.

Since the "A" horses are the ones facing the crowd they are more elaborate in their design and detail. The horses progressively get less intricate as they move toward the center. In addition, the side of the horse that faces out toward the audience whether it is "A" or "E" is more elaborate than the side that faces the center and is known as the "romance" side. It is very similar in concept to the set of a play or a movie. While the differences between the two sides of the smaller "E" horses are not as noticeably significant as the much larger "A" horses, the difference still exists.

Isle told me for a class I was teaching in 1998: "Each year between fifty to sixty horses are completely redone at a cost between $2500-$3,000 to refurbish each horse. All the horses are hand painted and everything that looks like gold really is gold. Only 23 karat gold leaf is used along with silver, copper and aluminum leaf. The antique wood horses of the Walt Disney carousel are valued between $20,000-$100,000 depending upon size, intricacy of carving and age."

The smaller horses can take two to three days to do but the more elaborate "A" horses can take a week or more. In addition, when the Disney Company obtained the carousel, almost all of the original wood working parts were replaced by metal, but the horses, decorations and band organ (from one of Italy's most famous factories) were saved.

While the Magic Kingdom was being built, Walt's brother Roy O. Disney was walking and inspecting the area. At the train station, he looked down Main Street and saw through the castle gate opening that the carousel seemed off center. Subsequent measurement showed he was right and the ride was re-centered. According to legend, the carousel had only been off a foot or two.

When the carousel opened, it was an "A" Ticket attraction. It was called *Cinderella's Golden Carrousel* (with the two "r"s to reference the French word for the original as well as the fact that it was the French version of the Cinderella tale that inspired the Disney animated feature). On the sign were the two mice, Gus and Jacques perhaps waiting for the Fairy Godmother to return and transform them again into white horses. Or perhaps it was a playful reminder that those magnificent white steeds may be mice and Gus and Jacques are visiting their friends who preferred to remain noble horses.

Ten years ago was when the urban myth that there was a "Cinderella horse" started to appear as cast members tried to create magical moments for guests. At the time, I asked Isle if there was a Cinderella horse and she laughed. She assured me that it was never planned for Cinderella to have a special horse. Cinderella never rode one in the animated feature. Remember, the horses on the carousel were all distinctly American steeds as well. If a Cinderella horse was desired, Disney would have created a special one or did extensive surgery on an existing horse so that there would be details (like Cinderella's crest on the saddle) to define it.

In addition, the horse with the gold ribbon on its tail that has been identified as Cinderella's horse is a "B" horse and certainly Cinderella would be riding a much more elaborate "A" horse where she could be seen clearly by her subjects, not hidden in the second rim on a less elegant steed. However, like most Disney urban myths, this myth persists with such intensity that it now sadly appears in officially approved Disney books and websites.

At Disneyland, there is a "Julie Andrews" horse called "Jingles" on the carousel. It does feature an elaborate emblem on the saddle (including Julie's initials and a silhouette of a flying Mary Poppins) and is one of the "A" horses where it can be clearly seen and found and there was a formal dedication ceremony declaring it the Julie Andrews horse.

Fortunately, Isle was still working when there was a "happy ending" story for *Cinderella's Golden Carrousel*. When the carousel was being prepared for Walt Disney World, the two authentic chariots were removed so that more horses could be installed for guests. As often happens, those chariots disappeared and Isle was unable to locate them years later.

Times change, and it was felt that very young small guests or guests with mobility issues might enjoy riding in a chariot. There was some discussion about creating fiberglass replicas based on some existing photos and artwork but Isle was adamant that she wanted the originals since everything else on the carousel was original. She posted pictures in her work area and tried everything she could to try to locate the chariots, including contacting as many people as she could.

In 1996, a cast member who was a friend of Isle and familiar with her hunt was walking through one of the Disney warehouses in California looking for something else. For some reason that he is still unable to explain, he decided to look up and behind where he was standing. There stored in the rafter area was what looked like one of the chariots, unlabelled and apparently "lost" on the books. He took a photo and sent it to Isle who immediately confirmed it was one of the missing chariots.

It was quickly recovered. Imagineer John Hench was involved in selecting the color scheme for it and it was repaired and painted and finally installed on the WDW carousel in 1997. When I asked Isle if she would use this original as a mold for a fiberglass model for the other side of the carousel, she looked at me firmly and said, "Only originals." She felt that the other chariot would still pop up somewhere in one of the many Disney warehouses. "After all, it only took twenty-five years to locate this one," she joked. The chariot took up the space of four horses so the carousel has eighty-six horses now and can be enjoyed by all guests.

Whatever the official name or re-invented storyline for the carousel, it still continues to provide enjoyment for guests of all ages who for two minutes are transported into a land of imagination where mighty steeds carried noble people on magnificent adventures.

## CIRCARAMA 1955

*"An advanced motion picture development, Circarama, consisting of a continuous image focused on a 360-degree screen, will be introduced at Disneyland Park on July 17 by American Motors Corporation, producer of Hudson, Nash and Rambler automobiles and Kelvinator appliances."* —*Disney press release from June 27, 1955.*

In 1960, Disney Legend Ub Iwerks was honored with the *Herbert T. Kalmus Gold Medal* from the Society of Motion Picture and Television Engineers (SMPTE) for his outstanding contributions to the technology in equipment and processes for the making of color-motion pictures. These achievements included creating the double headed optical printer, the color correction masking process, the xerographic process for animation and the 360 degree Circarama system.

Circarama! Like so many early Imagineering achievements for the Disneyland theme park, this was another innovative experience that has been taken for granted and poorly documented over the years.

The original film, *A Tour of the West* ran from 1955 to roughly the beginning of 1960 in the building at the entrance of Tomorrowland, just to the left of the infamous clock that could tell the time around the world.

As Iwerks remembered it, one afternoon, while working on the Disney live-action film *Westward Ho, the Wagons*, he paused in a hallway of the Disney Studios in Burbank to talk a little with Walt Disney about some of the challenges adapting some of the films to the Cinemascope process.

Supposedly, Walt encouraged Iwerks to give some thought to developing a new format for the presentation of movies that would involve a series of screens that completely surrounded the audience a full 360 degrees.

As Disney Legend Roger Broggie remembered it, Walt, after seeing the new theater process of Cinerama at the Hollywood Pantages theater, where three large screens were in synchronization to present motion pictures like *How the West Was Won* or *It's a Mad, Mad, Mad, Mad World*, called Broggie and special effects expert Eustace Lycett to his office and wondered: Since three screens could be put together, would it be possible to extend it so that there would be screens surrounding the entire audience?

The result of Walt's speculation was the creation of the first Circarama theater that was one of the few Disneyland attractions working properly for guests on Opening Day, July 17, 1955.

In 1901, at the World's Fair in Paris, one of the earliest versions of a 360-degree film debuted. However, this Disney process was so unique that Walt and Iwerks shared a patent on Circarama that was filed on the one-year anniversary of Disneyland and was granted four years later on June 28, 1960.

It was called "Circarama" not only as an allusion to "Cinerama" (that supposedly later resulted in the Disney process being renamed "Circle-Vision" in 1967 because the two words were too similar), but also because the film was sponsored by American Motors, who was not only using the Disney Studios to produce animated television commercials for its product but was also sponsoring the weekly Disneyland television show and the attraction. In fact, the original sign outside the attraction had the word "Circarama" in large dark black letters except for the word "car" which was in red.

American Motors Corporation (AMC) was an American automobile company formed on January 14, 1954 by the merger of the Nash-Kelvinator Corporation and the Hudson Motor Car Company.

To show you how casual correct nomenclature was at early Disneyland, contemporary paper documentation of the time, like newspaper stories, internal publications, maps and guides, etc. variously list the name of the attraction as "American Motors Circarama Exhibit," "American Motors Exhibit," "American Motors presents Circarama," and "Circarama, U.S.A."

No matter what it was officially called, it was evident that this was the American Motors show for Disneyland. Sponsorship from Richfield, Kaiser Aluminum, Monsanto and others provided funds for Tomorrowland, which was built only six months before the park opened. Without money from those lessees (as participants were known in those early days), Tomorrowland wouldn't have been built at all since Walt had spent all of his money and more on the rest of the park.

"This combination of photographic skills and entertainment talents promises an unusual spectacle for visitors to Disneyland. We're happy to have a part to play in making Circarama possible. As it represents added pleasure and value for the public, sponsorship of the Circarama is another forward step in our program to make American Motors mean more for Americans," said George Romney the then-President and Chairman of the company in the official June 27, 1955 press release.

On the floor inside the attraction were prominently displayed five AMC automobiles, as well as Kelvinator appliances. These appliances included the futuristic "Foodarama" refrigerator ("the last word in foodkeeping") that could hold 166 pounds of meat in its freezer, had a Breakfast Bar for eggs and bacon and two pitchers of juices, Cheese and Butter Chests, an aluminum foil dispenser, and even an un-refrigerated bin for bananas!

How was this unique movie experience filmed? Eleven 16mm Cine Kodak Special cameras with two hundred feet of pre-threaded film magazines were mounted on a circular platform covering 360 degrees of arc. The drive shafts of all the cameras were linked mechanically by means of a single sprocket chain.

The tachometer permitted precise control of the shooting speed of a full range of adjustments from eight to twenty-four frames per second. The driving power was supplied by batteries and a push-button control inside the car to start, stop and control the cameras. So basically, the push button controls for the camera were on the dashboard.

This unique camera set-up was strapped to the top of an American Motors Rambler to record a travelogue down the new Los Angeles freeways to Monument Valley, the Grand Canyon and even a visit to Las Vegas.

Disney Legend Peter Ellenshaw was the art director of the original show: "It was a travelogue in the round of Southern California and the West," Ellenshaw remembered. "They mounted eleven cameras on a circular platform atop a station wagon. I was the art director. My greatest problem is I would find this lovely composition, just beautiful, but the cameras behind this vista would show all this trash and junk. It was horrible. I had nothing to do with the mechanical side of the process. That was all Iwerks. On Wilshire Boulevard we ran the cameras at half speed so when it was run at normal speed it seemed like we were demons going at tremendous speeds and somehow amazingly stopping just in the nick of time. That's the scene that most people remember. That film lasted until around 1959 and then they replaced it."

The filming was plagued with challenges from the very beginning. On the way to Utah's Monument Valley, an unexpected bump sent the whole camera system lurching forward. Finding good, smooth roads in the desert was next to impossible. Pictorially, it was a challenge, as well, when in front of the crew was a magnificent mesa or butte but along the side or behind were electric power lines or billboards or similar visual disturbances.

There was a press preview at the end of June that was favorably reviewed in the *Los Angeles Times* that stated, in part: "Spectators located on a so-called island in the center of the stage where Circarama was shown at the Disney plant were able to look out in every direction and observe views of the Grand Canyon, Monument Valley, Las Vegas, Balboa Bay, and even the heavily traveled streets of Los Angeles."

The original design for the Tomorrowland theater was for a central gondola from which twelve images would be shown on as many screens surrounding the audience. With a working area only forty feet in diameter, extremely wide angle short focal length projection lenses would have been required which would probably have resulted in image distortion. A "doughnut" type of arrangement with an odd number of screens resulted in the 360 degrees of arc being serviced perfectly.

"George Romney (American Motors Chairman) and Dad (Romney's assistant) were hosts of the opening of the Circarama Exhibit which opened at 8 p.m. on the preview day. A line of people were standing at the door. Dad spotted Frank Sinatra and invited him in. A black man with Sinatra was hanging back. Dad invited him to come in, too. This man turned out to be Sammy Davis, Jr. After viewing Circarama, Sinatra remarked to Dad that this was the ultimate in motion pictures," remembered William McGaughey, Jr.

What was the experience like for *A Tour of the West?* Here's what Disneyland guests saw in 1955 after they surrendered their "C" Ticket worth thirty cents.

Throughout a twelve hour day, there were three approximately twelve-minute showings per hour, separated by eight minute intermissions during which the audience was loaded in and out of the theater. The film, of course, was shown in commercial Kodachrome.

The audience stood in an asphalt paved circular area forty feet in diameter with the eight foot high screens elevated about eight feet off the floor. There were no "lean" rails in those early days. As mentioned, there were AMC cars and Kelvinator appliances around the outside of the perimeter.

The circular screen was divided by 6-inch wide vertical black strips into eleven 8-by-11 foot sections onto which the continuous surrounding motion picture image was thrown by eleven Eastman 16mm Model 25 projectors with self-loading take-up reels, which required no rewinding in perfect synchronization.

Those projectors were equipped with a variable focus 15mm lens. Attendants were not needed to operate the projectors, merely to replace burnt out bulbs in automatic lamp changer, as well as torn film reels. The projection operation, as well as sound recording, was synchronized by Selsyn motor controls. The projectors were located between the black 6-inch wide strips dividing the eleven screen sections.

The black separating panels added to the illusion of continuity between adjoining sections of the picture, because they eliminated the disturbing jiggle between adjacent screen sections on the Cinerama three-screen image, as well as making it seem the viewer was in a car and looking out through the windows.

In addition, it was discovered that this early system had "blind spots." A person or landmark could suddenly disappear into one of these blind spots only to magically reappear on the adjacent screen. The strip of black between each screen helped solve that visual problem.

Since the projectors were about twelve feet apart, it was impossible to link them together mechanically as was done with the Cinerama system. Instead, the projectors were equipped with slotted-rotor synchronous drive motors that kept time with each other on the basis of the alternating cycles of the AC electricity that drove them. To compensate for voltage fluctuations, which might tend to slow down or speed up one or another of the projectors and also to synchronize the projectors with a four track sound reproducer, a Selsyn motor control unit was superimposed on the projector installation.

It automatically slowed down or sped up the out-of-phase motor's speed until perfect synchronism was achieved. All of that was accomplished in a matter of less than two seconds without causing the out of phase image to "bounce."

If the film should break in any of the projectors, the projector was instantly stopped and a warning light went on at the master control panel to alert the attendant that he had to replace the broken reel with one of the stand-by prints. That screen would be black until a replacement reel was installed.

Whenever a bulb burned out, an automatic bulb-changing mechanism on the projector swung the burnt out bulb out of position and replaced it with a fresh one, so that the picture goes on again in less than two seconds. As with a broken strip of film, a warning light is flashed to the master control panel alerting the attendant to put a fresh bulb in the stand by socket.

The sound was recorded on four magnetic channels and was fed into a bank of four six-inch speakers mounted beneath each projector. As a result, the theater could be flooded with sound from all the speakers or distributed in a directional pattern in just one section. Both formats were utilized during the screening.

The Ralke Company of Los Angeles was responsible for the installation and maintenance of the Ciracarama unit and the Urbran Engineering Company of Hollywood perfected the synchronization of the projectors and sound system. Kinevox Inc. of Hollywood engineered the audio portion of the presentation. Disney Legend Bill Anderson (credited as "William H. Anderson") was given credit for supervising the entire film.

As the show opens, a narrator explained the projection medium and introduces the line of Kelvinator appliances. James Algar wrote the narration for the attraction.

"In a few moments you will see the most unique motion picture presentation ever developed. You will be completely surrounded by the picture that you see. We hope that you will enjoy... Circarama."

Full-color slides of these modern AMC/Kelvinator marvels were projected in quick succession on each of the eleven screens and done in a way so the audience follows the progression of images until all the screens were filled and the audience had been conditioned to expect something on every screen.

Then the screens went black and a title appeared on one of the "forward" screens proclaiming *A Tour of the West*. From there the show began with all eleven screens filled with a continuous images of scenery observed from an automobile cruising through Beverly Hills onto Wilshire Boulevard and then on to the Los Angeles freeway system in route to the colorful Grand Canyon and Monument Valley sections of the Southwest as well as Las Vegas.

In the beginning of the movie, the audience had a tendency to look just straight ahead at the forward motion but, as the ride continued, people became accustomed to being in a "car" and started to look out the side and rear windows as interesting roadside objects passed by, an illusion reinforced by those black strips which seemed like the window separations in a car.

Probably the most memorable segment in the film was the "race" down Wilshire Boulevard. The car was driven at fifteen to twenty miles per hour. When they did the high-speed chase on Wilshire Boulevard, they achieved the high-speed effect with an old Hollywood trick of slowing the speed the film traveled through the camera meaning that fewer frames were shot, so when it was played back at normal speed, it looked like the car was racing. Basically, they shot at about eight frames a second and then projected the final film at twenty-four frames a second.

"The effect was astonishing," Ellenshaw said. "Suddenly we were hot rodders, racing down Wilshire at a hundred miles per hours, jumping out at green lights, and crashing to a stop only inches from the cars in front."

During the whizzing down Wilshire, a police car with siren wailing is in full pursuit. The camera car weaves in and out of traffic, swinging to the right and then to the left, alternately slowing down and speeding up, avoiding accidents by split-second maneuvers. It really was a virtual thrill ride for guests of the mid-Fifties and one they still talked about when they left the theater. The wail of the police siren was added in post production to the sound track to reinforce the illusion of danger.

The scene shifts to the desert wilderness and the feeling of not just watching this beautiful tableau but actually being in it.

To insure that audiences would scan all the screens, Disney employed some subtle audience manipulation. In the Las Vegas scenes which are set at poolside at one of the resorts, the camera films two charming young ladies in delightfully form-fitting swimsuits. With the cameras fixed forward, the bathing beauties walk separately with poise and confidence along paths on either side of the circle of cameras, meeting each other again at the rear screen. So much, if not all, of the male audience frantically tried to follow the action around the screen.

In a little more than eleven minutes, Disneyland guests got to journey through the West beginning on Sunset Boulevard in front of the Beverly Hills Hotel, then a high speed trip down Wilshire Boulevard and then along the Los Angeles Freeways to Monument Valley, Arizona. The adventure continued through Newport Harbor in California (with the cameras mounted on a speedboat instead of the car) and then off to Las Vegas and the Grand Canyon.

From a 1955 issue of *Popular Photography* magazine came the following review of the innovative Disneyland movie system: "Has Circarama a future? It doesn't seem likely as a story-telling entertainment medium. On the other hand, it has infinite possibilities in the form in which it made its appearance at Disneyland—as a travelogue device, to subject an audience to an unusual visual and emotional experience."

In 1958, Walt created a brand new Circarama film for the Brussels World's Fair, *America the Beautiful*. The new film showcased the entire United States. In June of 1960 the new film debuted at Disneyland sponsored by Bell Telephone.

In 1967, the film process changed with the opening of the New Tomorrowland and there was a 35mm print that was enlarged from the film of nine (rather than eleven) 16mm cameras. A few Bicentennial scenes were added in 1975 and the film ran until January 1984.

Other films including *Wonders of China* and *American Journeys* were shown in the theater until 1996. Then, *America the Beautiful* returned for the final year (July 1996-September 1997) when the theater was closed for good. However, it was *A Tour of the West* in Circarama that started it all with its first presentation on July 17, 1955.

"When the Circarama presentation was completed, Sinatra gave his verdict. He turned to Mr. Davis and said, 'This is the wave of the future. The motion picture single screen is obsolete and future movies will use this exciting new technology.' He was wrong, of course. Nevertheless, his words were encouraging and I felt somewhat redeemed that my Big Boss Romney had accepted my recommendation to pay the heavy rental cost for Disneyland exhibitions," remembered William McGaughey Sr. in 1998 when asked about the innovative Disneyland attraction he was in charge of in 1955.

# THE STORY OF STORYBOOK LAND

For countless millions of Disneyland guests over the decades, they have eagerly braved the menacingly wide open mouth of Monstro the whale from *Pinocchio* in order to be taken to a miniature land of enchantment known as Storybook Land.

Some might argue that the attraction actually opened July 17, 1955 with Disneyland since the attraction began as the Canal Boats of the World. The Disneyland souvenir guide of the time described it as "Boats of Holland, France, England and America travel through canals which pass the fabulous sights of Fantasyland."

On a trip to Paris, Walt had experienced a canal boat ride with a complex system of locks and channels raising the boat gently and then allowing it to cruise downstream. He even had a photograph taken of the ride but it did not show enough detail and the Disney Studio designers were forced to start from scratch. Eight separate barges were designed but due to economics, all the barges had the same molded hull with four different tops, two each for four countries including America.

The eight original Canal Boats of the World were named Nellie Bly, Lady Katrina, Lady of Shallot, Annie Oakley, Gretel, Bold Lochinvar, Lady of the Lake, and Lady Guinivere.

When Disneyland opened, the ride itself was merely a trough of muddy water with boats going by uncompleted muddy banks sometimes decorated with weeds. To this day, Dick Nunis who was in charge of Disneyland at one time refers to this version as "The Mud Bank Ride."

The original plan was to be a journey past miniature re-creations of the great landmarks of the world, but time and money were not available to make this vision a reality. Walt Disney was one of the first visitors to Madurodam, a tourist attraction that opened in the Netherlands in 1952. It was a miniature environment that still exists today that showcases the landmarks of the Netherlands with miniature buildings, streets, walkways, windmills, the countryside and more. Since he had suggested that Ken Anderson, the primary designer of Storybook Land, also visit Madurodam, it is apparent that Walt wanted a similar experience for Disneyland.

On the original Canal Boat ride, embarrassed cast members would tell guests: "The miniature landscaping is so small you can't see it!" There was no set spiel because there was nothing to talk about and, in addition, it was difficult to shout above the noisy outboard motors that often overheated and got vapor lock and had to be pulled by hand back to the loading dock.

The cast members driving the boats would shut off the engines occasionally so they could describe a variety of upcoming Disneyland projects, "both real and imagined". It was finally determined that a series of highly detailed miniscule buildings inspired by the classic Disney animated films would be best, but designed in a way to give the guests the feeling that the characters might appear at any moment or had just recently left the building.

The boats were built by the Robert Dorris Boat Works and the gas-powered outboard motors were unreliable to say the least. The Robert Dorris Boat Works replaced them with electric motors that were individually powered by direct chain drive from the propeller shaft to a General Electric motor for the opening of Storybook Land.

When the Storybook Land attraction opened during the Summer of 1956, four Mouseketeers (Darlene, Lonnie, Sharon and Bobby) joined a half dozen other children as the American Dairy Princess (remember there was a Dairy Bar in nearby Tomorrowland serving Carnation milk, an early participant at the new park) put on her tiara and christened the boats by pouring a pint of milk over their hulls.

The Storybook Land boats were named Cinderella, Daisy, Aurora, Alice, Faline, Flora, Fauna, Merryweather, Flower, Katrina, Wendy, Snow White and Tinker Bell. In later years, Belle and Ariel joined the fleet. The boats are almost sixteen feet long and move along a submerged guide rail very similar to the one used in the Jungle Cruise.

Walt was extremely pleased with the work of Ken Anderson on the early Fantasyland dark rides like *Snow White and Her Adventures*, *Peter Pan's Flight*, and *Mr. Toad's Wild Ride*. He was also aware that Ken not only had architectural training but also had worked as an animator and layout artist on the classic Disney animated features.

So it was natural that he turned over the task of converting the "Mud Boat Ride" to the Storybook Land ride to Ken. While Ken did the primary design work, he worked closely with others on this project, including Frank Armitage, Walt Peregoy, Harriet Burns and Fred Joerger.

Fred gained some notoriety by standing over the little copper roof of the miniature church each day right after lunch and 'aging' the copper be relieving himself in the most organic way imaginable. Fortunately, the paint shop soon came up with its own chemical formula for aging the copper so Fred's method was retired.

Imagineer Bruce Bushman had come up with an idea for a ride where guests, just like Pinocchio, would be swallowed by a huge Monstro the Whale. They would be lifted high in the whale's throat and then hurled down a watery path to a pond below. Walt rejected this idea just as he had the proposal to make *Mr. Toad's Wild Ride* a roller coaster because of his expressed concern that grown up family members would probably shy away from a too-thrilling white knuckle ride.

However no good idea was ever totally abandoned when Walt was alive, and so the concept of being swallowed by Monstro the Whale was later incorporated into the beginning of Storybook Land.

Walt demanded great attention to detail from tiny stained glass windows in Alice's church to small toys behind the frosted glass of Gepetto's toy shop to cobblestone streets that were paved with individually placed pebbles.

One contractor concerned about all the labor and expense of the details Walt was including in Storybook Land, in frustration at not being able to cut some corners, asked Walt, "Who'll know the difference?" Walt sternly replied, "I'll know the difference."

Ken later found out that Storybook Land was one of Walt's favorite rides, and while Walt rarely visited the site when construction was going on, he did make frequent visits to the model shop at the Burbank studio to provide comments and directions on the models.

Ken Anderson remembered when I interviewed him: "According to a press release, Storybook Land was a 'model maker's paradise.' I did all the design work. We had to get special permission on Cinderella's Castle. It was a nineteen foot castle. It looks like it was about ten feet at the most. We had to get special permission to bring it to Disneyland on the freeway because there were places you couldn't get it underneath the overpasses.

(The castle actually made the trip from Burbank to Anaheim on its side on the bed of a truck. Few Disney fans realize that Disneyland is the only Disney theme park that has both a Sleeping Beauty and Cinderella castle.)

*"Just because everything was small doesn't mean that they were easy to build. We had to grade the ground, lay the electrical wiring. Everything had to be done in the manner of a full scale house because these houses would never disappear. They were meant to be permanent structures.*

*"We made the houses out of wood siding and fiberglass over the top of it. The buildings were made of marine plywood or redwood covered with fiberglass to survive in the weather. The roofs and brick chimneys were modeled out of fiberglass and joined to the houses.*

*"Metal and concrete were used for the foundations to resist rot. Each little house or shop had openings so that the air could circulate through and prevent mildew. There were hundreds of tests to find the right transparent dye for the tiny plastic stained glass windows.*

*"Tiny lead doorknobs were installed on tiny doors that opened and closed on miniature hinges. Little thatched roofs were covered with plastic so the birds couldn't carry it off and make nests out of it. (Some of those roofs were removable and*

*the doors actually worked so that electricians had access to*
*change the light bulbs.)*

*"When the buildings were finished and painted, then we put in*
*landscaping: miniature trees, shrubs, mountains. Everything*
*had to be miniature because it was an inch to a foot.*

*"Snow White's cottage had these tall trees at twelve feet which*
*made them a hundred and twenty feet tall. Where do you find*
*small redwoods that would stay small? I found a place up*
*north in San Francisco called Van Damme State Park. There*
*was a redwood forest and an area where the redwoods had*
*starved to death because there wasn't enough space for them*
*to grow. It was on a platform of rock, these tiny trees. They*
*wouldn't let me have them or even go in there. We finally got*
*access to a place near there that was like it and we absconded*
*with some twenty trees and brought them down to Disneyland.*

(In fact, they were actually pine trees that grew about three
to four feet tall because they were unable to root properly into
a limestone shelf. Fifty feet away beyond the edge of the shelf,
the pine trees towered from sixty to eighty feet tall. A dozen
of the dwarf trees were taken to Disneyland where giant cranes
lifted them over the Storybook Land berm. Two of the trees
died in the process but were sprayed green during the next
two years until they could be replaced. Bonsai trees were not
considered because the cost of even a poor quality one at the
times was close to five hundred dollars apiece and the upkeep
was considered unfeasible.)

*"I got little daffodils from New Zealand that were an inch*
*across. Little, tiny daffodils but the trouble was they had stems*
*a foot and a half long so I had to bury the stems and just have*
*the daffodils on top. But they didn't last long enough. I had*

*to get things that would last. Walt didn't like anything fake. It had to be real. So we gave up the daffodils and got some little dinky flowers.*

*"All the little houses in Gepetto's Village started with some drawings Tenggren had done for the original animated feature. We enlarged on it. Tenggren had designed the original cottage. He was from the old country so it was stuff he knew. Those of us who worked on it we kind of enlarged on it and made it better we think.*

*"We had a pretty nice feeling for Swiss-Italian architecture of around 1500 or 1600. The buildings were all kind of katty-wompus and askew. Everything is cock-eyed. Nothing straight. Everything is like it has been there for some time. All the edges were round which gave it more character. There wasn't a flat roof or a t-squared top any where. They all showed the result of age and how aging had changed things. That is what happened to Gepetto's village.*

*"The challenge with Storybook Land is that each one was from a different country. You had Thaddeus Toad, Snow White, Cinderella and so on but they all had to go together. So we had to consider that. I had to consider the same thing for Fantasyland."*

---

Little remembered by most Disney fans is that the earliest cast members guiding the boats were all men in puffy shirts. It wasn't until around 1960 that the role was taken over primarily by attractive and charming young women.

Former President Harry Truman visited Disneyland in 1958 and refused to ride the *Dumbo* attraction because an elephant might be associated with the Republican Party. He did, however, board the Storybook Land boat but there was a slight delay. The canal boat was fully loaded, but, for some reason, the ride operator seemed unable to get it going. Finally, he turned to his noted guest.

"Pardon me, Mr. Truman," he said. "If you would lift your foot off the brake, we could start."

The former President of the United States instinctively lifted his right foot and the boat took off. He looked down at the brakeless floorboard; then joined the laughter at having fallen for this gag that operators on many of the Disneyland rides frequently pulled on unsuspecting patrons.

Walt insisted that the Casey Jr. train station be elevated so that potential riders could easily see that the train and the boats toured much of the same area. Over the decades, the little charms of Storybook Land brought large amounts of delight to guests of all ages.

## LIBERTY STREET 1959

*"Disneyland is dedicated to the ideals, the dreams, and the hard facts that have created America," stated Walt Disney in his dedication speech July 17, 1955.*

In a 1957 interview with newspaper columnist Hedda Hopper, Walt stated: "There's an American theme behind the whole park. I believe in emphasizing the story of what made America great and what will keep it great."

Even around the dinner table at his home, Walt would engage his family in discussions about the Constitution. So it is not surprising that Walt wanted a section of Disneyland devoted to the founding of America.

At Disneyland to the left of the Disneyland Opera House would have been a street that would have paralleled Main Street called Liberty Street. However, visitors wouldn't have been able to take the street to the Hub. It was to be a cul-de-sac. Only Main Street would have given visitors the option to visit other lands.

Publicity and signage at Disneyland announced that Liberty Street was scheduled to open in 1959 and the area remained on Disneyland park maps for several years as a "future development". Originally the street was going to be called International Street with a variety of buildings representing different countries from around the world. That project was announced as opening in 1958. However, by 1957, Walt had decided to use the land to showcase the founding fathers.

The release of the live action Disney feature film, *Johnny Tremain* (originally intended as merely a two-part episode for the Disneyland television show) in 1957 may have influenced Walt to consider the development of an area capturing that time period, especially since the first planning for Liberty Square officially began in 1957.

Liberty Street was to be an architectural mixture of several America cities as they existed during the Revolutionary War era. At one point there were to be thirteen buildings, one for each of the original thirteen colonies.

Cobblestones would pave the way down Liberty Street and into Liberty Square. There would be a blacksmith shop, apothecary, glassmaker, weaver, print shop, insurance office, silversmith and cabinetmaker. All the shops and exhibits would represent the types of enterprises that might be found in Colonial America. In fact, the shops were supposed to showcase people not only selling their wares but also practicing their crafts for guests to enjoy.

On an early Disneyland map, some areas were identified by name including Griffin's Wharf (supposedly the site of the infamous Boston Tea Party) with its tri-masted schooners in the harbor, Paul Revere's Silver Shop, Boston Observer Print Shoppe, and a Liberty Tree in the town square.

The original outline for the project stated that "the audience will walk around the street toward Independence Hall where the Liberty Bell would be constantly tolling." (Fortunately, in Florida, wiser heads realized a constantly tolling Liberty Bell would be more of an irritant than a joy when they installed their own replica of the Liberty Bell.)

One of the exhibits in Liberty Square would be a scale model of the Capitol building. Long-time Disneyland visitors might remember the model used to be displayed for many years at Disneyland in the pre-show area for the *Walt Disney Story* film. The model was personally purchased by Walt Disney himself from an artisan who had devoted twenty-five years of his life to carving it out of stone.

Liberty Hall (also called Independence Hall in some versions) was the centerpiece of the Liberty Square and was the entrance to the two major attractions in this land: *Hall of The Declaration of Independence*, and *Hall of Presidents of the United States*. A large foyer with dioramas depicting famous scenes of the Revolutionary War period would be the common entrance to the two big auditoriums.

The *Hall of The Declaration of Independence* was designed to present the dramatic story of the birth of the United States through three scenes that were based on three famous paintings. These scenes would be three framed settings with three-dimensional sculpted life-sized human figures in costume. It was hoped the figures would move realistically but in a limited fashion. Narration (sprinkled with quotes from the Declaration of Independence) would tell the story and historical significance of each tableau along with dramatic lighting and music. Theatrical curtains would open and close on each scene.

The first scene was inspired by the painting *The Drafting of the Declaration of Independence* by J.L.G. Ferris. The scene has Ben Franklin and John Adams in consultation with Thomas Jefferson as he drafted the Declaration of Independence.

The second scene would be based on the painting *Signing of the Declaration of Independence* by John Trumbull. The third scene would be based on the painting *Ringing of the Liberty Bell* by Henry Mosler.

Of course, the theater would try to capture the feel of the time period. There would be bench-like pews that could seat up to five hundred guests. Overhead, thirteen stars representing the original thirteen colonies would light the auditorium.

However, the main attraction in this area was to be the *Hall of Presidents of the United States.*

---

In 1963, Imagineer Wathel Rogers who was working on an audio-animatronics version of President Abraham Lincoln said, "Lincoln is part of a Disneyland project called *One Nation Under God.* It will start with a Circarama presentation of great moments in constitutional crises. Circarama is a special motion-picture technique Walt developed for Disneyland and the Brussels World's Fair. The Bell Telephone Circarama now at Disneyland tells the story of the great sights of America. It has a 360-degree screen. The audience is surrounded by the continuous action, as if they were moving with the camera and able to see in all directions.

"The Circarama for the *One Nation Under God* showing will have a 200-degree screen. After the Circarama showing, a curtain will close, then open again to reveal the Hall of Presidents. The visitor will see all the Chief Executives modeled life-size. He'll think it's a waxworks—until Lincoln stands up and begins to talk."

Walt assigned James Algar (who would later compose the final speech for *Great Moments With Mr. Lincoln* from a variety of Lincoln's speeches) to research information on the United States Presidents and in particular the Constitution that was to be the foundation for the show. The Circarama presentation would primarily feature enlarged paintings spotlighting key moments in the early United States history with the climax being a violent Civil War battle.

Imagineer Sam McKim recalled, "Walt wanted artillery that would fire from one screen across to the enemy on a screen on the other side and you'd see things blow up, and then you smell cordite. It was smell-o-vision!"

In the *Hall of Presidents of the United States* auditorium, the stage lights would brighten and the curtains would partially open to reveal life-sized sculpted and costumed figures of the presidents of the United States. They would all be in silhouette except for the main figure. The key U.S. President would not have been Lincoln but George Washington.

The show was entitled *One Nation Under God* and would be a theater presentation of "the mighty cavalcade of American History".

"Martial music would come up as lights played on the features of Washington, creating a feeling of reality. Narrations of the trials, decisions and formation of America's heritage were to be complemented by excerpts from presidential speeches. At the conclusion, all the nation's presidents (34 by 1957) would be seen on the enormous stage against a rear-projected image of the United States Capitol, as clouds panned across the sky and a musical finale closed the show," wrote Imagineer David Mumford several decades ago.

Obviously, this show would depend heavily on the development of audio-animatronics which still in its earliest of stages. WED had begun producing prototypes, including the head of an elderly Chinese man for a figure that Walt had originally intended for a Chinese restaurant that would have been in Center Street near the Market House. An elderly Chinese man wearing long flowing robes would have justified and concealed any shaky, slow, awkward movements when the figure came to life.

However, a good deal of money was needed for further development so in June of 1961, Walt Disney went looking for a sponsor in hopes that some company might want *One Nation Under God* for the upcoming New York World's Fair in 1964.

Imagineering compiled a presentation, which included a small model theater and a thirty-two minute slide presentation, which would hopefully entice potential corporate backers. There was a press package put together with little smiling Tinker Bell wearing a tri-cornered hat sitting on a sign proclaiming "Liberty Street in Disneyland!"

An excerpt from that proposal dated June 29, 1961 stated, "As presently planned, *One Nation Under God* will be a twenty-seven minute live action film dramatizing significant episodes in U.S. history, linked together with off-screen narration. Starting with the adoption of the Constitution, the film traces the development of our concept of government, through trial and tribulation, right up to the present.

"The technique is an extension of the Circarama idea, in that five projectors will be used instead of three—thus spreading the picture over an expanse of 260 degrees, or well beyond the field of human vision. As in Circarama, the audience enjoys the sensation of being right in the middle of everything. This feeling is enhanced by the use of multiple stereophonic sound tracks—and even 'smells' (e.g. the odor of gunpowder in battle).

"In a space age sequence, an extra dimension is added; the picture spreads up onto a dome overhead. For the finale, a 'Hall of Presidents' is unveiled. This consists of life sized moving and talking figures of thirty-four presidents—something brand new now being developed at Disney Studios."

The proposal went on for a few more paragraphs but unfortunately, the cost of such an attraction was prohibitive and even those sponsors who were impressed with the presentation felt that it didn't connect directly with their product.

Imagineering was working on a prototype of President Lincoln, a particular favorite of Walt's, for the *Hall of Presidents of the United States* attraction when in April 1962 Robert Moses who was promoting the New York World's Fair dropped by the Disney Studios to check the progress on the other attractions. He also got an impromptu demonstration of the Lincoln figure. Moses arranged for the State of Illinois to help pay for the development of the figure for its pavilion at the fair. Although crude by today's standards, the "winking, blinking Lincoln" as one reporter called it thrilled audiences. Many in the audience were convinced it was a live actor and suspicious children sometimes shot small ball bearings at the figure to try to disrupt the performer's concentration.

A second version of *Great Moments With Mr. Lincoln* was installed at Disneyland on July 18, 1965, mere feet away from where the entrance to Liberty Street was planned.

Instead of creating Liberty Street in 1959, Walt Disney used his money and expertise to update Tomorrowland with the Monorail, the Submarine Voyage and the Matterhorn.

However, Imagineering never fully abandoned Walt's dream. Walt Disney World's Liberty Square captures the spirit of Walt's plans for Disneyland's Liberty Street in 1959 including a *Hall of Presidents* housed in a building inspired by Independence Hall in Philadelphia as well as other Federal style civic buildings in Philadelphia at the time.

"The show was on and off at various times in the Studio, but when it came time to really firm it up for Florida, when I dug out the original script, it dated back to 1961. And the *Hall of Presidents* was very much Walt's baby. He had this great desire to present to an audience all of the Presidents of the United States on stage at once. He read into that single idea a feeling that it would have great impact and great audience interest and fascination and, in truth, it does," said James Algar who wrote the original script.

Walt Disney stated in May 1957, "As you know, Disneyland park is sort of a monument to the American way of life but after reading *Johnny Tremain*, we realized we had overlooked one major item in the blueprint…a memorial to the freedoms that made it all possible. We're putting it in right here off of Town Square. We're calling it Liberty Street. Everything is still in the planning stages, of course. In effect, Liberty Street will by Johnny Tremain's Boston of about 1775."

While that dream was never realized for Disneyland, the spirit of Walt's intentions finally came true with the opening of Liberty Square at Walt Disney World.

## SLEEPING BEAUTY CASTLE WALK THROUGH

Disneyland's iconic castle wasn't specifically designed to be Sleeping Beauty Castle. In early planning and written material, it is designated as "The Medieval Castle" and then "Fantasyland Castle" and even "Robin Hood Castle" to theme in with the Disney live action film. This may explain why some of Robin's merry men hung out in front of the castle on Opening Day and in the early years. On an early episode of his weekly ABC television show, Walt himself even referred to the castle as "Snow White's Castle."

However, by that fabled day on July 17, 1955, it was Sleeping Beauty Castle and it became an icon not only for the theme park itself but an icon almost as recognizable as Mickey Mouse to represent the entire Disney Company. The early guidebooks indicated that Princess Aurora was in the castle and "slumbers in her magnificent bed chamber" still waiting for Prince Phillip to free her from Maleficient's evil spell (even though a live action Sleeping Beauty was very active on Opening Day in the castle courtyard with Snow White, Alice from Wonderland and other Disney characters).

The legendary Van France, who along with Dick Nunis created Disney University and the original training programs for Disneyland cast members, was there in the middle of all the chaos when Disneyland opened that first day.

"Most of the day, I was outside the park on traffic detail, but I did go inside to check on things. I ran into [C.V.] Wood at the entrance to the Administration Building. This usually cool, calm and collected man was out of character. We had forgotten to lock the doors to Sleeping Beauty Castle. Internally, it was nothing but an incomplete shell. 'Van,' he yelled, 'there are people up in that castle. Get them out before they kill themselves.' Sure enough, here were some people at the top of the castle enjoying the show. They had found an open door and had climbed up on the construction platform. I found Larry Tyson, our finance director, who stood guard at one door, while we carefully helped the people down from their precarious perch before they killed themselves," France said with a chuckle.

Walt was keenly aware of what his guests wanted. He watched where they walked, what they did with their trash, and what they called things and all of those observations helped fine tune an already outstanding entertainment experience in the early years of the park.

It was definitely clear that the guests wanted to go inside the castle. So Walt called upon his fabled "jack of all trades", Imagineer Ken Anderson, to take a little visit to the park with him. Coming along was Disney Legend Emile Kuri who had designed the interior of the Nautilus for *20,000 Leagues Under the Sea* and had contributed significantly to the design of Disneyland's Main Street.

Ken Anderson remembered that fateful day in great detail:

*"One of the most entertaining things that happened was in Sleeping Beauty Castle. I had already finished* **Snow White**, **Peter Pan**, **Toad** *and all those things were all done.*

*"Walt came to me. Walt said, 'Hey, come with me. There's nothing in the castle, no room in the castle at all but I want you to look at things.' He wanted something in the castle and wanted me to come up with something.*

*"The castle was full of maybe a hundred or so feral cats. All these wild cats were living there. We climbed up this ladder to get to the first floor which was eighteen feet up. It was a high first floor. We were looking around.*

*"Another man who came with us loved to follow Walt around. He was a good man named Emile Kuri. He had an all white suit. Always wore beautiful clothes. Always white. I think he even had white underwear and socks. He was all white. He knew he had nothing to do with this thing Walt and I were talking about so he just stepped over to the side and there was a big box with a gunny sack in it where the cats had all slept in this thing.*

*"He lifted this thing. Walt was talking to me about what he wanted me to do. 'I want you to put Sleeping Beauty in here. You can do it. It's little but you can do it.'*

*"Emile pulled this sack out and I was looking at him and he went from white to gray. There he was standing in a gray suit. He burst into these terrible yells and jumped over the railing.*

*"I looked and Walt was all gray and I was turning all gray. We were crawling with fleas. So many fleas you wouldn't believe it. Thousands and thousands of fleas. Emil was jumping around and slapping himself pretty hard that it made this noise.*

*"Don't panic, fellers. Don't panic. I'll get somebody up here with the wagon," said Walt and he picked up a phone and called and I heard him yell, "Walt Disney! That's who!" Somebody must have said, "Walt who?"*

*"Send up a car right away!" yelled Walt and they sent up this motorcycle with a sidecar for just one person and that was Walt.*

*"Emile and I stood in the entrance of the castle and Walt got into the motorcycle and yelled back at us, 'Don't get into the crowd!' and he was off to wardrobe.*

*"Wardrobe was a long ways from where we were. We were supposed to wait for somebody to come but we couldn't wait because we were jumping around and slapping these fleas. We ran through the crowd leaving fleas behind us all the way. We got to wardrobe and got our clothes washed and changed. We were wearing spacemen suits for a week. We got all cleaned up.*

*"Walt enjoyed it. He laughed at us. "You didn't get through the crowd, did you guys?" he asked.*

*"Oh, no, Walt."*

*"Then how the hell did you get here?"*

*"One big leap, Walt, what do you think?"*

By the way, Walt arranged for bathing, grooming and eventual relocation of the "castle cats" and found them new families despite the recommendations of some of his staff to find a more speedy and permanent solution.

To help explain the story of Disney's interpretation of "Sleeping Beauty" to the guests, to promote the upcoming film and to allow guests an opportunity to go inside the castle, a narrow walk through diorama of miniature scenes was designed by Anderson.

Since the film wasn't complete, some of those scenes bore no resemblance to the final film even though Production Art designer Eyvind Earle, responsible for the distinctive look of the film in production, himself did some of the artwork for the dioramas. Sadly, Earle's work was replaced when the exhibit was re-designed in 1977.

This "A"-ticket walking tour costing a dime took guests up narrow winding stairs in the dark to view miniature dioramas concentrating on key moments in the story. Illuminated manuscripts in leather bound volumes helped guests follow the storyline as they walked from one end of the castle to the other over the archway. There was music and sound effects including an "echo" effect at one point.

The dioramas were dimensional plywood cutouts that had some elements of movement. For instance, Maleficent had Diablo the Raven on her shoulders and his wings slowly flapped thanks to a small motor mechanism. It was very similar to the sets and figures in the original Fantasyland dark rides.

There were almost a dozen scenes including "Burning of every Spinning Wheel in the Kingdom" (a series of flats with a lighted burning effect down in the courtyard similar to an effect later used in *Pirates of the Caribbean*),"Three fairies watching over the little Princess night and day" (the fairies would appear to float over the cradle using the "Pepper's Ghost" technique later used in the *Haunted Mansion* ballroom scene), "Meet Maleficent's demons" (where the guest could peak through keyholes to see the goons. This was a last minute addition since the original plans indicate that the guests at this point were to wander outside onto the rear balcony for a view of Fantasyland but that never happened.) and "Love's First Kiss" (when the prince leaned over and kissed the cutout of Aurora she fluttered her eyelids and opened her eyes)

To fit in all of these scenes and more, interior space of the two Fantasyland shops on the ground floor of the castle were reduced and portions of their ceilings lowered to help accommodate the stairwells. Cast member access had to be redesigned since it was still necessary for special celebrations to have costumed cast members and trumpeters appear on the battlements.

Imagineer Dick Irvine told Imagineer Randy Bright that he felt the dioramas looked like department store window dressing but praised Anderson for "great illusions and beautiful sketches." At this time, Anderson was working on a proposal for the *Haunted Mansion* and incorporated some of those effects that he was researching into the displays.

The official dedication of the new walk-through took place on Sunday, April 29, 1957 at three p.m. with the Disneyland Band playing "When You Wish Upon a Star" in the courtyard. Walt escorted actress Shirley Temple Black through a pathway created by the band led by Vessey Walker to the entrance of the walk through.

Walt, of course, was there to give the dedication speech. Jack Lindquist, who would later become the President of the park but at the time was involved in marketing, wrote Walt's speech and remembered it as one his favorite experiences.

Lindquist remembered in an interview with Scott Wolf, "One of the first times I got the chance to work directly for

[Walt Disney] was the opening of Sleeping Beauty Castle. I had the chance to write the speech for Walt. So I sat down at a typewriter and said, 'OK, now what the [heck] should I say?' So I wrote something, sent it up there and I'd heard from most everybody that Walt will change everything. So I was waiting for it to come back, I never heard a thing.

"He came down the day of the dedication and I met him over at City Hall about an hour before the dedication, and he took the speech out of his vest pocket and said, 'Who wrote this?' I thought, oh boy, next thing he'll say is 'You're fired.' So I said, 'I did.'" He said, 'Oh.' And didn't say a word. Put it back in his pocket, went to the opening and he read it and didn't change one word. So I was very pleased and proud of that."

The other person dedicating the new attraction was actress Shirley Temple, dressed as a princess wearing a gold crown and a floor length red velvet cloak and accompanied by her three children: oldest daughter Linda, son Charles Jr., and youngest daughter Lori. They stayed at the Disneyland Hotel and apparently enjoyed some time together at the park earlier that day before the dedication ceremony.

After Walt spoke to the crowd briefly, he introduced Shirley Temple Black who told the story of *Sleeping Beauty*. Then, with Walt, she cut the chest high ribbon to open the attraction and went inside. Later, she waved to photographers and guests from the upper balcony.

To tie-in with the new attraction, Disney produced a lavishly illustrated twenty-five cent booklet telling the story of *Sleeping Beauty* that could be purchased at the park. "A Free Envelope if you desire to mail this 'Sleeping Beauty Castle' booklet is available upon request at the Arts Crafts Store in the

Castle courtyard. Additional copies with envelopes 25 cents per book" claimed a perforated "for easy removal" coupon in the book.

Surrounding a color photo of Walt kneeling on the lawn in front of the castle with three small young boys was an introduction credited to Walt himself:

> *Imagination is the mold from which reality is created.*
> *Centuries ago men of vivid imagination created the fairytales*
> *which live to this day, even though in many cases the authors'*
> *names have been lost in the mist of antiquity. Of all these*
> *stirring legends of princes and princesses, of witches and*
> *fairies, and of the triumph of good over evil, none has ever*
> *been so inspirational to me as **Sleeping Beauty**. From the*
> *time I started making motion pictures I dreamed of bringing*
> ***Sleeping Beauty** to life through the medium of animation.*
>
> *But its scope defied us until recent years when our creative*
> *talent and technical advances made its production possible.*
> *Sleeping Beauty is the most beautiful and exacting picture we*
> *have ever made—and without doubt our costliest. It has been*
> *a definite challenge but thanks to our talented staff of artists*
> *and technicians, it has been met.*

Walt, the ultimate showman, then continued to tantalize guests' imagination not just about the new attraction but the forthcoming film as well. This was the first time in Disney history that an attraction based on a film opened prior to the film's debut. The castle opened four years before the release of the film and the walk through two years before the film debuted.

"And now as a result of our vast research and motion picture production efforts, Sleeping Beauty Castle in Disneyland has been completed. Through the medium of key scenes from our film, we have symbolized its timeless enchantments. Here behind these castle walls, in these towers and courts, may be seen the joys and tears of the beautiful Princess Aurora, mingled in her great adventure with the powers of good and evil. We hope the magic spell of these scenes and sounds will revive in every beholder's heart some image of his own most precious dreams—the dreams from which all enduring fairytales are made."

The Sleeping Beauty Castle Walk Through was redesigned in 1977 to increase the sophistication of effects now that Audio Animatronics made those earlier simple effects look ancient. In addition, it was felt that the displays should more closely mirror the actual finished film. New dioramas replaced the Earle originals. The 1977 dioramas were more three-dimensional and much more detailed and closely resembled the displays that decorated the windows of the Main Street Emporium.

The reason for that "look" was it was created by the same team that did those Main Street display windows. Bob Davis, Jim Dieli and Gene Camelot from Disneyland's Marketing Division were the artists who watched the films and came up with the set design and possible animation. According to Disney publicity at the time, "Gene, who was with the Studio's Animation Department during the production of Disney's *Sleeping Beauty*, lent his creative mind and hands to this project" of refurbishing the Sleeping Beauty Castle walk through. The actual creation of the sets and figures were in the hands of Eric Gatley and a team of craftsmen who then turned it over to Disneyland's Maintenance Division who completed the sets under the supervision of Disney artists.

The new scene pattern included such scenes as subjects attired in medieval costume approach King Stefan's castle to honor the newborn princess, Aurora dances with a make-believe Prince, Prince Phillip battles the fire-breathing dragon and the kingdom celebrating when Aurora awakes with love's first kiss. Over the years, additions were made to try and upgrade the attraction from the introduction of fiber optics, to changes in lighting to shimmering new fabrics for the sets and figures.

On October 7, 2001, the Sleeping Beauty Castle Walk Through was closed "for refurbishment." While there was speculation that the reason of the closure was for security purposes after the terror attack of September 11th that happened the previous month, the real truth was more mundane. While the castle gave the illusion of a rock structure, it was in fact made of wood that had not been maintained since the park opened just like the fabled Fantasyland carousel that required major attention. In addition, the popularity for the quiet experience had waned greatly over the decades.

The Sleeping Beauty Castle Walk Through, just like Princess Aurora herself, slumbered for many years. Quietly, the Disney Company redesigned the walk-through, retaining the spirit of the original Eyvind Earle designs. The walk through reopened on November 27, 2008. Unlike previous incarnations, visitors who are unable to climb stairs or navigate the passageways of the Castle can still experience the walk through "virtually" in a special room on the Castle's ground floor. Once again, Disneyland guests can delight in seeing true love's kiss bring magic back to the kingdom.

## ZORRO AT DISNEYLAND

For a certain generation, the Zorro theme song still stirs the blood and conjures up images of Halloween past when children dressed up as their hero. Ben Cooper costumes in 1958 announced that their Zorro costume was outselling all others by a ratio of three to one. Unfortunately today's youth is hopelessly unfamiliar with Disney's interpretation of the classic dashing character.

Walt considered many actors for the role of Zorro/Don Diego and the main antagonist in the first thirteen episodes, Captain Enrique Sanchez Monastario. Dozens of actors including Hugh O'Brian, John Lupton, Jack Kelly, Dennis Weaver, David Janssen, Henry Darrow and others were tested until it came down to Guy Williams and Britt Lomond.

Walt reportedly wanted Lomond for the part of Zorro since he had more theatrical experience, but writer-director Norman Foster preferred Williams in the role because he showed a greater flexibility and cast Lomond as the villain. Henry Calvin (as Sergeant Garcia) and Gene Sheldon (as the mute servant Bernardo) garnered almost as much affection for their roles as the two leads.

Today, the fabled Disney backlot where Zorro fought for justice (and Walt locked up Ken Murray's two daughters in a jail cell for their father to rescue them on Murray's home movies) is a parking garage.

Walt was famous for doing cross promotions like having the Mousekeeters and Fess Parker (as Davy Crockett) appear at Disneyland. As the half-hour *Zorro* ABC adventure show became a success, Walt had the cast appear at Disneyland for special appearances dubbed "Zorro Days" and publicized it with large local newspaper advertisements. Williams, Lomond, Calvin and Sheldon were announced. Missing from those announcements was Buddy Van Horn.

Stuntman Wayne "Buddy" Van Horn was hired primarily as Guy Williams' double. Wisely, at the urging of Britt Lomond, Van Horn practiced with Fred Cavens, who choreographed the fencing scenes (just as he had done with Douglas Fairbanks Sr., Errol Flynn, Tyrone Power and Basil Rathbone in many classic films) and coached the actors. Van Horn was also the stunt coordinator for any action other than fencing.

It is Van Horn who often doubled in the horseback riding scenes and any dangerous leaping off of walls, running across rooftops or swinging on ropes. While Williams was athletic and capable of doing much of this action, if he had been accidentally injured it would have delayed shooting and been a costly postponement. Ironically, the studio released some publicity stills of Van Horn dressed as Zorro, assuming the audience wouldn't know the difference between him and Williams, prompting someone to joke to Williams that he had better be careful because Disney could put anybody in the costume.

It was Van Horn, attired as Zorro, who did some of the daring stunts at the Disneyland shows like dashing over the rooftops of the Golden Horseshoe Revue. Later personal appearances had Van Horn accompany Williams for fencing demonstrations, taking on the role of the villain, and sometimes Van Horn performing as Zorro himself when Williams was unavailable like a Disney family night at the Hollywood Bowl in the Summer of 1958.

In the early years at Disneyland, there were five major Zorro appearances at Disneyland: April 26-27,1958 ; May 30- June 1, 1958; November 27-30, 1958; November 26-29, 1959; and, finally November, 11-13, 1960.

Lomond did not appear at the November 1958 appearance because of a conflict, but Williams appeared by himself for personal appearances at Disneyland around the Christmas season in 1958. The *Zorro* cast appeared on a float for the June 15, 1959 parade *Kodak Presents Disneyland '59* television special.

As Lomond remembered in his self published colorful memoir, *Chasing After Zorro* (2001), "Personal appearances for all the principal actors in the Zorro cast were always very important to Walt and to the other executives at the studio. They all felt that it was very important for the cast to always stay in contact with their admiring viewers. This was included in every star's contract and many of the featured player's contracts on the shows as well."

During "Zorro Days," the actors appeared in the parades each day and also performed in Frontierland for four shows daily. Three of the shows were a running battle between Zorro and Monastario over the rooftops of Frontierland, usually with a sword fight aboard the Mark Twain and some of Zorro's foes ending up in the Rivers of America.

The fourth show was in Magnolia Park, generally for autographs or sometimes an impromptu fencing match with guest volunteers. Williams and Lomond would again cross swords for the enjoyment of the guests, and Calvin and Sheldon would amuse the crowds with comedy and magic.

"I suggested we invite anyone from the audience the opportunity to fence, or 'sword fight' as we called it, with Zorro," said publicist John Ormond. "We always had two or three 'takers' at each show who wanted to take Guy on. This is a piece of audience participation that worked well at Disneyland whenever Zorro appeared. And by the way, we were using real swords. At Disneyland, we had a security and screening process so things couldn't get out of hand."

During an interview, Lomond recalled:

*"Disney always liked the casts of his shows to make appearances at Disneyland. It was great for attendance at the park and a lot of Zorro products were sold at the same time. Things like little Zorro costumes, play swords, puzzles, games and dozens of other items relating to the series. Money would pour into the Disney coffers. These personal appearances were a great moneymaker for the studio and Walt knew it certainly helped in the ratings which made ABC a very happy puppy.*

*"The Disney Studio's Production Coordinator, Lou Debney, set all the details of the appearance. The program Lou had for Guy and I at Disneyland was a very good one. There was a replica of a Mississippi steam boat called the Mark Twain. We were to perform in costume one of our spectacular fencing routines on the upper deck of the paddle-wheeler, at the end of which, I would be disarmed and go into my usual Monastario fist clenching and facial grimaces. Guy meanwhile would laugh at the commandant's disgrace and run down the gangplank to his trusty black stallion, leap onto the saddle, wave to the adoring crowd and ride off into the sunset (or the usual California smog). Every one of us would then join in a parade down the Main Street of Disneyland. Henry Calvin and*

*Gene Sheldon would sit in a car behind Guy and I riding on
our respective black and white horses. We would wave to the
adoring crowds that lined either side of the street, cheering us
as we passed by them.*

*"Everything sounded great—both Guy and I were very pleased
with the program that Lou had presented. We practiced one of
our fencing routines for the series for several days in the large
back yard of my house in Studio City. My house was easier to
work at because Guy still lived in an apartment in Hollywood.*

*"Finally the day came of our first personal appearance at
Disneyland. Everything went perfectly smooth...almost. Guy
and I did our fencing routine on the deck of the Mark Twain,
ending with my sword sailing into the air, as Guy disarmed
me. He then strutted down the gangplank and ran to his
black stallion where he was to leap into the saddle, lifting
his sword in victory and ride off. Great! However, when we
tried this routine for the first time at Disneyland, Guy missed
the horse's saddle and sailed completely over him, landing
on the pavement and sliding into a pool of muddy water on
the other side. A bit humiliating! The audience and I laughed
uncontrollably. I'm sorry but we just could not help it. The
picture of Guy's expression and the mud still dripping off his
nose was too much for everyone. I quickly raised my arm
in victory and bowed graciously to the applauding crowd.
This was the Commandante's one and only victory over his
nemesis, Zorro."*

To be fair, others don't necessarily remember that incident
(or at least as colorfully as Lomond recounted it).

Publicist John Ormond who handled the *Zorro* show as well as *The Mickey Mouse Club* was involved with the Disneyland presentations as well as some of Guy Williams personal appearances. Ormond wrote, "The Zorro show was mostly filmed at the studio, although we did have one lengthy spell down near Oceanside, shooting at an old Spanish mission. Walt came down for that four-parter, and brought his wife with him. Walt liked water cress sandwiches and Mrs. Disney made sure she brought a good supply while they were with us on location.

"As the weeks went by, I became close to Guy Williams, and we had a lot in common. He liked to play chess, and I liked gin rummy. So we alternated playing while we were on the set. Later, when we toured together for the *Zorro* feature, we always played (magnetic) chess on the planes. Guy was hard to beat at chess, but I outscored him with the cards."

Guy Williams made a host of other public appearances as Zorro, including the Pasadena Rose Parade in 1958 and 1959, state fairs, shopping centers and more. "The show has been a great experience, but Zorro is a role I both love and hate. It wasn't what I prepared for as an actor. I'm not worried about being typed as Zorro because the whole thing has had so many pleasant aspects to it. Besides, such typecasting buys a lot of groceries…" Williams said with a laugh.

## TOM SAWYER ISLAND

Tom Sawyer Island at Disneyland underwent a major transformation in 2007 and became the Pirate's Lair on Tom Sawyer Island, theming into the success of the *Pirates of the Caribbean* movie franchise, replacing the simple charm of Mark Twain's world. Tom Sawyer Island at Walt Disney World's Frontierland has remained the same for forty years and still showcases some of the original ideas Walt Disney had for the location at Disneyland.

"I put in all the things I wanted to do as a kid—and couldn't," Walt explained about the Disneyland Tom Sawyer Island to a *Reader's Digest* reporter in 1960. "Including getting into something without a ticket."

Tom Sawyer Island is truly the only part of Disneyland Park that Walt Disney single handedly designed himself. He always planned for there to be an island in the middle of the Rivers of America but he debated about what that island was going to be.

From Walt's 1953 sales pitch for Disneyland: *"Treasure Island.* Mickey Mouse, the best known personality in the world has his *Mickey Mouse Club* headquarters at Disneyland located on *Treasure Island* in the middle of the river, a fantastic hollow tree and treehouse serves as the Club meeting place. The hollow tree is several stories high, with interesting rooms and lookout spots for club members. There is a Pirate cove and buried treasure on the island…and direct from this location the Club presents *The Mickey Mouse Club* Television Show."

At one point, there were designs for the island that had included miniature reproductions of major American historical landmarks like Mount Vernon, Monticello, and Independence Hall that would have been viewed from the Mark Twain steamboat.

While many Disney fans know that Herb Ryman did the artwork of the original map of Disneyland and Peter Ellenshaw did the artwork for the huge map of Disneyland that Walt frequently used on the television program, few realize that it was Imagineer Marvin Davis who labored through dozens of map designs trying to find a workable pattern for the Disneyland that finally opened in 1955. He struggled over the contours of Tom Sawyer Island but his efforts failed to please Walt Disney.

"Give me that thing," Davis remembers Walt saying. That night Walt worked for hours in his red barn workshop in his backyard at his home in the Holmby Hills. The next morning, he laid tracing paper on Davis's desk and said, "Now that's the way it should be." The island was built according to Walt's design.

Marvin Davis stated, "The general shape of the island, the way it curves and so forth, was Walt's idea. The idea for Pirate's Cove on Tom Sawyer Island was also Walt's."

Imagineer Herb Ryman remembered, "I was originally called upon to name some of the nomenclature for Tom Sawyer Island. Walt came up to me and he said, 'Herbie, would you think up some names?' Obviously you think about Smuggler's Gulch and Robber's Cove and kind of inspiring names that little children would be excited about. And then later one day, Bill Cottrell told me, he and Walt rode around on the Mark Twain and Walt had this map in front of him where these names were allocated according to my designation. And

Walt said, 'Why should we let Herbie have all the fun and name all these names on the island? Why can't I name these?' And Bill said, 'Yes, I think you could.' So Walt re-named all these names."

"When you go to Frontierland, make sure that Walt takes you to Tom Sawyer Island," said Imagineer Dick Irvine to a *Reader's Digest* reporter in 1960. "Walt was brought up in Missouri—Mark Twain country—and that island is all his. He didn't let anybody help him design it."

Actually, Vic Greene, the original art director for Frontierland, worked with Imagineers Herb Ryman and Claude Coats to produce the first designs for the Island based on Walt's ideas, including the barrel bridge that appeared in 1957. Sam McKim did some finished renderings for the Old Mill and Fort Wilderness as well as the tree house. Bill Evans did the landscaping. Emile Kuri located some "second hand" animals at a museum to install on the remote end of the island.

During the second week of June 1956, advertisements appeared of a raft with a pirate skull-and-crossbones flag making its way to Tom Sawyer Island. It proclaimed:

"Now Open at Disneyland! Another NEW attraction! Tom Sawyer Island! Cross the river on A RAFT...explore INJUN JOE'S CAVE...with the SUSPENSION BRIDGE...visit FORT WILDERNESS...see the BURNING SETTLER'S CABIN. Relive exciting days out of America's lusty past. Explore all the magical mysteries of an island built just for FUN! Whatever you want to do, you will find fun and excitement for the whole family at this newest Disneyland attraction...Tom Sawyer Island."

A billboard during the construction announced that the island would open June 1st. It didn't. Opening ceremonies were held at noon on Saturday June 16, 1956 at the raft landing on the island. Two young guests were on hand in costume as Tom Sawyer and Becky Thatcher, and appeared in many newspaper and magazine photos with Walt.

The two children from Hannibal, Missouri, Perva Lou Smith and Chris Winkler, had won the very first of the now-annual "Tom Sawyer and Becky Thatcher" contests in Hannibal.

Although they did not know it when they competed, an added bonus for Hannibal's 1956 Tom and Becky was a chance to travel to Disneyland, stay at the Disneyland Hotel and together with Walt Disney himself preside over the dedication ceremonies of Tom Sawyer Island.

Perva Lou and Chris carried with them from Hannibal water from the Mississippi River and earth from Jackson's Island (the model for the island frequented by Tom and Huck in Twain's novels). With Walt's help, the two kids christened the raft with a jug of Mississippi River water and planted a box of soil from Jackson's Island near the foot of the landing pier. The island was "officially" made a part of Missouri.

After the dedication, there was a tour of the island, including Injun Joe's Cave (actually an above-ground building covered with earth and landscaping to give the illusion of descending into a cave), Huckleberry Finn's Fishing Pier (the area was stocked with 15,000 catfish, perch and bluegill for guests to catch with a bamboo pole and a worm and Walt caught a fish for the press that day but it got away before he could land it), Fort Wilderness, and other points of interest.

One of the biggest kids of all was Walt Disney himself, who once the island was officially opened, would often take a pole and fish from the dock with the other youngsters. One day, after fishing for some time without so much as a nibble, Disney turned to the dock attendant and said, "There's no fish in the river!"

The attendant replied, "There's fish there, all right, but the water's so muddy, they can't even see the bait."

Walt responded, "Well, I fished the Missouri River and it was a lot muddier than this, but the fish sure saw the bait!"

The fishing was soon eliminated because it became quite a challenge for guests to walk around Disneyland the rest of the day with their increasingly pungent catch that soon ended up discarded in some unusual locations.

After the dedication, everyone boarded the rafts and made their way across the Rivers of America to the Plantation House terrace, where an "old fashioned fish fry" was served, including thirty-eight pounds of authentic river catfish that had been flown in from the Mark Twain Hotel in Hannibal for the occasion.

The Hannibal Chamber of Commerce has made the Tom and Becky contests a regular feature of the Fourth of July celebration. Those winners who have been lucky enough to fill the roles during the years when the Disney Company dedicated a new theme park have been allowed to join in the dedication ceremonies for the other islands named for Tom Sawyer at the Magic Kingdom in Florida and at Tokyo Disneyland.

Perva Lou Smith and Chris Winkler are still very much alive
and returned to Hannibal in 2005 for the 50th Anniversary
celebration along with other Tom and Beckys over the years.
Smith still clearly remembers that lunch with Walt.

The Indian canoes were introduced July 4, 1956. In the
summer of 1957, Castle Rock Ridge, the Pontoon Bridge
and Tom and Huck's Treehouse (that for many years was
"the highest point in Disneyland") were added for guests to
enjoy. Originally, there were only two rafts *Tom and Huck* but
this expansion prompted the addition of two new rafts, *Becky
Thatcher* and *Injun Joe*. Each of these free floating rafts carried
up to forty-five guests. There were two landings on the island
and there were even occasions when the *Mark Twain* was being
refurbished that the rafts would carry guests all the way around
the island.

Fort Wilderness was built entirely backstage and then
disassembled, trucked to Froniterland and floated across the
river, log by log, to be totally reassembled on the island. There
was even a mocked up, full-size wood skeleton framework put
up on the island first so that Walt and his Imagineers could
determine if the fort would look good in its proposed location,
and whether it would be visible from any places it shouldn't
be.

What was it like in those early years? While cast members
were scattered about the island to keep an eye on the youngsters,
Walt has given strict orders to let the kids enjoy themselves.
One security officer took his job too seriously and tried to keep
the kids quiet and orderly. Within a week he was transferred to
a gate-watching job on the night shift.

*The Saturday Evening Post* (June 28, 1958) and other magazines including *Parade* (April 7, 1957) spotlighted a teenaged boy named Tom Nabbe who waylaid Walt in 1956. Nabbe had been selling the *Disneyland News* newspaper in the park since the day Disneyland opened.

"I found Walt and told him I looked just like Tom Sawyer and he should hire me to be Tom Sawyer on the island," remembered Nabbe. "He didn't hire me on the spot like I had hoped. But the key thing is he didn't say "no". So that left the door open. He said that he'd think about it. Anytime I could find Walt in the park, I would ask him if he were still thinking about it. He finally said, 'You know, I could put a mannequin… or was it, a dummy?...I could put a mannequin, I think it was, that wouldn't be leaving every five minutes for a hot dog and a coke.'"

Referred to in articles as "the luckiest boy in the world", Nabbe was eventually hired to lead other kids through Injun Joe's dark and scary cave, bait guests' fishhooks and answer questions. During the summer and weekends, Nabbe worked full time but during the week he had to attend school and maintain a "C" average.

Here is an excerpt from an article about Disneyland from *the Saturday Evening Post* June 28, 1958:

> *"Mr. Disney comes to me for advice now," brags Tom Nabbe as he sits barefoot on the dock at the island, clad in dungarees and faded green shirt. "Why, when he wanted to put in a slide, I told him it would be bad because a lot of the kids who come here are dressed in their best clothes. So he didn't put the slide in."*

Tom Nabbe lived near Disneyland, and he and his mother who was an autograph collector were outside the gates of Disneyland on opening day July 17, 1955. When Danny Thomas exited the park early, he gave two of his complimentary passes to Tom and his mother, and they went in and enjoyed themselves.

The next day, the twelve year old got a job as a newspaper boy hawking The *Disneyland News* to guests coming to the park. If he sold a certain number of issues, he was allowed to come into Disneyland for free.

Hearing that Tom Sawyer Island was going to open, Nabbe kept approaching Walt about playing the part of Tom Sawyer. At first, Walt believed that children visiting the island should imagine themselves as Tom Sawyer, but eventually, Walt gave in to the persistent pleas of Nabbe. As a Disneyland press release explained, "It wasn't an easy task, working all day long in the hot sun, but it had many rewards, including the envy of all the other youngsters who came to visit and the attention of national magazines and news writers."

One important job requirement was that Nabbe had to keep a "C" grade average in school. So every quarter, the boy brought his report card directly to Walt for inspection.

After outgrowing the role of Tom Sawyer, Nabbe went on to manage other attractions. In 1964, he met his wife, Janice, who was working at a concession stand in the Park and they married in June 1968. He continued working for the Disney Company for nearly fifty years (mostly at Walt Disney World) and was made a Disney Legend in 2005.

## Tom Nabbe recalled:

*"Unfortunately, that opening was all scheduled around the winners of the Tom Sawyer and Becky Thatcher contest from Hannibal, Missouri. But from that point forward, I was the one and only Tom Sawyer. They gave me a title as 'guest aide.' That was my occupational title. I started working in Entertainment but they didn't know what to do with me so they gave me over to Operations. They had stocked the Rivers of America will blue gill and catfish and we had 25 fishing poles on each of the two piers so a total of 50 fishing poles. I had to ensure the fishing poles were put out each morning and had hooks and sinkers and corks on them. And worms. I had to make sure worms were out in the cans and available for people to bait their hooks and if they didn't want to bait their hooks, I had to bait the hooks for them.*

*"And I would pose for pictures with them. When you get down to it, I really looked more like Huck Finn who had the fire red hair and freckles and some guests thought I was Huck Finn. Tom Sawyer didn't have red hair. The guests fished on the island through about mid-1960. The only change was, when the Tom Sawyer Island opened it was catch and clean the fish, but the dead ones that the guest left behind didn't smell to good, so we went to catch and release for the end of the first summer and I was happy about that decision because I was the one who cleaned the fish.*

*"I worked through junior high and high school as Tom Sawyer. When I was seventeen or so, they didn't know what to do with me. I was a little too old to be Tom Sawyer but not old enough to be a ride operator. When I turned eighteen, I became a ride operator. Very little training. I had already operated the rafts*

*and things early in the morning when guests weren't in the*
*park. So I stepped into that role."*

Over the years, the island has seen not only changes, but
tragedy and turmoil including the drowning death of a young
boy who hid out on the island past its closing time and then
tried to swim back to shore with his brother on his back and
a six year old girl who lost part of her index finger when she
caught it in a rifle trigger in one of the guns at Fort Wilderness.
Security checking was increased and the rifles eliminated.

Fort Wilderness was closed after the island re-opened from a
refurbishment in 2003. In 2007 Disney demolished the original
1956 Fort Wilderness due to long-neglected termite and weather
damage. A new Fort Wilderness facade was constructed from
standard milled lumber but was not accessible to guests and is
used as a break area for cast members and performers.

Today, Tom Sawyer Island bears only minimal resemblance
to Walt Disney's original vision but that is also due to changing
times where some activities have become legally hazardous.
Still, parts of the island continue to conjure up the memories
of Tom and Huck and the rustic playground that delighted
children for decades.

# EPCOT FOUNTAIN

*"In a ceremony signifying international understanding and cooperation, representatives of the performing groups gathered around the Fountain of World Friendship in CommuniCore Plaza and added water from their own countries into the fountain." ---EYES AND EARS (a Walt Disney World cast newspaper) reporting on the ceremony in the October 28, 1982 edition*

The Fountain of Nations? The Fountain of World Friendship? The CommuniCore (Community Core not Communication Core) Fountain? Innoventions Fountain? Over the years, the fountain in the middle of Epcot has been called many different things both on websites and on official Disney Company press releases.

Whatever guests and cast members call it, it is often used as a meeting place landmark and photo location with SpaceShip Earth in the background. However, one of the things that makes the fountain memorable is the story of its dedication.

On Sunday, October 24, 1982 at precisely 11:00 a.m., double Westminster chimes signaled the beginning of the Grand Opening Dedication Ceremonies at EPCOT Center.

A group of sixteen herald trumpeters and six drummers joined by the West Point Glee Club soon followed the chimes as did the four hundred and fifty piece All-American College Marching Band assembled by Walt Disney World from 146 colleges.

There were over four thousand invited guests including Walt Disney Productions executives Donn Tatum and Card Walker along with Mrs. Lillian Disney (Walt Disney's widow), corporate executives, foreign and American political figures and many other VIPs.

There was a flag raising ceremony with an American flag that was a gift from President and Mrs. Reagan and had been flown at the White House.

---

This activity was followed by what was called the "International Ceremony of the Waters". This ceremony was inspired by a similar event during Walt Disney's lifetime where the dedication of the *it's a small world* attraction at Disneyland included children of many nations pouring water from the waterways of their countries into the attraction flume.

The attraction opened at Disneyland on May 28, 1966. It involved 10,000 balloons, 500 costumed children and 1500 foreign dignitaries. At the opening ceremony, a liter of water from each of the one hundred countries represented was poured into the canal, which is called the Seven Seaways. This inspired the similar ceremony at the Epcot fountain.

International performing groups surrounded what was then known as the CommuniCore Fountain and one by one, they poured a vessel of water into the fountain. Each vessel was unique to represent the country and each was stored under tight security in Cash Control so that the integrity of the water being from that particular country could be maintained. The water was gathered from the lakes, rivers, and oceans of the twenty-three countries and was to "signify the international understanding and cooperation that Epcot Center stands for." Publicity photos claimed to show the acquiring of the water in the actual locations.

CEO and Chairman of Walt Disney Productions Card Walker walked to the podium and said:

> *"It is a great thrill, really a wonderful thrill. Lilly, thanks for being with us. Joining us around this magnificent fountain are representatives of nations from around the world. They have brought with them waters from the great oceans, the seas, the rivers, and the lakes on our planet, spaceship earth. These waters will flow together as a symbol of the oneness of humankind and the hope for peace among nations, making this truly a fountain of world friendship.*

> *"And now it is my great pleasure to read the bronze plaque officially dedicating EPCOT Center. I'll read it right here: 'To all who come to this place of joy, hope, and friendship, welcome. EPCOT Center is inspired by Walt Disney's creative vision. Here human achievements are celebrated through imagination, the wonders of enterprise, and concepts of a future that promises new and exciting benefits for all. May EPCOT Center entertain, inform, and inspire, and above all may it instill a new sense of belief and pride in man's ability to shape a world that offers hope to people everywhere in the world.' Thank you."*

As Card Walker led Lillian Disney off the stage, he said in an undertone: "Well, we've done it."

Mrs. Disney, who was known for her shyness, did not officially speak at the event.

The countries represented who poured urns containing one gallon of water into the fountain were: Canada, Denmark, Italy, Korea, Japan, Africa [several countries included in group], Egypt, Morocco, Colombia, Mexico, Barbados, Puerto Rico, China, Philippines, Belgium, Czechoslovakia, Finland, France, Germany, Spain, Switzerland, U.K., Yugoslavia.

Water came from as far away as the Arctic Ocean, the Nile River in Africa, and the Yangtze River in China. Those urns were kept under lock and key and strict security and scrutiny before the ceremony. Afterwards, they were tossed aside into dumpsters rather than preserved as historical artifacts.

At the conclusion, an aerial salute of fireworks created "The Colors of the World" immediately followed by a jet flyover by the Florida Air National Guard.

Preparation for these festivities began nearly four years earlier with the minute-by-minute planning starting in March 1982. Twenty different committees were involved in creating the Dedication ceremonies from design of invitations to finance to talent booking to transportation and more.

Dennis Despie, then Vice-President of Entertainment for Walt Disney Productions said that he hoped this celebration would become an annual event because it was one of the few opportunities for this type of international celebration in the United States. One thousand, five hundred folk festival performers from twenty-three nations performed during the weekend of October 22-24. They performed in and around the nine international pavilions.

Today, every fifteen minutes, the fountain showcases water ballets where over two hundred shooters propel over fifty gallons of water up to one hundred and fifty feet in the air. Once upon a time, human cast members actually measured the wind and controlled how high the water shot in the air so as not to soak guests on windy days.

There are seven different musical selections that rotate: Instrumental from the *Air Battle* sequence from *Surprise in the Skies,* a former daytime lagoon show at Epcot, *Day One* by John Tesh, Main title selection from the Disney live-action feature film *Iron Will, Mickey's Finale* selection from a proposed Epcot show tentatively titled *Around the World with Mickey Mouse,* Selection from Disney's animated feature *The Rescuers Down Under,* Selection from the Disney live-action feature film *The Rocketeer,* and *Standing in Motion* by Yanni.

It took three months of computer programming to design the seven different water ballets and at night, over a thousand colored lights highlight the streams of water. It is the largest fountain on Disney property. The fountain holds approximately one hundred and fifty thousand gallons of water with computer controlled pumps sending almost thirty thousand gallons of water per minute cascading down its tiered walls.

The fountain uses almost thirty-five miles of electrical wire. Chloride is too corrosive for this fountain so Disney uses bromine to keep it clean and to ensure there is no algae. The coins that are retrieved from this fountain, like others on property, are donated by the Disney Company to local charities.

Running underneath the entire fountain is an underground work area that houses the pumps and computer systems, as well as a workshop for cast members who maintain the Epcot fountains. There is also a space with special lifts that are used beneath the stage area for performers and equipment. The underground work area was built and then the fountain placed on top with no planning on how to get new equipment down into the area. Over the years, the fountain has been damaged like when a temporary stage for performing elephants was put on top of it when Epcot showcased a daily circus.

In the 1980's the fountain team at Walt Disney World included a young civil engineer whose thesis was on the behavior of turbulence free water. That engineer, Mark Fuller, later founded WET Design. This company became the premiere fountain company in the world. Mark Fuller is also responsible for other Disney fountains including the leapfrog fountain at the Imagination pavilion. His greatest creation to date may be at the Bellagio Hotel in Las Vegas.

---

At 10:01 am (that time was selected to indicate the month and the day) on Monday October 1, 2007 at Epcot, there was an official 25th anniversary rededication ceremony at the "Fountains of Nations Plaza" as it was called according to the official Disney press release. Present at the ceremony was Imagineer Marty Skilar who while reminiscing about the opening month of Epcot stated, "One of the things I remember the most was a water pouring ceremony to start the Comunicore fountain behind us. Don't you think it would be wonderful if we could do something like that today?"

Tracy Wui, Rededication Ceremony Hostess, took over the microphone at that point and said: "Today we have the incredible privilege of having our own cultural representatives right here at Epcot. It's time to meet the representatives of the countries of World Showcase. The cultural representatives are carrying colorful banners representing the countries of World Showcase: Japan, Morocco, France, United Kingdom, Canada, America, Italy, Germany, China, Norway and Mexico. The cultural representatives are carrying many different types of water containers, representing famous rivers or bodies of water."

For each country, the name of the container and the body of water was announced as the processional continued with the water from each poured into the fountain.

The story of the fountain being a representation of the harmony between countries of the world adds to the beauty and understanding of this wonderful Epcot landmark that has provided such joy and wonder for countless guests over the years.

# CAPTAIN EO

With Michael Jackson's tragic death in June 2009, there was a flood of special magazines and media tribute projects that detailed the life and achievements of the innovative singer/ dancer. With all those achievements, his involvement with *Captain EO* was considered so uneventful that it often wasn't even mentioned.

Even in Jackson's own autobiography, *Moon Walk*, published just two years after the premiere of *Captain EO*, there are barely three paragraphs devoted to the project. One paragraph described Jackson's affection for Walt Disney while another described briefly the plot of the film, and, finally, a mention that Jackson flew up to Skywalker Ranch to consult with George Lucas on the project. That's all.

Jackson's affection, some might even say obsession, with Disney was well-known. He often visited the Disney theme parks (sometimes in disguise), the entrance to his Neverland Ranch was inspired by the entrance to Disneyland, and he had a large collection of Disney memorabilia (some of it exclusively created by Disney artists).

"Jackson was a huge fan of our parks, sometimes visiting several times a month, in and out of disguise," said former CEO Michael Eisner. "He knows more about Walt Disney than anybody who ever existed. He certainly knows more than I do."

Michael's older brother Jackie once stated: "[Michael] always studied Walt Disney. He loved Walt Disney. He read books on him every day on the road. He worshiped the guy."

*Captain EO* returned for a limited engagement at Disneyland and Walt Disney World in 2010 over a decade after it officially closed. The story behind the creation of this unique film experience involved some of the top creative people in the film industry.

A month after Eisner took over as CEO of the Disney Company in 1984, he arranged for filmmaker George Lucas to take a tour of Disney's Imagineering facilities in Glendale and encouraged Lucas to create some new theme park attractions. Having a good relationship with Eisner when he was at Paramount and supported *Raiders of the Lost Ark*, Lucas was very open to coming on board, especially on developing a flight simulator ride based on his popular *Star Wars* franchise.

Soon afterward, Jeffrey Katzenberg, who had just come on board as Chairman of the Disney Studios, took Michael Jackson around the Imagineering facility in Tujunga, California and first opened discussions with the pop star about appearing in a Disneyland attraction.

The Imagineers had prepared a mock-up of a dark ride attraction that would feature Jackson. Supposedly, it was to be in 3-D. Jackson liked the mock-up, but didn't want to be involved in a ride attraction. There were also discussions about a 3-D film that would be housed in the Carousel of Progress building and that suggestion caught his interest.

In 1984, Jackson had been considering developing several movie projects as he discovered he enjoyed the process of filmmaking. David Geffen had suggested that if Jackson was serious about starring in a movie that he should make a movie for Disney. Geffen called his long-time friend, Katzenberg with the idea. Katzenberg and Eisner countered with the idea of creating a 3-D movie/rock video for Disneyland to duplicate the unprecedented success of the innovative *Thriller* music video that had been released about two years earlier and was still popular.

"We wanted to create something with Michael Jackson, who appealed to teenagers, but also to young kids, and even their parents," Eisner said.

Jackson liked the idea, but to protect himself, insisted that either George Lucas or Steven Spielberg be a part of the project.

Imagineering's Rick Rothschild drew up three different storylines. The first had Michael as a Pan-like character in a magical forest with mythological beasts. The forest would be threatened by an Ice Queen and Michael would eventually melt her cold heart with the power of music. The second proposal had Michael hiding inside Disneyland after the park had closed for the night and his adventures including a dance number with the audio-animatronics figures in *Pirates of the Caribbean*.

However, everyone involved was excited by the third concept known as "Intergalactic Music Man" which evolved into *Captain EO*. It was only a one page proposal, barely four paragraphs but had the basic concept that Michael's music would transform ugliness into beauty. The name EO comes from the Greek Goddess of the Dawn—EOS. According to legend, her rosy fingers open the gates of heaven to the chariot of the sun.

Rothschild became the Show Director. In addition to many other credits, Rothschild would later head the teams for other Disney 3-D attractions including *Honey, I Shrunk the Audience*,

*It's Tough To Be A Bug* and *Mickey's Philharmagic* at Walt Disney World.

Jackson wanted a director he could trust and Steven Spielberg was unavailable, working on the film *The Color Purple*. John Landis was suggested because of his work on *Thriller* but there was some apparent concern about Disney not being able to control him and that he would go over budget.

On the other hand, George Lucas was already working closely with the Disney Company on *Star Tours*. Lucas had been assured that he would be involved in all the new projects for Disneyland's Tomorrowland, making it a non-Disney universe. One proposal was of a space craft crashing into the then empty Carousel of Progress theater with the passengers on the ship performing a musical show for the Disneyland guests as they awaited rescue.

---

Lucas brought in Francis Ford Coppola, Rusty Lemorande, and Angelica Huston for the film. Coppola, a longtime friend of Lucas, needed to repair his reputation after the recent box office failure of the film *The Cotton Club* so he was brought on as the director. It was believed at Disney that even though Coppola was the director of record and would bring some publicity to the project, that Lucas would probably step in and do most of the directing.

That didn't happen as Lucas was not on the set a lot and was getting frustrated at the typical Disney politics surrounding the project. Lucas had become used to working independently and not being answerable to others after his *Star Wars* success.

Coppola said, "*Captain EO* is like one of those little children's stereo reel masters that spins while the viewers see beautiful three-dimensional fairy tales making you wish you could just step in and sit down next to the white rabbit. I think it happens like that here."

There was indeed three weeks of principal photography with Coppola at the helm but when he left the Second Unit spent nearly six months trying to fill in holes in the story to make the entire thing work with additional filming.

Lemorande, who had produced and scripted a recently released science-fiction-themed film with comedy elements, *Electric Dreams*, was to script *Captain EO* with input from Coppola and Lucas. Lemorande had also recently produced *Yentl*, so he would be the on-site producer. He later did uncredited work as a second unit director and film editor. Lucas would be credited as the executive producer.

"It was a collaborative process where a good deal of the storyline came out of the characters that were already created so really there is no single author to the piece," Lemorande said. "We were doing some construction at WDI, we were on stages at Laird Studios in Culver City, we had special effects at Disney and at important moments in time we all came together."

Huston, who would win the Oscar for her performance in *Prizzi's Honor*, which was released in 1985, would play a spider-like H.R. Giger Alien-version of the Evil Queen from Disney's classic *Snow White and the Seven Dwarfs*, suspended in the air by web-like cables.

In later years, Lemorande shared that one of the factors that made *Captain EO* a troubled production was the resentment that Disney Imagineers had about "outsiders" being brought in to handle a Disney theme park attraction. In fact, the high hourly rates charged by Imagineering resulted in Katzenberg giving some of the work on the film to outside contractors.

Tony-award winner John Napier, who had just been recognized for his work on the musical *Cats*, was brought in and he built a miniature theater in scale to demonstrate the interactive effects for the show. That model greatly impressed Eisner and later, when Napier wanted to lift the ceiling of the theater to eliminate an interfering beam, Eisner quickly approved the additional expense.

Napier worked on the costumes that not only had to represent the evil nature of the dark planet and its twisted metal and steaming vents, but still had to have the flexibility of movement for the dancers to showcase Jackson's style of movement.

"What I am doing with the costumes is trying to make people able to move in these things, where they won't fall apart in these robotic characters," Napier said. "I put in a lot of detail that should work well in 3-D."

Most of the project was supervised by Katzenberg but Eisner occasionally dropped by to see the work in progress and felt that this was "his" project that would demonstrate how he could revitalize Disneyland.

Jeff Hornaday had done the choreography for *Flashdance* (1983), and had recently worked with Paul McCartney and Jackson on the *Say, Say, Say* music video so he seemed a natural addition as choreographer.

"We wanted the dances to be a storytelling element, directly connected to a character," said Hornaday, who was supervising the other dancers. "Working with Michael for me has been a unique experience in that usually a choreographer will devise sequences of dance and then give it to the dancers to do. Michael's talent and approach is so unique that you are limiting yourself by just giving him what you do."

"I'd have Michael dance improvisationally to the music and tried to expand it into something that forty dancers could do," recalled Hornaday. "Michael was a composer, a co-choreographer, a dancer, a singer, an actor , a collaborator on every level and in each case, he collaborated with an amount of passion unequaled by anyone else on the show."

Rick Baker who had done the makeup for Jackson's *Thriller* video was brought in to supervise the makeup for *Captain EO*. Tom Burman (who had done work on the infamous *Star Wars Holiday Special*) did the makeup design for Huston's character and it took three hours each day to apply that detailed makeup.

Lance Anderson, who among other credits was a creature designer on the recently released *Ghostbusters* is credited as the co-designer for *EO*'s ragtag crew of Hooter, the Geex, and Major and Minor Domo. Baker was credited as being responsible for Fuzzball.

James Horner, who had recently scored Disney's *Something Wicked This Way Comes* (and decades later would score *Titanic*) provided the original score for the film. Jackson himself wrote the two songs featured in the film: *We Are Here to Change the World* and *Another Part of Me*. *Another Part of Me* later appeared on Jackson's hugely successful *Bad* album (1987) but *We Are*

*Here to Change the World* was not officially released until 2004 as part of *Michael Jackson: The Ultimate Collection.*

Pre-production on the project began March 1985. There was three weeks of principal photography. The same big blue screen from Disney's sci-fi film *Black Hole* was used for filming the scene where Michael Jackson danced out over the audience's heads.

It was not surprising that this production, with all this high-profile talent, quickly ran over the budget. While Disney never confirmed the actual cost, it was reported that the seventeen minute film ended up costing somewhere between $17 million and $30 million, or roughly more than one million dollars a minute, making it at the time the most expensive film ever made. The original budget was ten million dollars.

"*Captain EO* ran over budget. The biggest factor was special effects, some one hundred and fifty of them, more per minute than Lucas had used in *Star Wars*," Eisner said.

For years, people have estimated that the final budget for *Captain EO* was around $17 million dollars with some estimates going as high as $30 million. The actual cost according to the WDI final billing of *Captain EO*: $23.7 million dollars.

Why did the project run almost $14 million over budget? Certainly, the talent and technology were expensive (although that was supposedly addressed in the original budget) but the real cause was that the project went into production without a firm story. In fact, Michael Jackson would come in each day with different versions of the songs. This was one of the first examples of a park project where "everybody had to approve everything" whether they knew anything about that aspect or not and that ran into time and money.

---

The film tells the story of Captain EO, the leader of a spaceship's "ragtag crew", which included a dwarfish, clumsy green elephant-like creature called Hooter who plays musical notes through his flute-like trunk; a small, long-tailed orange haired flying creature called Fuzzball sometimes described as a monkey with butterfly wings; two shaggy haired conjoined creatures know as the Geex (Idy and Ody) who served as the navigator and pilot; and a silver metal officious robot security officer named Major Domo who had a smaller robot, Minor Domo, attached as a module to his back.

Commander Bog (a holographic head performed by the talented comedian Dick Shawn who was never on the set) was displeased by the bungling of this group of misfits and has given them one final mission to redeem themselves.

They are to follow a "homing beacon" to a forbidding, dark industrial planet of sinister twisted metal and to give a gift to the Supreme Leader (Angelica Huston). Crashing on the planet, the crew finds its way to the palace of this witch queen creature and are captured by her army and threatened with torture for their unauthorized visit.

Captain EO agrees to that punishment, but also tells the queen that she is beautiful, but without a key to unlock that beauty. His crew transforms into a musical band, but before he can share his magical song, Hooter accidentally stumbles into the equipment rendering it momentarily useless, angering the queen who orders her guards to capture Captain EO and his crew. A short battle ensues before Hooter repairs the equipment. EO's song transforms the dark, mechanical inhabitants into agile and colorful backup dancers.

EO is able to defeat the queen's Whip Warriors and change not only the queen into a beautiful woman, but also her palace into a peaceful, vibrant Greek temple. The planet is transformed into a verdant paradise reminiscent of the work of artist Maxfield Parrish. EO and his crew dance off back to the ship and leave the planet as the grateful inhabitants wave good-bye to them. At the time it was described as the EO crew using the power of music, dance and light to fill the planet with all the shades of the rainbow.

The finished footage was not as impressive as hoped. Jackson lacked a commanding presence as the lead character, Huston's role had been trimmed severely and the attempts at humor and urgency felt flat and forced. Even the staging of the 3-D effects seemed to pale in comparison to Kodak's *Magic Journeys* that had previously run in the theater.

By this point, Coppola was already involved in his next film, *Peggy Sue Got Married* that would open a month after *Captain EO*, and Lucas was struggling with *Howard the Duck*, which would open one month before *Captain EO*—and work on the *Star Tours* attraction was facing some challenges.

Reportedly, Lemorande and Jackson did some re-shooting and re-cutting for the film (at one point using a spray painted ball cock from a toilet as a stand-in for the head of the Minor Domo puppet that couldn't be found). While there had been plans for Disney's Imagineering to work on the special effects (the talented Harrison Ellenshaw is listed in the credits), Lucas gave the film to Industrial Light and Magic to "fix" and delays on giving the film to Disney was credited to Lucas's notorious "perfectionism."

One Imagineer who worked closely on the project described the raw footage of the three weeks shooting to be "a mess." To make matters worse, there were three moments in the film where it was out of sync: two audio moments and one instance of 3-D. Those problems, by the way, were not fixed when the film opened. The last effects shot for *Captain EO* was that of the logo that juts out into the audience

However, it could have been the worse film ever made and it would have made no difference, because it was done at the height of "Jackson Mania" and the opportunity to see Jackson singing and dancing to two new songs he had composed guaranteed its success.

*Captain EO* opened at Epcot on September 12, 1986, but the big premiere was scheduled for its Disneyland opening on September 18, 1986. The film would later open in Tokyo Disneyland in 1987 and Disneyland Paris in 1992.

Although built for *Captain EO*, Disneyland's Magic Eye Theater, that seated about seven hundred guests, opened in May 1986 with the amazing *Magic Journeys*, the original 3-D movie from Epcot's Imagination pavilion, in preparation for the *Captain EO* debut. Live theater special effects were added for the *Captain EO* presentation including lasers, fiber-optic stars, fog effects and more that were all painstakingly synchronized with the action on screen.

Frank Wells renegotiated Kodak's contract so that Kodak agreed to pick up some of the costs of producing the film, building a theater at Disneyland and renovating Epcot's 3-D Theater to accommodate the new special effects.

The week of the grand opening, the *National Enquirer* printed the infamous photo of Jackson lying inside a hyperbaric chamber. It was theorized that, in order to live to be 150 years old, he slept in it each night to get that influx of oxygen. In reality, several biographies of Jackson pointed out that Jackson himself leaked the picture purposely at that time to draw attention to the premiere of *Captain EO,* especially with its "sci-fi" aspect.

There were more than two hundred members from the international press who attended the Disneyland premiere and were herded into the Tomorrowland Space Place eatery, where they were given a press kit containing nine separate releases, six photos and a commemorative *Captain EO* T-shirt. Surrounded by free coffee, soft drinks and croissants, the press could watch a trailer about the making of the film on an endless loop.

The big parade of celebrities started around two o'clock in the afternoon. Over a hundred celebrities attended the grand opening of the film at Disneyland and were chauffeured down Main Street to a cheering crowd. There were so many celebrities from Jack Nicholson to John Ritter to Annette Funicello that the parade did not end until an hour and a half later.

By five o'clock, the rising heat had made things uncomfortable and the children brought by their celebrity parents were beginning to show how tired they were, but it was still not time to see the film. Jack Wagner introduced the Pine Bluff High School and Washington High School Marching Bands and Gregg Burge, from *A Chorus Line* who some speculated had been chosen because he was a young male

African-American with a singing and dancing background to perhaps represent the absent Michael Jackson. Burge burst into an original Disney song about "Let's make way for tomorrow!" followed by a float featuring costumed character versions of Hooter, the Geex and Major Domo.

At the end, CEO Michael Eisner smiled and addressed the crowd, "Michael Jackson is here." The crowd got very excited but Eisner continued, "But he is disguised, either as an old lady, an usher, or an Animatronic character."

Nobody in the audience, especially the journalists, believed Eisner. While there is still debate whether Michael Jackson showed up for the official premiere (although his mother and two sisters did attend), he did indeed pop in to watch the "test" shows at Disneyland. Since he had taken to wearing the surgical mask, he was often easy to spot by guests. When that became an issue, Jackson sought sanctuary in the projection booth to watch the film and the reactions from the audience.

After a speech by Kodak's vice chairman, Coppola, Lucas and Angelica Huston gathered at a red ribbon drawn across the entrance of the theater. Nearby were Coppola's nephew Nicholas Cage and the newest Jackson superstar, Janet.

Reading from cue cards, they proclaimed:

Huston: "For all those who still believe in the magic world of fantasy and imagination…"

Lucas: "For all those who are still moved by the wonders of music and dance…"

Coppola: "For all those who share Walt Disney's dream and delight in the promise of the future, we cut this ribbon signifying the opening of the 3-D musical motion picture space adventure, *Captain EO*!"

Animation Historian Charles Solomon, reviewing the film in the *Los Angeles Times*, October 9, 1986 echoed the feelings of many people when he wrote: "For all its wondrous imagery, *Captain EO* is nothing more than the most elaborate rock video in history, like a hollow chocolate Easter bunny, it's a glorious surface over a void... given that list of credits and the film's lavish budget, audiences have a right to expect more than empty flash."

As expected, the show opened to long lines of crowds but over time, the film attracted fewer and fewer guests and odd behavior by Jackson in public certainly didn't help encourage guests to attend the show. *Captain EO* closed quietly and without fanfare at Disneyland April 1997. It had closed July 1994 at Epcot, September 1996 at Tokyo Disneyland, and lasted until August 1998 at Disneyland Paris. Captain EO returned for a limited engagement at Disneyland and Walt Disney World in 2010 over a decade later to eager crowds once again anxious to see the production and celebrate the talent of Michael Jackson.

## MICKEY MOUSE REVUE

In the December 31, 1962, issue of *Newsweek* magazine, Walt Disney talked about plans of creating an attraction at Disneyland for "all of the Disney characters, so everyone can see them... I have in mind a theater, and the figures will not only put on the show but be sitting in the boxes with the visitors, heckling. I don't know just when I'll do that." Almost a decade later, *The Mickey Mouse Revue* opened at Walt Disney World.

On May 25, 2009, the charming Audio-Animatronics show *The Mickey Mouse Revue* closed at Tokyo Disneyland after nearly twenty-six years of delighting Japanese guests and was replaced by *Mickey's PhilharMagic*. When the attraction was removed from the Magic Kingdom, some of the figures were recycled years later in other attractions.

Imagineer Tony Baxter took the mold for the character of Alice (from *Alice in Wonderland*) from this show and made a lightweight fiberglass model and painted it to look like Tinker Bell. He installed equipment inside so that it would operate like a radio controlled model helicopter and actually fly down Main Street during the parade. A successful test was done in the Imagineering parking lot, but the project was abandoned over fears that that the twelve pound figure might malfunction and drop on a guest.

Imaginer David Mumford, show designer for the *Alice in Wonderland* dark ride at Disneyland, claimed in a 1999 interview that the Alice figure added during the 1984 renovation came from the *Mickey Mouse Revue*.

"The Alice figure was a last minute addition, after some debate over showing the character," Mumford said "There was a set of Alice figures in storage from the 1971 *Mickey Mouse Revue* attraction in Florida. Included were some Flower Garden heads, the Mad Hatter, the March Hare and Alice, so we used them at Disneyland in 1984."

The Seven Dwarfs figures and their organ were reused in the 1994 *Snow White's Scary Adventures* ride renovation.

*The Mickey Mouse Revue* show opened as an "E" Ticket attraction at the Magic Kingdom on October 1, 1971, and ran until September 14, 1980, when it was closed and dismantled and sent to Tokyo Disneyland where it was an opening day attraction in April 1983. The entire show, including the pre-show, was re-recorded in Japanese and a few small cosmetic enhancements to a handful of the characters were made.

The theater at Walt Disney World was renamed the Fantasyland Theater and hosted several other shows over the years including *The Legend of the Lion King* and *Mickey's Philharmagic*.

From the end of the eight-minute pre-show that covered Mickey's career and the use of sound in animated film:

Narrator: "Join us now in a presentation of the latest colossal achievement in Mickey's illustrious career. Mickey Mouse, bigger and better than ever, appears in a completely new dimension, leading his friends in a medley of Walt Disney musical highlights."

Mickey: "Come along folks! It's time for the *Mickey Mouse Musical Revue!*" (The theater doors open.)

Originally, this almost ten minute show was going to be called *Mickey Mouse Musical Revue* and that name appeared on some early posters as well as that last announcement in the preshow. An Audio Animatronics figure of Mickey Mouse conducted an all-toon orchestra of twenty-three characters, and the show itself showcased scenes and songs from some of the memorable Disney animated films that were staged around the orchestra.

There were a total of seventy-three different Disney animated characters who performed in the show from the Fab Five to Humphrey the Bear, Timothy Mouse, Winnie the Pooh, Baloo, Scrooge McDuck and many, many more that filled the 86-foot-long stage. (However, there were a total of 81 figures since some characters appeared at different places on the stage, like the Three Caballeros, or in different costumes. Several characters planned for the show like Horace Horsecollar, Clara Cluck and the Big Bad Wolf didn't end up in the final production. However, a shadow of the Big Bad Wolf did appear before the song *Who's Afraid of the Big Bad Wolf?*)

Songs included *Heigh Ho, Whistle While You Work, When You Wish Upon A Star, Hi Diddle Dee Dee, Who's Afraid of The Big Bad Wolf, I'm Wishing, The Silly Song, All In The Golden Afternoon Bibbidi-Bobbidi-Boo, So This Is Love, Zip-a-Dee-Doo-Dah,* and *Mickey Mouse Club March.* None of the voices in the show were from the original soundtracks, perhaps for legal reasons or the need to compensate those performers.

Imagineer Bill Justice had a long and illustrious career with the Disney Company from being the primary animator of Chip and Dale to an experimenter in stop motion animation in *Babes in Toyland,* and the opening credits for Disney live-action films to the first designer of character costumes at Disneyland to one of the original Audio-Animatronics programmers on attractions like *Pirates of the Caribbean*. That's only the tip of his many achievements. He also directed the opening animation for the original *Mickey Mouse Club* television show, for instance.

*The Mickey Mouse Revue* was the original brainchild of Justice although, of course, others were involved including John Hench and Blaine Gibson. About the time work was beginning on the Magic Kingdom in Florida, Justice had an idea. Justice first wrote about the creation in his limited edition memoir, *Justice for Disney* (1992). I conducted two lengthy interviews with Bill when he visited the Disney Institute and performed with me at Give Kids the World. Here are some of those comments.

*"WED had designed some imaginative shows for the parks, but we seemed to be getting away from our heritage. **Pirates of the Caribbean** was a big hit, but what did it have to do with Disney? What we needed was a reminder of what Walt had accomplished. I pulled out a sheet of paper and got to work.*

*"Mickey Mouse would have to be the main figure. Yet some mention must be made of our great animated classics. I made sketches of all the characters I thought should appear. Then, I called upon my modeling skills to build a one-16th-inch scale paper cut-out model of what I wanted. This was before photo-copying machines with reducing capabilities, so I had to make all the drawings in scale. Many of the figures had to be drawn, a quarter-inch high. The entire set was about 18-inches long by 3.5-inches high. But this model was a good tool for planning the show sequence and experimenting with different scenes.*

*"Once I thought I had a winner, it was time for a bigger model. I recruited some craftsmen and we built a room size*

*miniature theater with a stage about twelve feet wide. Blaine
Gibson and his assistants sculpted all the figures to one
quarter inch scale from my drawings. Everything worked
except the figures themselves—lighting, turntables, curtains,
sound tracks. When we were done, I notified my bosses. They
invited Roy O. Disney to see the results of our work. The show
we had in mind was this:*

*"Mickey Mouse would lead an orchestra of Studio characters
through a medley of Disney tunes. Then on the sides of the
stage and behind the orchestra, scenes from our most popular
animated features would appear one by one. Mickey and
his orchestra would close the performance. Roy looked the
model over, then paid me the best compliment I ever had in my
career: 'This is the kind of show we should spend our money
on.' That's how* **The Mickey Mouse Revue** *was born.*

*"I monitored the show's progress until it opened. Blaine and
his sculptors made full-size characters to serve as models for
the Audio-Animatronics figures. The figures were built and a
theater was designed. One problem surfaced: Mickey. With
thirty-three functions crammed into a 42-inch body, he was
the most complex figure to date. He also became my biggest
programming challenge because he was supposed to lead the
orchestra.*

*"I finally discovered I should program Mickey's arms to raise
as high as possible, then immediately drop as low as possible.
Same thing with his wrists and elbows—bend back and forth
as quickly as he could to the extremes. This is the only way
Mickey could appear to keep up with the tempo.*

*"As the show's theater in the Magic Kingdom of Walt Disney World was being constructed, someone came up with the idea of having a pre-show. They designed an area just outside the main theater where guests could watch a film on Mickey while they were waiting to enter. Good idea, except there was a glitch. The theater seated 504 people, but the space available for the pre-show could only accommodate 300. Unfortunately, there was no time left to make further changes. It came as a shock when I was told my pride and joy was being moved to Tokyo Disneyland. 'Because it never played to full capacity'. Of course not! How can you fill 504 seats with 300 people?"*

Of course, another reason for the attraction to move to Japan was not only the Japanese love of cute things (since it made the list of what the Oriental Land Company wanted for its park) but it also saved the Disney Company money because it was the only attraction that was shipped directly to Japan rather than being replicated. It would have been time consuming and expensive to build it from scratch in Tokyo.

Bob Mathieson (who held many positions including Vice President of Operations at Magic Kingdom) recalled to David Koenig, "It was a very big fight. We screamed like crazy on that one. It was a very popular attraction, and it was so much of our culture. It was what people really loved. But they didn't have time to build their own. They had to take it."

At the Magic Kingdom, the attraction had already been downgraded to a "D" Ticket amidst the Disney Company's concerns that it had not become a signature attraction for the Magic Kingdom. It was the first attraction to be removed from the Magic Kingdom.

PART FOUR:  THE OTHER WORLDS OF DISNEY
STORIES

There are some wonderful untold stories about Disney history that just don't fit as comfortably into the other three sections of this book but still deserve to be told.

Disney has been involved in so many different areas over the decades from merchandise to music to projects for other companies that the list seems endless. There were many people involved in Disney activities that never received proper credit or any credit at all. There are a lot of great stories in all of these topics.

Animation historian John Culhane wrote a fascinating book that went into great detail about the making of the animated feature *Fantasia* (1940). There have been several extensive documentaries about the film made for the DVD releases. However, the following story that originally appeared in the *Philadelphia Inquirer* newspaper was never recounted in any of those exhaustive resources.

When Leopold Stokowski was recording the music for Walt Disney's *Fantasia* with the Philadelphia Symphony Orchestra, the complex recording system set up in the basement of the Academy of Music (also known as the American Academy of Music and is the oldest opera house in the United States still used for its original purpose) was declared a fire hazard and work was ordered stopped.

On the advice of friends, Stokowski called Joe Sharfain, then city solicitor for Philadelphia and an ardent music fan. Sharfain quickly withdrew the stop order and recording proceeded. Later, Stokowski expressed his gratitude and asked, "Now, what can I do for you?" Sharfain said jokingly that one of his greatest wishes was to be rich enough to engage Stokowski and the orchestra for a single performance at which he would be the sole audience. (The price at that time would have been at least $10,000.)

Stokowski asked, "When did you have in mind?" Sharfain answered, "Oh, that's a long time away." Stokowski countered, "How about tomorrow at two o'clock?" The incredulous Sharfain appeared at the side door of the Academy of Music the next afternoon, to be escorted by a deputy of the maestro into the hall, empty except for the orchestra and conductor. The maestro turned to make sure Sharfain was there, raised his arms and conducted for four hours—all the music of *Fantasia*—just for Joe Sharfain.

An amusing anecdote but never included in either the book or the documentaries because there was so much more important information to cover about *Fantasia* including all the sequences for future planned versions.

This section covers some personalities and projects that never get discussed in the bigger picture of Disney history but are still highly entertaining and offer a richer perspective into the wonderful wide world of Disney.

## KHRUSHCHEV AND DISNEYLAND

For those who grew up during the Cold War, Khrushchev was the "boogeyman" who was going to bury the United States. Nikita Khrushchev served as first secretary of the Communist Party of the Soviet Union from 1953 to 1964, following the death of Joseph Stalin, and chairman of the Council of Ministers from 1958 to 1964. Khrushchev's party colleagues removed him from power in 1964, replacing him with Leonid Brezhnev.

Khrushchev was removed from power partly because conservatives in the Communist Party found his flamboyant and dramatic gestures embarrassing on the world stage. Supposedly, Khrushchev pulled off his own shoe to pound it on a desk to make a point at the United Nations. He threatened America, saying "we will bury you," at the time when nuclear war was a very real possibility.

Other than the total destruction of capitalism and the triumph of communism, what did Khrushchev really want? He wanted to go to Disneyland.

Nikita Khrushchev, premier of the Soviet Union and a fiery opponent of American capitalism, arrived in the United States on September 16, 1959 for an extended eleven day visit to the United States, finishing with a long summit meeting with President Dwight D. Eisenhower. During his trip, he visited several American cities including New York and San Francisco.

The Russian leader had indicated a desire to see Hollywood and a visit was arranged. Khrushchev had also apparently indicated he and his family wanted to visit Disneyland during his time in Los Angeles. He was not informed until his plane was flying to the Los Angeles airport that while his wife and children might be able to go to Disneyland that other plans had been arranged for him.

Major General Nikolai S. Zakharov of the Soviet Security Police had come to Los Angeles three weeks before Khrushchev's visit to review security arrangements with Los Angeles Police Chief William H. Parker.

Parker was adamant that his department could not guarantee security because the motorcade would have to travel more than thirty miles to get to Disneyland and in addition, Anaheim was part of Orange County and therefore outside his jurisdiction so that he could not assure the necessary protection.

Other Los Angeles police escorts to Disneyland had been provided for former President Harry Truman and other visiting Soviet dignitaries. Kings and queens, princes and princesses, presidents, heads of state and a host of other dignitaries had already visited Disneyland over the first few years without incident.

Parker was probably aware that there were heated feelings about Khrushchev's visit to the Los Angeles area. Even before the Soviet leader arrived, there was a huge anti-Soviet rally held at the Rose Bowl and President Eisenhower had to personally urge calm. When Khrushchev did arrive in Los Angeles, his motorcade was bombarded with tomatoes on the ride from the airport to the 20th Century Fox studios.

Parker firmly advocated dropping a Disneyland visit from the schedule altogether. However, since the Khrushchevs had indicated a desire to see the theme park, there were two different alternate security plans prepared. One plan was devised if just Mrs. Khrushchev and her children decided to visit and another in case Mr. Khrushchev decided at the last minute to come along.

On September 19th, Khrushchev and his wife arrived in Los Angeles. The day began with a tour to a soundstage at Twentieth Century Fox Studios where the movie *Can Can* was being filmed.

At the studio, Khrushchev saw the cast members perform a musical number from the film. Superstar performer Frank Sinatra was an unofficial master of ceremonies for the visit, and the Soviet premier lunched with dozens of Hollywood celebrities from Marilyn Monroe to Shirley MacLaine to Maurice Chevalier before his arranged housing tour later than afternoon.

Supposedly, at lunch, comedian Bob Hope was seated near to Mrs. Khrushchev and, in trying to make polite conversation, told her something along the lines of "You should really try to go to Disneyland. It's wonderful."

Hollywood columnist James Bacon remembered, "Mrs. Khrushchev was lamenting to Frank [Sinatra] that their trip to Disneyland and been nixed because of security reasons. 'It's the only place I really wanted to see here,' she told Sinatra in accented but good English. Frank told her: 'Why Disneyland is the safest place in the world. I'll take you there myself if you want to go.' David Niven who was sitting nearby chimed in and said the same thing." (Actually, one report from that luncheon recalls Sinatra leaning over to Niven and saying, "Tell the old broad that you and I will take her there this afternoon if she wants to go that badly.")

At that point, Mrs. Khrushchev wrote a note in Russian and had it delivered to her husband on the podium. In the note, she wrote about how disappointed she was that the Khrushchevs, for security reasons, would not be allowed to visit Disneyland. Khrushchev reportedly confirmed this with the Secret Service near him.

The *New York Times* (September 22, 1959) reported that the Moscow newspaper, *Izvestia*, wrote that Khrushchev felt during the trip like he was under arrest because of the strict security measures. The newspaper also informed the Soviet citizens that the real reason Mr. Khrushchev was not allowed to go to Disneyland was that it was a Saturday, a day on which tens of thousands of ordinary American citizens and their children would have filled the park and that U.S. authorities did not want them interacting with the Soviet premier.

Khrushchev's son-in-law, who was a writer for the newspaper, later wrote a 700-page book about Khrushchev's trip titled *Litsom k litsu s Amerikoi* (*Face to Face with America*).

Still fuming from an earlier comment by Twentieth Century Fox President (and strong anti-communist) Spyros P. Skouras who tried to goad the Soviet premier with a reference to a previous speech about burying American capitalism, Khrushchev's famous temper probably got the better of him. He stood up and in a voice shaking with emotion, took the opportunity to complain about the level of security that prevented him from visiting Disneyland.

*"We have come to this town where lives the cream of American art. And just imagine. I, a premier, a Soviet representative, when I came here to this city, I was given a plan. A program of what I was to be shown and whom I was to meet here.*

*"But just now I was told that I could not go to Disneyland. I asked 'Why not? What is it? Do you have rocket-launching pads there?' I do not know.*

*"And just listen—just listen to what I was told—to what reason I was told. 'We, which means the American authorities, cannot guarantee your security if you go there.'*

*"What is it? Is there an epidemic of cholera there or something? Or have gangsters taken over the place that can destroy me? Then what must I do? Commit suicide?*

*"This is the situation I am in. Your guest. For me, this situation is inconceivable. I can not find words to explain this to my people."*

The State Department later said that Mrs. Khrushchev and her daughters were free to attend Disneyland but that Mrs. Khrushchev decided "at the last minute" to remain with her husband instead. Supposedly, Mr. Khrushchev had said that if Disneyland wasn't safe for him to visit, then it wasn't safe for his family to do so.

Imagineer Marty Sklar remembered that everyone was waiting at Disneyland in case any of the Khrushchevs decided to come.

"We were all set. We were ready. We had, I would guess, over a hundred Highway Patrol motorcycle cops and Anaheim police. So we invited them all in [to the park] and fed them all," said Sklar.

Walt Disney was eager for the Khrushchevs to visit, especially because of the worldwide publicity it would generate for Disneyland that was barely four years old. Walt had no sympathy for communists, but his wife was interested in meeting Mr. Khrushchev.

Later, after lunch at 20th Century Fox, an apologetic Khrushchev supposedly told some of the performers in *Can Can* that the studio commissary had been too hot and probably put him in an ill humor. He later denounced in the press the Can Can dance he had seen in rehearsal as "decadent."

Instead of visiting Disneyland, Khrushchev was driven behind a large police escort through shopping centers, housing developments and the UCLA campus. Sirens howled. Helicopters hovered overhead. Shouting people lined the streets.

Khrushchev was told he could stop anywhere to get out and visit but the Russian leader chose not to stop anywhere and reportedly, in a petulant mood, hardly looked out the window of his closed limousine.

"Putting me in a closed car and stewing me in the sun is not the right way to guarantee my safety. This [not being allowed to go to Disneyland] development causes me bitter regret. I thought I could come here as a free man," said the Soviet premier.

Ironically, four Russian newsmen who were reporting on Khrushchev's trip did slip away to visit Disneyland and spent four hours enjoying the experience. They told American reporters they believed that Khrushchev and his family would have really enjoyed Disneyland.

The newspaper reports focused on Khrushchev's outburst at not being allowed to visit Disneyland instead of the prepared speech he gave later that evening. Soon, even political cartoons were commenting on the tantrum.

The following morning, many people saw Khrushchev's train leave from the Glendale train station and then pass through the San Fernando Valley on its way to Santa Barbara and San Francisco. The Soviet leader continued his trip through California without further incident and returned to Washington for his meeting with Eisenhower.

Author Herman Wouk (*The Winds of War*) commented at the time: "I don't blame Khrushchev for jumping up and down in rage over missing Disneyland. There are few things more worth seeing in the United States, or indeed anywhere else in the world."

Later, that year, comedian Bob Hope used the incident as a springboard for a gag when he was entertaining troops in Alaska during one of his Christmas tours when he joked: "Here we are in America's 49th state, Alaska. That's halfway between Khrushchev and Disneyland."

Walt apparently got a kick out of the whole situation and the publicity it generated. Years later, he talked with Bill Walsh about creating a live-action comedy screenplay about the incident. Disney Legend Walsh had a very successful career at the studio including writing and producing many top films including *Mary Poppins*.

Walsh teamed with another top storyman, Don DaGradi, to write *Khrushchev at Disneyland*. The screenplay dealt with an excited Khrushchev coming to America to visit Disneyland under the guise of meeting with the President of the United States to resolve Cold War issues. When Khrushchev discovers that due to safety concerns, he won't be able to visit the Happiest Place on Earth, he comes up with a wacky scheme in the Los Angeles-area hotel where he staying.

Khrushchev disguises himself and slips by both Russian security and the U.S. Secret Service to sneak out to go to Disneyland. However, the security officers are soon in hot pursuit. "He gets mixed up with the animals down there and dresses up as a bear or as a wolf or something as I remember," said Walsh. "Walt liked Peter Ustinov. He also liked the idea of Ustinov playing Khrushchev going to Disneyland. It was somebody's idea who sold it to Card Walker and Card thought maybe we'd better just take it out of circulation because somebody would do something with it or would do something wrong. So, I said, 'Yeah, I'll do it.' I like stories where there's a gimmick like that. I immediately knew that that would be fun, doing that with Ustinov playing it."

This would have been only the second theatrical film up to that time to use Disneyland as a setting. The first film was *40 Pounds of Trouble* with Tony Curtis. It was released in 1962 from Universal. Curtis played a Lake Tahoe casino manager who inherits a five year old girl who was abandoned by her debt-ridden father. The film was based on the Damon Runyon story that inspired previous films like *Little Miss Marker* (1934) and *Sorrowful Jones* (1949). Curtis ends up taking the girl and his love interest (played by Suzanne Pleshette) to Disneyland where a detective hired by his ex-wife ends up chasing Curtis throughout the Happiest Place on Earth. It was the first entertainment feature film to be shot at Disneyland and the park segment lasts about twenty minutes.

Actor Peter Ustinov was to play the part of Khrushchev. At the time, he was filming his first Disney live-action film, *Blackbeard's Ghost* with producer Walsh and director Robert Stevenson who were also both connected to the *Khrushchev at Disneyland* project. In fact, the last Disney live-action film Walt saw in production was *Blackbeard's Ghost* and on his final visit to the set before he returned to St. Joseph's hospital for the last time, Walt joked with Ustinov and Stevenson about the upcoming film project.

An excited Ustinov told Walt that he intended to shave his head to look more like Khrushchev and that his mother resembled Khrushchev.

Walt quipped, "I didn't know your mother was bald."

The Disney Studio wasn't as confident about the project as Walt. When Walt died in late 1966, the initial work was shelved and still gathers dust in the forgotten files.

Walt reminisced about the incident in a 1963 conversation:

> *"We didn't refuse him permission. No, we were all set. You see, we work according to what the State Department wants to do when they come in and they have guests. Khrushchev was a guest of the government. So, I mean we were ready to receive Khrushchev. But it so happened that the security problem here in Los Angeles...because, actually, Disneyland is in another county, you see ... and the chief of police, we can't blame him. He had quite a chore there to carry out. He just was a little worried about somebody maybe walking in Disneyland with a shopping bag and what they might have in it. You'd never be able to know, you know."*

Although Walt was avid anti-Communist, he did see the potential for publicity and fun of Khrushchev coming to visit Disneyland.

*"But we were ready for him. The press was ready. Both the State Department security and the Soviet security had come and cased Disneyland and they were all set. And I was all ready. In fact, we've had a lot of dignitaries down there and he was one that Mrs. Disney wanted to go down and meet. So, she was disappointed he didn't come.*

*"I had...we had different shots, places where we'd take pictures with Khrushchev and I had one that was my favorite. We'd be lined up in front of my eight submarines, you see, and I thought, well, it'd be nice. I'd be pointing to Mr. Khrushchev and saying, 'Well, now, Mr. Khrushchev, here's my Disneyland submarine fleet.' It's the eighth-largest submarine fleet in the world."*

Robert Wormhoudt, Disneyland's chief protocol official at the time stated, "Our job is to receive heads of state and royalty in accordance with their official stature. We always grant protocol admissions to individuals who are guests of the American President. Actually, Disneyland was not on Chairman Khrushchev's official itinerary. It was Ambassador Henry Cabot Lodge who accepted the responsibility for deciding against the Chairman's impetuous decision to come. After the incident, Disneyland had an unusual number of Soviet visitors. I guess they are all trying to outdo the boss."

## A/K/A THE GRAY SEAL

Artist and storyman Floyd Norman once mentioned that, in an early storyboard meeting on *The Jungle Book*, Walt's dissatisfaction with the direction of the story was summed up by him telling the storymen that the story was "too dark, like Batman." What did Walt know about masked mystery men? Ah, that is the mystery that has been solved!

By the time Superman, Flash Gordon, Buck Rogers and Batman and their peers first appeared, Walt was already in his thirties and had been struggling for many years with the adult responsibilities of his animation studio so these types of characters didn't capture his boyhood "sense of wonder" as they did so many others. It is interesting to speculate on the effect they might have had on Walt if he were twelve years old when they appeared.

As a young boy, Walt supposedly read all the works of Mark Twain as he told at least two interviewers and that he also read books by Charles Dickens and Robert Louis Stevenson, which was all probably standard reading for most youngsters in those days. He told author Bob Thomas that he liked reading Shakespeare as a boy but only the "fighting parts".

Walt Disney's brother-in-law Bill Cottrell mentioned in an interview that Walt loved the fictional character, Jimmie Dale, Alias the Gray Seal, and as a boy, Walt would re-enact those adventures with his boyhood friend, Walt Pfieffer.

In the Fifties, Walt purchased the rights to all the Jimmie Dale books in the hopes of developing a television series based on the character. A copy of a document from the Copyright

Office of the United States located by animation historian
Michael Barrier helps provide another piece of the story.

Originally signed April 2, 1952 and filed for record on May
19, 1952, Marguerite Pearl Packard, acting on behalf of the late
author Frank Packard, freely gave "for valuable consideration
paid to the undersigned by Walt Disney Productions" the "sole
and exclusive" rights to make "motion picture, photoplay,
television, radio and/or any other adaptations of every kind
and character" as well as the right to "obtain copyright in all
countries upon said work and upon any and all adaptations".

This document was for the rights to "All stories which were
written by Frank L. Packard, deceased, utilizing the fictional
character, JIMMIE DALE." Want to look it up? It is in volume
832, pages 120-123 at the Copyright Office.

So just exactly who the heck was Jimmie Dale?

Jimmie Dale, the infamous "Gray Seal," was created by
Frank Lucius Packard (February 2, 1877 - February 17, 1942),
who was a Canadian novelist born in Montreal, Quebec. He
worked as a civil engineer on the Canadian Pacific Railway and
his first stories were railroad stories but he earned a living by
writing other "pulp-ish" stories including several Westerns. If
he is remembered at all today, it is for his work on "Jimmie
Dale."

Those adventures first appeared in 1914 in serial installments
in *People's Magazine* (and later magazines like *Short Stories
Magazine* and *Detective Fiction Weekly Magazine*) before they were
later compiled and published in novels: *The Adventures of Jimmie
Dale* (1917), *The Further Adventures of Jimmie Dale* (1919), *Jimmie*

*Dale and the Phantom Clue* (1922), *Jimmie Dale and the Blue Envelope Murder* (1930), and *Jimmie Dale and the Missing Hour* (1935).

When the stories first appeared, the *Saturday Review* called them: "Stories of excitement, intrigue, etc., which have no equal."

The *New York World* said: "These tales are abounding in 'pep'! Beyond doubt the most polished narratives of the underworld yet published."

In fact, the character was so popular that Broadway actor E.K. Lincoln (not to be confused with actor Elmo Lincoln) starred in a sixteen chapter silent movie serial titled *Jimmie Dale Alias the Gray Seal* from the Monmouth Film Company distributed through the Mutual exchanges. Directed by Harry McRae Webster and written by Mildred Considine (based on Packard's stories), the film was released March 23, 1917 and fairly closely followed Packard's concepts including using the mystery woman.

But who was Jimmie Dale? Well, writer Walter Gibson who created The Shadow claims that he "borrowed" elements for that famous character from Jimmie Dale.

As Disney Legend Donn Tatum told author Bob Thomas in an interview on May 24, 1973: "He (Walt) also used to talk about... He loved The Gray Seal stories. Do you ever remember that? Jimmie Dale Alias the Gray Seal? He used to compose that as a television show. The "Gray Seal" was really an amateur private eye who lived in Boston. His name was Jimmie Dale and Walt used to act them out all the time. Jimmy Dale was a disguise artist. In every story he'd put on a different disguise and find the criminal. And if he didn't find the criminal he prevented someone from committing a crime. And his trademark was a gray seal pasted somewhere. Walt had bought all the books. There were a number of them and he owned all the rights to them."

According to the Disney Archives, there was a story number (1764) assigned to the "Jimmie Dale project" on December 26, 1951, and John Lucas headed the story crew. This was several months before Walt actually got the rights to the character. However, no other information that can be easily found about the project exists at the Disney Archives other than the project was eventually abandoned within the following decade.

Part of Walt's agreement with ABC and later NBC was that the networks had the right of first refusal on any new television series that Walt wanted to produce. For ABC, of course, those series included the original *Mickey Mouse Club* and *Zorro*.

One of the projects that Walt proposed to NBC was a series to be called *Jimmie Dale, Alias the Gray Seal* but the network felt the concept was not what the public expected from Disney and rejected the proposal.

Jimmie Dale was the son of a wealthy New York City family. He spent his teenage years working at his father's safe manufacturing factory and later entered Harvard University where he spent a lot of time reading detective fiction and amusing himself with amateur theatrics.

After graduation, he joined the exclusive St. James Club and lived the life of leisure that only a gentleman could. To amuse himself, he created the identity of the "Gray Seal", a two-fisted masked mystery man, who broke into homes, stores and public buildings and opened even the most tightly guarded safes just to prove that no safe was safe. He always left his calling card, a gray diamond paper seal, and never took anything.

He lived alone in his mansion except for his faithful older butler, Jason, and his devoted but rough chauffeur, Benson. In addition to being the "Gray Seal," he also adopted another secret identity, "Larry the Bat", a disreputable dope fiend who could more easily maneuver through the underworld of crime to obtain information. Later in the series, he creates yet another persona, "Smarlinghue," a junkie-artist.

He kept all his equipment including his disguise kit at a secret hideout on the third floor of a tenement in the worst part of New York, the Bowery. This fortress of solitude is called the "Sanctuary" and it also serves as a refuge for the foppish playboy. As the Gray Seal, his attire includes a "wide leather belt filled with small pockets," each with the tools of his trade.

Unfortunately, Jimmie made a mistake on one of his playful capers and ended up being blackmailed by a mystery woman known only as "the Tocsin." She later turns out to be Marie LaSalle, a young and beautiful woman, who uses Jimmie's skills to put an end to the crime bosses controlling New York City's criminal organization known as the Crime Club. After many years of flirtations, Dale and LaSalle walk off into the sunset together once the Crime Club is destroyed.

During these adventures, the Gray Seal developed an adversarial relationship with Herman Carruthers, a former Harvard classmate of Jimmie Dale and editor of the *Morning News-Argus* newspaper.

Packard describes Jimmie's physical appearance in this paragraph: "Six feet he stood, muscular in every line of his body, like a well-trained athlete with no single ounce of superfluous fat about him--the grace and ease of power in his poise. His strong, clean-shaven face, as the light fell upon it now, was serious--a mood that became him well--the firm lips closed, the dark, reliant eyes a little narrowed, a frown on the broad forehead, the square jaw clamped."

Jimmie had an unusual aptitude for all things mechanical and his memory is phenomenal. He is also an accomplished painter, disguise artist and mimic among other talents.

A thief who uses his talents for good? Well, that was the Saint. A gentleman safe cracker? Well, that is probably Raffles. A special utility belt with the tools of the trade? Well, that was Batman. Multiple secret identities? Well, that's the Shadow. A secret lair? Well, that was Doc Savage. Leaving behind a signature icon? Well, that could be the Spider or even the Scarlet Pimpernel (who never left behind flowers in the book version but did in his first film outing made long after Jimmie Dale's success) or maybe even Zorro who left the famous "Z".

However, the Gray Seal stories first appeared in 1914 when Walt Disney was about thirteen years old and almost two decades before the era of the pulp hero and all these other characters previously mentioned. The only pulp-like hero to precede the Gray Seal was probably Baroness Orczy's *The Scarlet Pimpernel* (1903).

Jimmie was, in many ways, a model for later classic heroic characters who made use of secret identities (especially the ineffectual wealthy playboy who secretly becomes a masked two-fisted man of action), secret hideouts, special gadgets, beautiful mystery women who helped them in their endeavors, costumes and disguises, battling with the local newspaper editor, and so many other iconic elements. Apparently, these stories captured Walt's sense of wonder.

There is a picture of Walt sitting behind his desk at the Hyperion Studio from the mid-Thirties. There are stacks of books, some in foreign languages including four written by Brüder Grimm. One of the few American books in the stacks, and in fact at the very top of the stack under a revolver that was probably a cigarette lighter, is a copy of *Jimmie Dale and the Blue Envelope Murder* published in 1930.

"Walt never got around to doing it. Every time he'd see Leonard Goldenson (founder and chairman of ABC, the network that presented the first Disney television programs) he'd tell Leonard the story of the Gray Seal," recalled Donn Tatum. "Leonard wasn't interested. Walt was very disappointed about that."

Unfortunately, except in his very vivid imagination, Walt never had the opportunity to bring to life the adventures of his boyhood hero, the man of mystery called Jimmie Dale, also known as The Gray Seal.

## MICKEY MOUSE THEATER OF THE AIR

There is a newspaper column reportedly written by the famous radio comedians Amos and Andy titled *Amos'N'Andy, From Toothpaste to Soup: First Men of Radio Change Sponsors this Weekend* from the *Los Angeles Times* of Saturday, January 1, 1938. The column, done as a humorous letter to "Norm," details how the show is changing sponsors from Pepsodent toothpaste to Campbell Soup.

What does this have to do with Disney history? Well, the newspaper article features a photo of actor Charles Correll (who played Amos) handing over their "lucky radio horseshoe" to a smiling Walt Disney who would take over their sponsor and radio slot with the *Mickey Mouse Theater of the Air* while actor Freeman Gosden (who played Andy) looks on approvingly. In the picture are stuffed three-foot tall Charlotte Clark made dolls of Mickey Mouse and Donald Duck.

The caption to the picture reads: "Lucky New Year…Amos (left) and Andy (right) turn over their lucky radio horseshoe to Walt Disney (center). Disney is going to work for their former sponsor, while Amos'n'Andy continue on the air for a new boss. Mickey Mouse is pleased. Donald Duck is trying to look the same way, too."

One of the many forgotten aspects of early Disney history was the short-lived (only twenty episodes) radio show, *Mickey Mouse Theater of the Air* produced by the Disney Studios in 1938 to showcase Mickey Mouse and his friends and to help promote the release of the animated film *Snow White and the Seven Dwarfs*.

Once upon a time radio was king. It was not just the home for music and countless talk show hosts. During the Golden Age of Radio, listeners could tune in the dial on their huge radio (that was actually a piece of living room furniture) and hear programming of adventure, comedy, drama, horror, mystery, musical variety, romance, thrillers, as well as classical music concerts, Big Band remotes, farm reports, news and commentary, panel discussions, quiz shows, sidewalk interviews, sports broadcasts, talent shows, weather forecasts, and more.

The Golden Age of Radio lasted from the early Twenties until the invasion of television in the late Fifties. In the beginning, American radio network programs were presented almost exclusively live, since the national networks prohibited the airing of recorded programs until the late Forties. As a result, prime-time shows would be performed twice for both coasts. However, some programs were recorded as they were broadcast during this period, typically for syndicated programs or for advertisers to have their own copy.

Thankfully, the estate of Felix Mills, the musical director of the *Mickey Mouse Theater of the Air* donated all his original discs of the show to the Pacific Pioneer Broadcasters for future researchers to enjoy and study.

"I remember Walt being very excited about doing the show, and I thought he believed his characters had to be seen because he planned the production as a children's radio show. He was constantly amazed by how much grown-ups loved and admired his work," Betsy Mills Goodspeed, daughter of Felix, wrote. "My father thought *Snow White and the Seven Dwarfs* was the most marvelous film that was ever produced. As far as I know, he didn't go to the Disney Studios to discuss the music for the radio show but went to Disney's house, or Walt came to ours. Walt obviously believed that Felix was the best choice for the job, and Felix thought the radio program was a fantastic endeavor by all those who were involved. He felt highly honored to have been awarded the contract."

Walt Disney and his animated friends were no strangers to radio. Walt (often doing the voice of Mickey Mouse and sometimes accompanied by Clarence Nash voicing Donald Duck) popped up on several radio shows during its Golden Age.

In the summer of 1937, Lever Brothers (who made products like Rinso and Lifebuoy) were looking for a half-hour program to precede and build an audience for their Al Jolson's Lifebuoy Show on CBS that was being massacred in the ratings by its competition on NBC, Jack Benny. Looking for additional funds and publicity for the almost completed *Snow White and the Seven Dwarfs*, Walt Disney hesitantly agreed in September to do an audition record for a weekly Disney radio show.

It was hoped that the show would air beginning on October 5, 1937. Written by comedy writer Ken Englund, the premise was that Mickey Mouse would host the half hour and present a weekly guest star (actor Leslie Howard was chosen as the first guest) but that Donald Duck would mess things up.

Deeply involved in the final months of making *Snow White*, Walt wouldn't be available to do the voice of Mickey Mouse so actor J. Donald Wilson was selected. One newspaper at the time reported that it was "the first time anyone other than Walt Disney himself was allowed to speak for Mickey." Clarence Nash, of course, did the voice of Donald Duck and the musical chores were handled by Meredith "Music Man" Wilson.

Roy Disney flew to New York in September to close the deal but it fell apart because of a dispute over monetary terms. Some news stories including one in the *Hollywood Reporter* also hinted that "Disney is afraid [his characters] may sour on him if they [air] every week" and that Walt "refuses radio because he doesn't think his Mickey Mouse and others would broadcast well." Reportedly, at one time even Lucky Strike cigarettes tried to woo Walt into a weekly radio children's show. Eventually, Lever Brothers decided to sponsor instead a dramatic program, the popular *Big Town* with Edward G. Robinson.

Shortly afterward, Pepsodent (thanks to a guarantee of a budget of somewhere between $10,000 and $12,000 weekly and some other concessions) lured Walt into committing to doing a radio show to fill the gap left by *Amos and Andy* on NBC on Sunday afternoon. (*Amos and Andy* at this time actually ran six times a week.) Walt probably agreed because the show coincided with the release of *Snow White* and he saw it (just as he later did with television) as an opportunity to publicize his latest film.

The original option was for thirteen weeks with Walt doing the voice of Mickey Mouse until a suitable replacement could be found. Despite what it says at other sources, Walt only did Mickey's voice for the first three weeks. From the fourth show on, the voice of Mickey was comedian Joe Twerp whose comedy relied on being an excitable, stuttering person who confuses words. He had been considered for the role of Doc, a similar personality, in Walt Disney's *Snow White* but Roy Atwell was chosen to supply the voice instead.

The writers for the show were Bill Demling (who had supplied material for big name radio comedians like Ed Wynn and Joe E. Brown) and Eddie Holden ( a radio actor who supplied the voice of the giant in the Mickey Mouse short *The Brave Little Tailor* and did incidental voices in *Dumbo* and *Bambi*).

Music direction was by Gordon "Felix" Mills, one of radio's most active orchestra leaders of era who directed thirty-three musicians for the show. Six of those musicians also performed as Donald Duck's wacky novelty "gadget" band, the Webfoot Sextet, who used cowbells, bottles, a meat grinder, auto horn, a Bob Bums-style bazooka, and a "syrup-cruet hurdy gurdy." Amazingly all of this cacophony sounded pretty good and funny.

In his unpublished memoir, Felix Mills remembered, "I called in a young drummer from the (Eddie) Cantor show when one of our drummers had the flu, and for several weeks he hung around at rehearsals. [His name was Spike Jones.] Spike asked what I was going to do with the Duck's music and I said, 'I'll never use it again; do you want it?'" Soon the City Slickers appeared on the scene playing a wild arrangement of *Cocktails for Two*."

There was a twelve voice female choir (who had four members who specialized in bird whistling so they also performed as Minnie Mouse's Woodland Bird Choir) and an eight-voice male choir. The opening theme song for the show was the still popular *Who's Afraid of the Big Bad Wolf?* and the closing theme was *Heigh Ho* from *Snow White*.

Broadcast from a theater studio on the RKO lot (remember that RKO was releasing the Disney animated films), Joe Twerp did the voice of Mickey Mouse. Minnie Mouse was performed by Thelma Boardman who would later supply Minnie's voice in the some of the Disney cartoons of the Forties. Pinto Colvig had left the Disney Studio by the time the show started so the role of Goofy was done by Stuart Buchanan, who was the official "casting director" at the Disney Studios and had supplied the voice of the huntsman in *Snow White*. Donald Duck was voiced by Clarence Nash and Clara Cluck was Florence Gill. Both of them had performed the same roles in the Disney animated cartoons.

The announcer was John "Bud" Hiestand (who appeared in many movies in 1938 as a radio announcer besides his regular radio announcing). In addition, he also supplied the voice of the Magic Mirror, which was the primarily form of transportation that allowed Mickey and the gang to journey through time and space to meet everyone from Long John Silver to Mother Goose to Robin Hood. While the Disney version of the Snow White character showed up on at least two episodes (and in one episode Walt danced with Snow White), the gang also got to visit Cinderella and Sleeping Beauty almost two decades before those films were made.

Incidentally, on some of the later shows, Walt was too busy to attend rehearsals and performance so Hiestand had to impersonate Walt himself when the script called for an appearance. In addition, Glanville Heisch, the creator of the popular radio show the *Cinnamon Bear* and Hiestand's brother-in-law, was on board as a writer and director on the show. His skill at writing verse and songs is evident in the Disney radio program.

There were other voices on the show as well supplied by popular performers including Billy Bletcher (the voice of Peg Leg Pete in the cartoons who popped up as Old King Cole and Judge Owl in the show), Hans Conreid (still many years from voicing Captain Hook who did a comical turn as the Pied

Piper), Bea Benaderet (portraying Miriam the Mermaid in the kingdom of King Neptune), Walter Tetley, and many others including Mel Blanc.

Mel Blanc? The voice of Bugs Bunny, Daffy Duck and countless other cartoon characters who always told the story that the only voice he did for Disney was the voice of Gideon the Cat in *Pinocchio* and it was later cut out except for a hiccup? (Or course, Blanc also supplied the voice for the Audio-Animatronics Cousin Orville in the *Carousel of Progress* as well.)

Yes, the then twenty nine year old Blanc was a regular on the show portraying a variety of characters as well as one of his earliest continuing characters, a man who gets so excited that he starts hiccupping so violently that he can't stop. Perhaps this performance gave Walt the idea to use him in the production of *Pinocchio* that was in development at that time.

Initially, Walt Disney tried to be excited about the show. He wrote in a 1938 issue of *Radio Log* magazine: "I'm letting Mickey and the rest of my gang go on the air, although I've been advised against it. We consider this a good omen, for we were also strongly advised against ever creating Mickey, doing our pictures in sound, branching into Technicolor, and creating a feature length picture."

Despite this optimistic statement, Walt had deep concerns that the success of his cartoon characters depended primarily on their visual antics and not their distinctive voices. He once joked that part of Donald Duck's popularity in foreign countries was the fact that no one could understand what he said and had to use their own imagination.

"Many sponsors have whispered the siren song of (radio's) riches in our ear. Several tried, but none of them had the feeling for our characters. Then we realized that what we had begun to suspect was true: if Mickey went on the air we'd have to build the program ourselves."

However, Walt was greatly distracted by the release of *Snow White* and other issues at the Studio. He took the chance on radio because he hoped it might prove to be a good way to advertise his films and might indeed spark the creation of some new characters or ideas that could be utilized. No new characters were created from the venture but perhaps this foray into radio gave Walt some insight on how to handle later his entry into television.

"It's a rather logical direction in which we can expand. We expect to develop new ideas and personalities we can use in our pictures. We look upon radio as a new stimulus, a challenge—something which will give us fresh ideas and a better perspective on our work."

When the contract ended after thirteen weeks, Pepsodent did renew the show for the remaining seven weeks of that season, but then the show quietly disappeared as so many other radio shows did that didn't capture the imagination of its audience.

As always, Walt had been right. He had been quoted as saying before the show even premiered that, "I don't think this show will work. You have to see the characters to fully appreciate them. "

Contemporary critics agreed. Aaron Stein of the *New York Post* wrote: "All the strength, the vigor and logic of the Disney films lies in the pictures. The voices, the music and the sounds are usually funny and effective, but they register only as sound effects which point up the pictures. On the air they offered only disembodied sound effects."

---

Let's take a brief look at the final twenty-two page, half hour episode from May 15, 1938 where Mickey and the gang try to save Old MacDonald's farm. After all, as it was pointed out in the script, Old MacDonald HAD a farm so how did he lose it and can the Disney characters help him save it?

Old MacDonald was voiced by Cliff Arquette, who may be best remembered today for his character of Charley Weaver (the old man with the little round glasses, squashed hat, baggy pants and suspenders from Mount Idy who would read a letter from his mama) who often popped up on *Hollywood Squares* —or for the fact that he is the grandfather of actors Patricia, Rosanna, and David Arquette.

The farmer's daughter was voiced by Blanc, who did his hiccupping bit to help reveal why she never married in almost thirty years. The villain, Squire Perkins, who is foreclosing the mortgage on the farm, was voiced by Bletcher.

The show begins with Hiestand announcing "The Pepsodent Company presents Mickey Mouse!" (The show was never referred to as *The Mickey Mouse Theater of the Air.*)

After some banter between Mickey, Donald, Goofy and band leader Felix Mills, Hiestand does a commercial for Pepsodent which is constantly being interrupted by Donald Duck urging listeners to try either the toothpaste or tooth powder themselves especially since Pepsodent is packed with "Irium" that helps brush away stubborn surface stains on teeth.

Goofy sings *Old MacDonald Had a Farm* and it turns out that Goofy and Donald have found the old farmer himself. When asked how he lost his farm, he replies it is a "long story" but that basically Squire Perkins had a mortgage on the place and foreclosed. "I often think, if I had that one day to live over again, I might have been able to save the old homestead," sighs Old MacDonald who reveals that he had a daughter who was "half an orphan" since her mother died.

The idea of a "real genuine farmer's daughter" excites both Goofy and Donald and the decision is made to call the Magic Mirror so they can all go back to the day that the villain foreclosed on the farm thirty years ago.

When they journey to the past, Old MacDonald introduces them to his daughter, Priscilly, who is milking the cows and singing "Whistle While You Milk" that includes the phrase: "When trouble troubles you, don't cry and go 'boo-hoo' (Cow goes "Moo"), Remember that the teensty pigs are rooting just for you—hoooo-hoo, so whistle while you milk."

Old MacDonald explains that her name is Lucinda Arabella Priscilla "but folks jest call her Silly." While Mickey and Minnie explore the farm with Old MacDonald, Goofy and Donald try to comfort Priscilly who is so upset about the foreclosure that she is crying against a cow. Donald's Webfoot Sextet plays a raucous version of *Let Me Call You Sweetheart* to cheer her up.

Priscilly asks if Donald is a traveling salesman because "you see, my father once told me to look out for traveling salesmen and so I've been looking out for one ever since (giggle)." Then Goofy and Donald find one of the reasons that Priscilly never married. She gets so excited that she starts hiccupping out of control. Priscilly thinks it must be the heat making her do it because she feels very warm.

Donald replies: "Oh year? Phooey. You're not so hot, sister! (running away when Mickey returns) Is she terrible! Fooey! Lemme out o' here! Lemme out o' here!" And Goofy adds: "Out o' my way, Duck! Here I go—hurry up, Donald!"

Before they can leave, they are stopped by Mickey who informs them that Old MacDonald has trained all his animals how to sing and they do, led by Clara Cluck who somehow must have come along, as well.

After the concert, Abner the hired hand (also voiced by Twerp) comes and lets the group know that Perkins is coming but it takes forever to do so because he is so excited he keeps messing up the words: "Dister Mock Manold—Moster Dick Minald—Dooster Mack Monald—Hey, boss—come quick!"

Old MacDonald pleads with Perkins not to foreclose for the sake of his little daughter. Perkins mistakes Minnie Mouse for the farmer's daughter and being quite taken with her cuteness suggests a compromise: "Give me your daughter's hand in marriage and I'll tear up the mortgage!"

MacDonald has Perkins put it in writing and then tears up the mortgage and calls in his real daughter. Perkins is appalled at the real hiccupping daughter and as she grabs him, Perkins finally offers MacDonald $1,000 to tear up the contract. MacDonald agrees and Perkins leaves while over apple cider, everyone else sings parodies of public domain songs.

At one point MacDonald sings to his daughter: "And you're nobody's sweetheart now. You can't get a man no how. Piano legs—banjo eyes—You'll never win no beauty prize so harness yourself to a plough because you're nobody's sweetheart now" followed by the stage direction that the entire cast laughs!

To the tune of *Turkey in the Straw*, Minnie sings "Mickey, Mickey, I've been thinking that his daughter won't look glum if she only starts in using Pepsodent with Irium!" again with the stage direction that the entire cast laughs!

This verbal abuse of Priscilly goes on for seven choruses but apparently that is more than enough fun because the Magic Mirror appears and announces to Mickey: "Master, your time is up I fear. Return at once or dwell forever here!"

Mickey and the gang return to the present (with Donald and Goofy telling the farmer to hang on to his daughter so she doesn't follow them) and have some fun with the announcer before he does the closing commercial. Apparently, it is time for summer vacation and Mickey says: "I haven't time to think about it. I've been so busy with this radio program and making movies for Walt Disney and…"

The Magic Mirror suggests: "Perhaps I can help. At my command, I'll take you all to Vacation Land."

Mickey: "Gee, Mirror, that'll be swell. Come on, gang---Vacation Land!"

With the tune *Heigh Ho* playing in the background, the announcer says: "And so with Mickey and the Gang headed for Vacation Land we bring to a close the last program in the present series. This program has come to you from the Disney Little Theatre on the RKO lot."

That was the end of the twenty episode adventures of Mickey and the gang during the Golden Age of Radio. Obviously, Walt was distracted by his attention to *Snow White* to devote his storytelling skill and his famous attention to detail and innovation to the show but it remains an interesting if little known footnote in the history of Disney.

Here is the list of all twenty episodes of The *Mickey Mouse Theater of the Air*:

January 2, 1938: *Robin Hood*
January 9, 1938: *Snow White Day*
January 16, 1938: *Donald Duck's Band*
January 23, 1938: *The River Boat*
January 30, 1938: *Ali Baba*
February 6, 1938: *South of the Border*
February 13, 1938: *Mother Goose and Old King Cole*
February 20, 1938: *The Gypsy Band*
February 27, 1938: *Cinderella*
March 6, 1938: *King Neptune*
March 13, 1938: *The Pied Piper*
March 20, 1938: *Sleeping Beauty*
March 27, 1938: *Ancient China* (with a guest appearance by Snow White!)
April 3, 1938: *Mother Goose and the Old Woman in a Shoe*
April 10, 1938: *Long John Silver*
April 17, 1938: *King Arthur*
April 24, 1938: *Who Killed Cock Robin?*
May 1, 1938: *Cowboy Show*
May 8, 1938: *William Tell*
May 15, 1938: *Old MacDonald*

## GOLDEN OAK RANCH

Many California elementary school students were taught that one of the key events in California history was the big Gold Rush that started in 1849 where thousands of the Forty-Niners flooded into the Sacramento Valley area to seek their fortunes.

The textbooks never seem to mention the story of rancher Francisco Lopez who, in 1842, first discovered gold in Southern California. The legend goes that Lopez fell asleep under an oak tree and dreamed of finding gold. When he awoke, he was so hungry that he pulled a nearby wild onion up to eat. Surprisingly, Lopez found gold flakes (or small nuggets depending upon who is telling the story) in the roots of the onion and that discovery sparked a modest gold rush nearly seven years before Sutter's discovery at that Sacramento sawmill.

A plaque at the Golden Oak Ranch says the oak next to the church building is that famous "Golden Oak," and that "Under this tree, gold was first discovered in California by Don Francisco Lopez, March 9, 1842." Over a hundred years later, the site produced gold of a different kind when it was purchased and used by the Disney Studios as the site for filming many of its live action productions.

However, the Golden Oak Ranch in Newhall, California, wasn't always called the Golden Oak Ranch. Originally it was called the San Francisquito Rancho, and was part of Mission San Fernando.

When pioneer filmmaker Trem Carr owned the property, he called it the Placeritos Ranch as early as 1915. His set designer,

Ernie Hickson, created a Western movie town location using buildings he imported from Nevada for Carr's productions.

Carr sold the ranch around 1930 and Hickson moved the sets westward in Placerita Canyon, creating what would become the Monogram Ranch for filming B-movies featuring upcoming stars like John Wayne. It was later called the Melody Ranch Movie Studio, the home of singing cowboy Gene Autry, a long time friend of Walt Disney. At one time, there were fifteen active movie ranches in the Southern California area.

Meanwhile, Carr's one-time movie property reverted to a working horse and cattle ranch that was occasionally used by filmmakers.

Walt Disney Productions found a different kind of gold there when they needed a place to film the Triple R Ranch scenes for *The Mickey Mouse Club's Spin and Marty* serials for three years in the mid-Fifties.

Annette Funicello's mother, Virginia, recalled that filming the *Spin and Marty* serials at the location was enjoyed by all the young performers. "They loved it. They wore cowboy outfits. They rode horses. They swam. They didn't want to go home at night. It was wonderful!"

Prior to that time, the Disney Studio had been traveling long distances to do location shooting for live-action films including Arizona for *Song of the South* and Tennessee for *Davy Crockett*.

When Disney began doing television shows as well as more live action flims, it became necessary to find a more economical outdoor location site close to the Studio. The Golden Oak

Ranch located on Placerita Canyon Road in Newhall, California, roughly twenty-five miles north from the Disney Studios in Burbank, seemed a perfect choice.

The Disney Studio made arrangements to use the Golden Oak Ranch, now named for the gold that Francisco Lopez discovered at the base of the oak tree.

About that same time, many of the ranches that other movie studios had been using to film their exterior scenes were gradually being sub-divided, and Walt Disney feared that the motion picture ranches and the opportunities they provided might cease to exist.

Disney liked the varied topography of the area. So, on March 11, 1959, he purchased the 315-acre Golden Oak Ranch for $300,000. It was joked that this was more than three times the amount of gold that was found on the property that amounted to close to $80,000.

The first movie that was filmed on the ranch after Disney purchased it was *Toby Tyler or Ten Weeks With A Circus* in 1959.

Walt assigned his art directors William Tuntke and Marvin Aubrey Davis (who was a master planner for both Disneyland and Magic Kingdom) the job of converting the area for filming. Davis installed an irrigation system to keep the area green year-round (on some days almost one million gallons of water can be used) and created two lakes and a waterfall to be used for filming. The waterfall is designed so it can be turned on and off.

Davis designed one lake to look like a river from certain angles so it could be used for river crossings where it is approximately two feet deep in some areas and other areas where it is five feet deep. The artificial current was created by using water pumps. The lake can be drained in approximately eight hours and refilled completely in roughly forty-eight hours. Davis also developed portions of the landscape, planting thirty foot tall pine trees brought in from Lake Arrowhead.

Over the years—thanks to additional purchases of adjacent land needed to prevent the sights and sounds of modern life like television antennas, cars, condominiums or other items from intruding upon the movies shot at filming locations on the ranch—the area of the ranch increased to approximately eight hundred acres. The added acreage was necessary to insure unhindered vistas in all directions, especially for projects set in the Old West.

The prediction Walt Disney made in 1959 came true in just over two decades. The large Fox and Paramount ranches near Malibu were sold, and the once-popular Albertson Ranch is now covered with houses. The Golden Oak Ranch has become practically the only surviving movie ranch, and other Hollywood production companies have made use of the ranch for productions ranging from *Bonanza* to *Roots* to *Lassie* to *Back to the Future* and countless others.

Even while Disney was using it for filming, the Golden Oak Ranch doubled briefly as a working cattle ranch for a time. Three real cowboys ran herd on about fifty head and took them to market each winter to be sold for beef.

In 1960, Disney purchased a small herd of eight American buffalo and used them in several productions. Within two years the animals proved not to be worth the trouble since they wandered into shots, broke fences, and were more than a little "ornery" according to Walt. Walt, rather than sell them for slaughter, was convinced to donate them to the County of Los Angeles which put them out to pasture down the road at William S. Hart Park in Newhall.

At one point, Walt wanted to build a residential community at the ranch, an eighteen hole golf course and a shopping village and they were all to be connected by a train.

"He [Walt] was very fond of the ranch. He liked it so much that Walt seriously considered building a house and living there," remembered Bob Gibeaut who was Vice President of Studios Operations.

Walt had Marvin Davis design a home for himself and his wife and another for his brother Roy and his family and yet another for his daughter Diane. However, that plan was halted when Walt's wife decided she didn't want to live that far from Los Angeles.

In 1965, thirty-eight acres were set aside by Walt Disney for construction of the California Institute of the Arts campus, but eventually the school was built in Valencia instead. It was announced to the press in 1965 that work on construction was expected to begin immediately with the first classes to be held in the Fall of 1967.

Within the ranch's boundaries, there are permanent rural town sets, "Roots Street" an Old West street which was built for *Roots II*, several houses and barns, a lake with a covered bridge, sprawling meadows, majestic oak trees, creeks, and water falls.

The ranch even has its own wildlife including beautiful peacocks (originally purchased by Walt) that run wild, ducks swimming in the lake, a few horses who live in the stables and natural wildlife like rattlesnakes, bobcats, mountain lions and some rabbits (or more likely their offspring) that supposedly have survived from the Disney live action classic, *Old Yeller*.

Diamond Decorator, who played Tornado, Zorro's black horse in the popular television series was the only horse from that series that was personally owned by Walt. After the series, Diamond Decorator lived at the ranch until his death around 1987.

The ranch manager is Steve Sligh. The day-to-day caring of the ranch is by Pat Patterson, the twenty plus year ranch foreman, and his assistant, Jesus "Garcia" Guerrero, who has been living at the ranch since 1963. They are responsible for keeping the ranch in working order, mowing its meadows, pruning the trees and bushes, caring for livestock, and keeping those who utilize the site in proper bounds.

The property continually changes like the addition of Pine Lake, a twelve-foot-deep, man-made lake that was added to the property several years ago. The lake took a crew two months to make and forty-eight hours to fill. Today, it is home to freshwater fish and it is a popular spot to film.

Thanks to Walt's vision, the Disney Company and other movie studios still have a beautiful diverse wilderness area for their exterior filming needs. However, the ranch is private property so don't plan a visit without an invitation.

## DISNEY GOES TO MACY'S

A special Sailor Mickey Balloon, about six-stories tall, made its maiden voyage in the 83rd Macy's Thanksgiving Day Parade in November 2009 and will continue to appear through 2011. It represented the Disney Cruise Line, which had announced the launching of two new ships: the Disney Dream and the Disney Fantasy.

Mickey, perched upon an anchor, added to his iconic red shorts, white gloves and yellow shoes, a sailor's cap and a nautical blazer. It was Mickey's first appearance in the Macy's Thanksgiving Day Parade since 2000, when he was dressed as Bandleader Mickey.

Jeff Ebersol was a very talented Disney artist working for the Disney Design Group that produces artwork for merchandise like pins. Ebersol came up with the design for the Sailor Mickey balloon

He didn't want a stuffy-looking captain, so he reviewed early Mickey Mouse shorts and was taken by *Boat Builders* (1938) and based Mickey's outfit on that cartoon. He went through a variety of designs from Mickey tied to an anchor to a life preserver around the mouse's midsection. None of those concepts seemed like a good idea for a cruise ship emphasizing safety. So, it was determined that Mickey would be saluting and riding on an anchor as if it were lifted from the water for the ship to set sail.

Like too many other Walt Disney World cast members in March 2009, Ebersol was surprised to find himself laid off from the Disney Company. The responsibility of finishing the Sailor Mickey project fell on the shoulders of another very talented Disney Design Group artist, Brian Blackmore, who would need to go to New York to approve the clay sculpture for character integrity and, later, the color approval.

"I draw Mickey every single day so it becomes second nature," remembered Blackmore recently. "I had to remind myself that I was representing the Disney Company and the heritage of Mickey." (It is Brian's Mickey that decorates the WDW Disney Magical Express buses and is on the front of the Disney Dream cruise ship.)

Blackmore was impressed by the work of the Macy's sculptors and that it was a pretty good job for a first attempt at Mickey. However, there were a few changes that needed to be made.

"The buttons were not as round and the nose was not positioned correctly," he recalled.

John Piper, who directs the Macy's studio where the balloons and floats are designed and made, suggested that Blackmore get his hands dirty and make the corrections himself which he did willingly, although occasionally glancing at his watch so that he didn't miss his returning flight to Orlando. He had taken pictures of the sculpture before and after the changes and e-mailed them to the Disney Design Group in Florida, who discussed them over a conference call before the final approval. Blackmore made his plane, even in rush hour traffic.

Then, there had to be approval of the coloring which was assisted by the Pantone system where colors are assigned numbers.

"I do this so often I know that Mickey's face is 162, pants 485 and shoes 130. I have nightmares about all this," Blackmore said with a laugh.

Using that information, a full-sized balloon was created and Blackmore was flown out to the super secret location of Vermillion, South Dakota, where the Macy's balloons are built and tested. Inside the Mickey balloon was an intricate mass of ropes to make sure it kept the shape of everything like the head and the nose. Each balloon is hand-painted, as well.

"It takes approximately three hours to blow up the balloon and maybe three minutes to deflate it," Blackmore said. "When they were maneuvering it in the Dakota Dome, someone had brought along their four year old child who was excitedly yelling 'Mickey!' I realized at that moment how powerful this balloon was to send a message of goodwill."

Unfortunately, Blackmore couldn't immediately approve the finished product.

"I looked at the eyes and they were stark as if Mickey was in a coma", he said.

"After drawing Mickey so often, I knew it could be corrected by putting a little heavier line at the top of eyeballs. Imagine my surprise when I said this that they pulled the balloon down to the ground and got me a stepladder and I climbed up since the eye was about six feet high and I marked off the change on one of the eyes so they could make the change on both eyes. They did and I signed off on the balloon."

On November 27, 1924, the first Macy's *Christmas* Parade (as it was originally called) stepped into the streets of New

York with more than four hundred Macy employees (dressed as clowns, cowboys, knights and sheiks) accompanied by animals from camels to elephants (borrowed from the Central Park Zoo) and bands and floats. There was an audience of more than a quarter-million people!

Conceived by Macy's employees (many of whom were first-generation immigrants who wanted to celebrate the American holiday with a similar traditional festival popular in their homelands), the parade ended with Santa Claus unveiling Macy's Christmas windows on 34th Street and attracted children and their parents to Macy's newly expanded toy department.

The famous balloons did not make their appearance until 1927 (to replace the real animals which were frightening young children) and they were in fact not the balloons that are so familiar today. They were air-filled bags of rubber that were held upright with sticks. The first cartoon superstar in that 1927 parade was Felix the Cat.

Those first balloons which for a while were called "balloniacs" (and the later helium filled airborne ones) were the designs of Tony Sarg. Most histories of the parade refer to Sarg as "the artist behind Macy's fabulous window displays" but that is only the tip of the iceberg. Sarg was one of America's premiere puppeteers, as well as an illustrator. Disney had also licensed Sarg to produce Disney character marionettes during the 1930s, including Mickey, Minnie, Pluto, Donald and Snow White and the Seven Dwarfs.

In 1934, Sarg teamed with Walt Disney to produce the first Disney balloons to appear in the Macy Parade.

The advertisement for the 1934 parade proclaimed "See Gigantic Balloons designed by none other than Walt Disney creator of Mickey Mouse Himself. Mammoth Mickey Mouse a Colossus 40 feet high!!!! Pluto the Pup!! The Happy howling canine. Horace Horsecollar filled with fun and helium. 12 ½ feet high. The Big Bad Wolf!!! Held down by thirty marchers!!!!! See the Big Bad Wolf 34 feet high. See the Pig 31 feet high!!!"

That pig balloon was a very bad version of the Fifer pig from the popular cartoon *The Three Little Pigs* (1933). The press laughed at the portly pig's difficulty at the elevated train line at 65th Street and again at 53rd Street. Canvas was quickly placed on the street to protect it from the rough pavement. He was slowly glided under the structures on his back to successfully rise again and finish his parade trek. Following the pig was the Big Bad Wolf with a white star on its chest.

Why was Horace only twelve and a half feet high? Because six Horaces pulled Santa's sleigh!

The star balloon debuting in 1935 was Donald Duck. Returning was Mickey, Horace, the Big Bad Wolf and Pluto. Mickey was in a "Superman-style" pose with his hands on his hips and elbows out in the air while more than a dozen balloon handlers, who were dressed in black sweaters, baggy shorts, black tights and Mickey Mouse masks, held on to ropes and guided the helium-filled mouse down the street. Mickey's face had been painted in Akron but the rest of his body was painted in a huge warehouse in New York.

For two consecutive years, Whitman Publishing Company (responsible for producing Big Little Books featuring the Disney characters) printed two special Mickey Mouse premiums for Macy's Department Stores. Macy's Santa handed out copies of *Mickey Mouse and Minnie* at Macy's to children during the 1934 Christmas season. The following Christmas season in 1935 saw Macy's Santa handing out *Mickey Mouse and Minnie March to Macy's*. Both of these special Big Little Books (3 7/16" x 3 9/16" and 144 pages long) told the story of Mickey and Minnie attending the Macy parade. Like other Big Little Books, one page had text while the facing page had a black and white drawing. Kay Kamen, the genius behind Disney marketing beginning in the Thirties, was the instigator behind these unique promotional books.

After 1939, Mickey Mouse as a balloon disappeared from the parade for several decades, until 1970, when an updated Mickey appeared just in time to help promote the upcoming opening of Walt Disney World. (In 1971, gale-force winds grounded all the Macy balloons and television viewers had to settle for watching clips of the balloons from the 1970 parade. Mickey was back flying high in 1972.) This was a colorful Mickey wearing an opened collared, short sleeved yellow shirt, his famous red shorts, yellow shoes and white gloves and pupils that were so close together that Mickey looked cross-eyed.

The 1973 parade celebrated the 50th anniversary of Walt Disney cartoons (since the Alice Comedies premiered in 1923) with the Mickey Mouse balloon and costumed Mickey, Pluto, Goofy and Pinocchio near the Disney Circus wagon float. Other Disney floats were devoted to *Alice in Wonderland* and Captain Hook's ship, as well as the Walt Disney World Castle showcasing that year's animated release, *Robin Hood*.

Manfred Bass, who was the designer of the parade for forty-one years beginning in 1960, remembered about the castle float: "That was really a lot of fun, working with the Disney people. They wanted us to reproduce the castle and celebrate it in the parade. We were in a sweat about the whole thing, but it was an exciting project."

After being given some general information and "a little thin sketch," Bass and his crew began to develop the castle float design not only from a creative perspective, but also for its technical needs.

"Our goal was to make the castle look as big and grand as possible," he said.

"And yet, all parade units have to be transported from Hoboken, New Jersey, into Manhattan on the night before the parade. That means no unit can be more than 12 1/2-feet high or 8-feet wide in order to fit through the Lincoln Tunnel under the Hudson River. So how do you capture the majesty of the actual Disney World Castle given these physical restrictions? You have to create a 'magical box'!"

So various parts of the float were designed to fold up, fold down or telescope into position. The sides of the castle were folded out, and various elements were put in place, including the three telescoping turrets.

Mickey Mouse again disappeared from the parade for a period of time but was re-invented for the 74th Macy's Thanksgiving Day Parade in 2000, as Bandleader Mickey Mouse led the parade into the new millenium. The red and gold outfit was inspired by Mickey's bandleader outfit from the 1950s *Mickey Mouse Club* television show (although the balloon Mickey's baton in his right hand was significantly different).

Today it takes from six to nine months to create a new Macy's parade balloon like Bandleader Mickey. After several sketches of possible designs, designers build two models of the new balloon. One model has numbers over it to help figure out how to cut the pieces of fabric and where to attach the ropes. The second model shows what colors to paint the balloon. Disney makes sure those colors are accurate.

The balloons are made in many sections and each section is inflated separately, so, if there is a leak, the entire balloon won't deflate. Today, there are forty-five to seventy trained rope handlers (usually Macy's employees) for each balloon like Bandleader Mickey.

More than seventy-five years after the first parade, the Macy's Thanksgiving Day Parade continues to be a magical Thanksgiving morning experience for both children and adults and Mickey Mouse has been a significant contributor to those magical memories.

## TINKER BELL TALES

The little pixie, Tinker Bell, is one of the most popular Disney characters and currently stars in her own straight-to-DVD feature films (voiced by Mae Whitman) and appears in person at the Disney theme parks, often in an area dubbed "Pixie Hollow". For over fifty years, she has brought her special magic to the Disney Company.

James Barrie's first draft of his famous story of the magical boy who never grew up, *Peter Pan*, originally christened the world's most famous female fairy as "Tippy-Toe." Fortunately, by the time the play was first performed, the little pixie had been renamed "Tinker Bell" and has remained so ever since. She appeared on stage as a spot of light reflected from an offstage hand held mirror and when she spoke, it was a tinkling sound created offstage by a collar of bells with two special ones that Barrie had purchased in Switzerland to create just the right tone.

Over the years, the fairy's name has been spelled a variety of ways including "Tinkerbelle" but Disney Archivist Dave Smith has determined the official name is Tinker Bell because in the film Captain Hook refers to her as "Miss Bell," indicating that Bell is her last name. A tinker was an itinerant tradesman who mended pots and pans. He rang his distinctively high pitched "tinker's bell" to announce he was in the neighborhood.

Barrie pictured the fairy with fiery red hair because she was so small she could only have one emotion at a time, and the red hair seemed to reflect her most common emotions of anger, passion and embarrassment.

In 1924, Barrie wrote a screenplay for a possible movie of *Peter Pan* but it was never used. From that unpublished screenplay, here is the description of the first appearance of Tinker Bell:

"The fairy, Tinker Bell. Now we have the outside of the window, with swallows still there. The fairy music comes now. The fairy, Tink, flies on and alights on the window sill. The swallows remain. She should be about five inches in height and, if the effect can be got, this should be one of the quaintest pictures of the film, the appearance of a real fairy. She is a vain little thing, and arranges her clothes to her satisfaction. She also keeps shoving the birds about so as to get the best place for herself. There should never be any close-up pictures of Tink or the other fairies; we should always just see them as not more than five inches high. Finally, she shoves the swallows off the sill."

When the animated feature was first released, the Disney publicity department insisted that this would be the first time that Tinker Bell would be visible as more than just the little spot of light flitting around the scenery that was familiar to audiences from the many stage productions of the play.

In actuality, a silent movie version of *Peter Pan* released by Paramount in 1924 had a live actress appear briefly in some close-ups as Tinker Bell. Her name was Virginia Brown Faire, and she had appeared in silent films for over three years before she won the role of Tink.

Through the special effects of Roy Pomeroy using "in-the-camera matte photography," Tink was seen as a real person for the first time. The director wanted audiences to believe she was very much alive so that the film audience would understand why it was necessary to clap their hands to save her life near the end of the film. For most of the film, she remains the familiar ball of light.

A film magazine of the time, *Exceptional Photoplays* (Dec.-Jan. 1925 issue), was delighted by the final effect: "What could be more delightful than the picturing of Tinker Bell as a brilliant ball of light, flitting swiftly through the air and which, when alighting, is disclosed to the wondering audience as a tiny creature in the wind-blown draperies—all flame and unreality and beauty?"

Herbert Brenon, who directed that film version, was still around when Disney released its animated feature. He was very complimentary about the Disney interpretation of Tinker Bell. "Tinker Bell is absolutely magnificent. That was something we had to do most of the time with just a light on the end of a wire. Cartoon is the ideal medium for portraying the role," he stated when the film was originally released.

For the Disney version, actress Margaret Kerry (who also modeled and provided a voice for one of Neverland's mermaids) was the model for Tinker Bell. Miss Kerry had to audition in pantomime for the film's directors and had previously played a fairy in the Warner Brothers' film adaptation of *A Midsummer Night's Dream*, besides a host of other professional acting credits beginning from the time when she was only four years old.

"One of the greatest misconceptions about Tinker Bell is that she was modeled after Marilyn Monroe," claimed animator Marc Davis, who was responsible for designing and bringing the pixie to life. "There is no truth whatsoever to this. Margaret Kerry was our only live action reference and she was a tremendous help in allowing us to rough out the action."

*"I had an agent who sent me over for the Disney audition for **Peter Pan**," remembered Kerry. "How do you audition for animation and for a character who doesn't speak? At home I had a room set up... my dance room... with all these mirrors and a bar, etc.... so I got this little record player and put on an instrumental record and I worked up a pantomime to the beat of the record of making breakfast. You know, carrying eggs and maybe dropping one, etc. So the next day I went to the studio and took the record player and put on the record and did this mime I had created. I believe there were three people there... probably Marc Davis and Gerry Geronomi and somebody else I can't remember right now. Anyway, they gave me some direction of 'look up as if you see such and such', etc.*

*"The sessions were very exciting. There were all kinds of props for me to interact with including an oversized keyhole which I had to pretend to squeeze through. They also had a pair of twelve-foot scissors which I had to move. It's difficult to do a pantomime if you don't have a rhythm so I did a lot of action with songs like The Donkey Serenade going through my mind.*

*"They called me 'Two Take Tink' because I would get it right the first time and then they would have me do it a second time for 'safety'. I was so young and foolish. I could have made a lot more money messing things up so they would have to do it over and over. When I showed up that first day, I was in a bathing suit....and tennis shoes! You can see it in a publicity photo or two and they offered to get me ballet slippers and I told them I had those at home and I would bring them in the next day and I did."*

Disney publicists did take great pains at the time to point out that Tinker Bell's personality characterized by jealousy, anger, vanity and more was entirely different from Margaret Kerry's personality.

"Our intention was always to make (Tinker Bell) attractive," recalled Marc Davis. "She is basically a jealous woman and that is what motivates all her actions. The pouting aspect of her personality was suggested by Barrie."

More time and money were spent on the development of Tinker Bell than any other character in the animated feature, including Captain Hook. One press release claimed she was on the drawing board for twelve years and during that time her hair changed from blonde to red to dark brown, and finally back to blonde. One interpretation had her as a cool, sophisticated, ballerina-like fairy. In the final film, her wings were animated on a separate cel level to give them a more translucent appearance.

Disney Legend Ollie Johnston said that Tinker Bell is "a prime example of how much an artist can do with a character that doesn't talk by simply using pantomime. Marc made the character much more memorable than if she had some kind of voice."

When the film was released, critics were not kind to little Tink. Bosley Crowther in his review for the *New York Times* described her as "a bit of vulgarity, with her bathing beauty form and attitude" and Francis Clarke Sayers called her "a vulgar little thing, who has been too long at the sugar bowls."

The official Disney coloring instructions for the original animated Tinker Bell list the color of her outfit as "dreiss."

That name may puzzle art students because that term only existed at Disney. Legendary Disney ink and painter Phyllis Craig first started to work at the Disney Studio during the production of *Peter Pan*. She stated that "dreiss" was "a color named after a lovely woman who worked there who always wore this distinctive chartreuse green" that was selected for the famous pixie.

Audiences immediately fell in love with Miss Bell and she was featured on a variety of products including clothes, jewelry, comic books (including two issues in the Dell Four Color Series illustrated by Al Hubbard), dolls, games, night lights, sunglasses, and many more items like a number of different souvenir bells that were available at Disneyland.

One of the first Disneyland-specific products sold at Walt's new theme park for twenty-five cents was a glow-in-the-dark "Tinker Bell's Enchanted Wand" that after being held under a light bulb for several minutes and then going to a darkened location, Tinker Bell's star mounted on the top of the wand would glow faintly and mysteriously.

There were even a series of commercials produced by the Disney Studios in the mid-Fifties where Tinker Bell was the spokes-pixie for Peter Pan Peanut Butter, one of the major sponsors of the weekly Disneyland television series.

The primary director for these commercials was Charles Augustus "Nick" Nichols. Nichols, who began his Disney career as an animator on the Disney shorts, and had most of his responsibility as a director on the Pluto cartoons from 1944-1951.

The commercials provided work for some of the Disney animators who had been working on the short cartoons that were being phased out of the theatrical schedule. Phil Duncan, Volus Jones, Bob Carlson, Bill Justice, Paul Carlson and others contributed to this new endeavor.

One of the greatest Disney storymen of all time, Bill Peet, remembered when he butted heads with Walt Disney on a segment of *Sleeping Beauty*, that the "next day, I was sent down to the main floor to work on Peter Pan Peanut Butter TV commercials, which was without a doubt my punishment for what Walt considered my stubbornness. I toughed it out for about two months on peanut butter commercials, then stubbornly decided to return to my room on the third floor whether Walt liked it or not."

The commercial work also provided jobs for other talent at the Disney lot. Sterling "Winnie the Pooh" Holloway and Cliff "Jiminy Cricket" Edwards narrated the Peter Pan Peanut Butter commercials. Tinker Bell was mute in those days and had to pantomime her delight at the peanut butter that could be put on hot toast because it melted like butter and was so smooth that it could even be spread on "crispy potato chips."

Tinker Bell would fly around huge jars of Peter Pan Peanut Butter while the theme song would remind audiences that "your eyes know and your tummy knows... best of all, your taster knows... Peter Pan Peanut Butter is so grand—the smoothest peanut butter in the land."

These commercials often appeared on the weekly Disneyland television show. The popular television show opened each week with Tinker Bell introducing audiences to the four lands of Disneyland. The memorable animation of Tink was done by Disney Legend Les Clark.

She became so associated with the new theme park that one of the most frequently asked questions of cast members was "Where is Tinker Bell?" Walt came up with a solution to that problem in the Summer of 1961 by having a real life Tinker Bell fly over Sleeping Beauty Castle during the nightly fireworks display.

That first Tinker Bell was Tiny Kline. Tiny Kline came to America as a Hungarian immigrant at the age of fourteen as part of a dance troupe. She caught the attention of a renowned Wild West trick rider whom she married shortly thereafter. Five weeks after the wedding, he fell off of his horse and died, leaving Kline to begin her own career in the circus. Her trademark act when she performed with the Ringling Brothers Circus was an aerial iron jaw act where she was suspended in the air from a metal bit in her mouth on a long glide wire where she slid from the top of the tent to the ground.

On August 1, 1958 at a special "Disney Night at the Hollywood Bowl", Walt was impressed with a spectacular one thousand foot glide from the top of the amphitheater, over the audience, that ended on the stage that was performed by Kline dressed as Tinker Bell.

Kline, at age seventy, became the very first Tinker Bell at Disneyland in 1961. Suspended nearly a hundred and fifty feet up in the air, she glided down a long wire from the Matterhorn to Sleeping Beauty's Castle to signal the beginning of the fireworks. At the time she was four feet ten inches tall and weighed ninety-eight pounds.

"Tiny Kline wanted to fly as Tinker Bell with the 'jaws of life' device where she would use her teeth to hold on to a harness because she didn't want to look down. She'd hit two mattresses. The harder she hit the better she liked it. She took the bus in each night and had to run to catch the last bus going back to Los Angeles," remembered William Sullivan, who was a supervisor at Disneyland at the time.

"I have become a part of the most joyous experiment the world has ever known," gushed Kline at the time. "It's like the frosting on the cake."

Kline performed for three summers but in 1964, health problems required her to hand over the wand (and harness) to nineteen-year old Algerian circus acrobat Mimi Zerbini. Zerbini was also a circus family veteran but only performed as Tinker Bell for that one summer. Kline passed away in 1964.

In 1965, Judy Kaye began a career of more than a decade of flying across the night sky at Disneyland. Kaye stood five foot, one and seven-eighths inches tall. She was born into a circus family and paid her first visit to a circus arena when she was barely three weeks old.

She said, "I love doing Tink because of the flying. I'm partially a ham anyway. I enjoy my work...I wouldn't otherwise do it. In show business I can put forth what I've been observing and learning all my life. I like satisfying people. Show people stay young-Tiny Kline was a classic example of that."

Kaye's father, Terrell Jacobs, worked with lions and tigers for the Ringling Brothers Circus. Her mother, Dolly, was a dancer and an aerialist who eventually became grounded due to a series of falls and eventually turned to working with animals as well.

When Walt Disney began making films featuring live animals, many of the animal stars were owned and trained by Judy's mother. Walt even included some of the animals in the old Disneyland *Mickey Mouse Club* Circus that only ran from November 1955 to January 1956.

Judy remembered that in those days they had a young Indian elephant owned by her mom. Walt walked up to the baby pachyderm and exclaimed: "That's Dumbo!" Judy's mom corrected Walt, "But her name's Dolly." "From now on," proclaimed Walt, "she's Dumbo."

When not performing as Tinker Bell, Judy still trained and worked with animals as well as designing and making circus costumes. Her husband, Paul V. Kaye, had his own circus that toured internationally. Judy and her husband also were co-partners in a talent agency and booked some of the talent that toured the U.S. and Europe as part of the *Disney On Parade* show.

Shortly before nine o'clock each night during the summer, Judy Kaye would go into the Entertainment Office that was then above the *America Sings* attraction dressed in her street clothes. With some assistance she was transformed into Tinker Bell. Wearing a long coat and her head covered, she was moved through the park to the Matterhorn where through a series of stairs, elevators and ladders, she was taken up to her position.

She was helped into her harness that resembled a parachute-like contraption, her wings attached and then was hooked up to the cable. Her "launcher" would hold her ankles in position as they waited for the signal. Her "catchers" waited behind the Fantasyland break area with a large mattress or two.

At the end of the night parade, the park announcer directed guests to look into the skies over Sleeping Beauty's Castle where Tinker Bell would light up the night with *Fantasy in the Sky*.

A recorded "click track tape" counted off the seconds before take-off. At the highest point, Tinker Bell is on a wire about one hundred and fifty feet in the air while most high wire acts in the circus are done no more than fifty feet above the ground.

Approximately thirty seconds from the time she left the mountain top, she 'landed' at the tower, sometimes coming in easily, sometimes rapidly and packing a real wallop, depending on a number of factors such as weather, weight and speed of flight. At that end, the other half of her crew 'catches' her in a large, padded body mitt, calls the mountain to let them know she made it and how, unhooks her from the cable, de-wings her, and she's down and off in a waiting van, back to the Entertainment Office where she becomes Judy Kaye once again.

Tinker Bell's nightly flight was sidelined when her landing tower had been torn down to build the new Fantasyland in the early Eighties. Gina Rock at the age of twenty-seven auditioned for the role when Fantasyland re-opened in 1983.

For two years, she had performed with Ringling Brothers Circus and then spent another three years on the flying trapeze at the Circus-Circus casino in Reno, Nevada. Eventually, Rock returned to her home in the San Fernando Valley where she married a trapeze artist. In need of work, she recalled her Grad

Night at Disneyland when she first saw Tinker Bell fly and had thought: "I want that job!"

The only stipulation from the Disney Company was that she not get pregnant. "Two weeks after they put that wand in my hand ...," Rock laughed. She flew through that first summer anyhow in the early stages of pregnancy, with no one the wiser. (In fact, she flew two summers as Tink while she was pregnant.)

"It was like launching a rocket," she said, "What I would do is close my eyes right before I flew. On top of the Matterhorn, especially on a full-moon night, it was so beautiful. I would listen to the story, and become the character"

With a spotlight on her, Rock traveled thirteen miles per hour, as high as one hundred and fifty feet above the park for the length two football fields. Her actual shift lasted about twenty-three seconds, depending on the wind. After twenty-one years (and sharing the last eight with another Tink) at the age of forty-eight, Rock retired from the role.

"She's a pure pantomime character," stated animator Marc Davis about the character of Tinker Bell shortly before his passing. "She had to be a visual character, not just a spot of light, in our medium. For the most part, everybody has liked the character and the Disney Company has used her in so many different ways. I feel really good about that."

## FBI'S MOST WANTED: THE MICKEY MOUSE CLUB

At the same moment that the following telegram was sent, Walt Disney was also officially deleted as an FBI SAC contact.

*"Indeed sorry to learn of passing of your husband and want to extend my heartfelt sympathy. I know words are most inadequate to ease your grief, but it is my hope that you will derive consolation from knowing that his outstanding contributions will be a lasting memorial to him. His dedication to the highest standards of moral values and his achievements will always stand as an inspiration to those who were privileged to know him. John Edgar Hoover, Director of Federal Bureau of Investigation."* —Western Union Telegram sent to Lillian Disney on December 15, 1966.

In an official memo to J. Edgar Hoover dated December 16, 1954, Los Angeles agent John Malone of the Los Angeles Field Division had recommended that Walt Disney be made a Special Agent in Charge (SAC) Contact. Walt was approved for that role on January 12, 1955 by the Bureau.

According to the FBI's Office of Public Affairs, that designation did not entail undercover, cloak and dagger spying. It was primarily an indication that the person was acceptable and reliable to be used as a source of information by FBI agents. If field agents needed information or advice about a particular industry or area of expertise, then a SAC Contact could supply that information or point them in the right direction without the FBI agents always starting from scratch.

While an honor, Walt's status was not unique. For instance, at the same time Samuel Engel, who was a producer at 20th

Century Fox and then current head of the Screen Producers' Guild, was also a SAC Contact, as were many others. Walt was never paid for this work, nor is there any indication in any of the FBI documents of what information was ever requested or confirmed by Walt during his decade in this position, which is a trifle odd since even the most insignificant things appear in the files.

That memo from Agent Malone on December 1954 included the following statements: "Because of Mr. Disney's position as the foremost producer of cartoon films in the motion picture industry and his prominence and wide acquaintanceship in film production matters, it is believed that he can be of valuable assistance to this office and therefore it is my recommendation that he be approved as a SAC contact. Mr. Disney has volunteered representatives of this office complete access to the facilities of Disneyland for use in connection with official matters and for recreational purposes. No derogatory information concerning this individual appears in the files of this office."

However, if obtaining a copy of those documents through the Freedom of Information Act (and there are hundreds and hundreds of pages dealing with Walt and the Disney Studio), there will be sections that are "redacted," meaning that they are blacked out to make them unreadable.

This was done to prevent an unwarranted invasion of personal privacy (like when Lillian's home address was redacted on the copy of the telegram Hoover sent), might expose the identity of a confidential source, or of course, might endanger National Security. It has always been a matter of curiosity why so many FBI documents including the ones on Walt are so heavily redacted.

Of course, some know that Walt's relationship with the FBI became strained around 1961 with the production of the live-action comedy, *Moon Pilot* that would have featured inept FBI agents. The FBI protested vehemently, even going so far as to threaten the studio with Public Law 670, a Federal statute that prevents the commercial exploitation of the name of the FBI or its use in any way that implies an endorsement by the Bureau.

To further aggravate things, Disney planned to make a film of the book *Undercover Cat* by Gordon Gordon, a former FBI agent who had challenges with the Bureau over the years because of his literary portrayals of FBI agents. The film was released as *That Darn Cat*. (By the way, in the book, the name of the cat "D.C." stood for "Damn Cat".)

Disney did reassure the Los Angeles agents that "any portrayal of the FBI or its agents in this picture would be done in a dignified and efficient manner" but FBI documents from the time period kept emphasizing "just another instance where Gordon Gordon is trading on his former affiliation with the FBI to further his own personal motives. Certainly any production or book authored by Gordon is not going to do the Bureau any good."

If Walt was in hot water, apparently, he started the pot boiling back in 1958 with *The Mickey Mouse Club*. In those days, the highly popular *Mickey Mouse Club* was televised weekly over ABC at 5:30 p.m. PST.

One of the segments on the MMC was a short documentary-like newsreel segment, sometimes shot by independent companies. These were inexpensive to purchase or make and were popular with viewers according to surveys.

In January 1956, a Disney Studios representative in Washington, D.C. named Jerry Sims, took a public tour of the FBI's headquarters and thought it would make an interesting segment for the MMC. The senior agents at the FBI vetoed that request.

A year later, a new Disney representative in Washington, Hugo Johnson, pursued that request again. This time, a March 1, 1957 memo reveals that Johnson, along with MMC producer Bill Walsh, met with agent Malone in Los Angeles to once again pitch the idea of an FBI segment for the MMC.

Initially, correspondence indicates that the Bureau preferred an hour-long show about the history of science in law enforcement on the more prestigious Disneyland television show on Wednesday night, following the format of previous shows on atomic energy and aviation that combined animation and live-action to tell the history of the subject. Using that same combination of animation and live-action, the program would trace law enforcement practices from the Dark Ages through the establishment of the FBI's laboratory in 1932 that would be celebrating its 25th anniversary in 1957.

Walsh informed the FBI that Walt "is interested in filming the show on the FBI, but feels that a production on the Laboratory would be impossible at this time because of the amount of work which would be involved, and the limited time available between now and the Laboratory anniversary."

Walsh pointed out that it took more than a year and a half to produce *Our Friend the Atom* and that "this type of film is usually not profitable for the Disney company" but Walt "likes to do films of this type occasionally as a public service."

A month later, Walt brought up the subject again with Malone in Los Angeles. A memo from Malone again met with disapproval from the senior agents. Johnson continued to pursue the request through a friend of his, Louis Nichols, the assistant to the director. Nichols recommended to Hoover's protégé, associate director Clyde Tolson that the Bureau should cooperate with the Disney Studio. Tolson finally agreed after some prodding.

Since segments for the MMC could be produced quickly, and that the Disney Studio was so eager to feature the FBI, were the deciding factors to agree to proceed with the project so that the FBI Laboratory anniversary could be widely publicized.

The Washington series for the MMC would feature young Dirk Metzger in Washington, D.C. Four parts dealt with the FBI, two parts on Congress, three parts on the making of money and two parts on the White House. These were each edited down to ten minute shorts.

EXTERIOR DAY—Dirk Metzger is against backdrop of Washington, D.C. with Capitol Building in foreground, as seen through window. Desk is in foreground. OPEN Close Up on window, pull back to find Dirk in Medium Shot partially facing backdrop. He speaks before turning. FADE IN.

"Washington, D.C.! Quite a place! Believe me! I'm Dirk Metzger. Maybe some of you will remember me as a *Mickey Mouse Club* foreign correspondent from a couple of years ago. Well, Walt Disney has now assigned me to cover Washington… not from the tourist angle, as we just saw…but Washington from the inside. What goes on behind those big doors? As a *Mickey Mouse Club* reporter I did a little exploring, and for the next two weeks, I'm going to show you what I saw…where I went…what I did. Follow me!"

Friday, January 24, 1958 episode: Dirk was photographed with J. Edgar Hoover on May 15, 1957 by Hugo Johnson using a handheld camera and one light in a matter of minutes in the Director's outer office. After that meeting, Dirk goes right to Quantico and there is a sequence with firearms training.

Monday, January 27, 1958 episode: Dirk visited the FBI Identification Division.

Tuesday, January 28, 1958 episode: Dirk visited Quantico for a crime scene search, followed by a visit to the Laboratory to see the examination of evidence.

Wednesday, January 29, 1958 episode: Dirk followed up the Tuesday episode with more time in the Laboratory.

In 1958, Dirk Metzger was fourteen years old and a freshman at Wakefield High School in Arlington, Virginia. His filming would take place in the afternoons after school in several establishing shots and then during the day the rest of the scene was shot around him.

He was going to an American school in England three years earlier when his father, Marine Colonel Louis Metzger was stationed in London. From the seventh grade class of twenty-eight boys, Dirk was picked by the Walt Disney Studios to make twenty 15-minute travelogues for the MMC.

One of the MMC newsreel segments in the first and second seasons featured Metzger as a correspondent in England.

(There were also Italian, Mexican, Danish and Japanese correspondents.)

For a year and a half, Dirk spent his weekends being filmed in and around London as he visited secret tunnels of a pirate's cove, took a lesson in roof thatching, watched wild ponies in the west of England and talked to what he remembered as a "grizzly sheepherder with a mouthful of teeth. But the most fun was riding a canal boat from Manchester to London."

Dirk was asked to continue and stay in England and make more segments when his family returned to the United States, but he declined saying, "London is an adult town. America is better in every way." Robbie Serpell replaced him.

However, when Disney decided to do a series based in Washington, D.C., they were delighted Dirk was living in Arlington. For the series, Dirk got to meet President Eisenhower, Vice President Nixon, J. Edgar Hoover and other government officials as he visited various Washington landmarks.

"I waited a couple of weeks in the President's outer office," Dirk told a newspaper reporter in April 1958, "Then the President talked to me for eight minutes instead of two. He asked me quite a few questions like what does my family do. The President was really terrific and so nice—nothing but the best. He told me about his Bureau of the Budget. I wasn't too interested in that. He also said two of his grandchildren watched the Mickey Mouse show."

Dirk was flown out for two weeks to Hollywood to record his commentary. The FBI liked the fact that Dirk was a Boy Scout.

"This young man makes an exceptionally fine appearance and is the son of a Marine Corps Colonel assigned here to the Fiscal Section of U.S. Marine Corps Headquarters. Metzger is not a professional actor and he has greatly impressed the Bureau personnel with whom he has come in contact during the course of films shot at Quantico last week" stated a memo from May 15, 1957. (In that same memo, it was revealed that the FBI investigated Dirk's father and found nothing negative.)

However, his fame did bring him some teasing at school. As he told a reporter, "I didn't advertise too much. Sometimes I sort of get it in the face. There's always some Mickey Mouse show viewer at school who yells 'Hey, you forgot your ears!'"

The FBI reviewed the initial rough cut footage and composed a memo on October 22, 1957 of twenty-two things they wanted changed in the four episodes. Some were as elaborate as "the scene of the Agent firing two revolvers simultaneously and breaking the clay targets does not show the targets themselves breaking. This footage is available, and it is felt that if the scene is used at all, it should show the Agent's bullets breaking the clay targets" to simple phrase changes like "in line 3 of the narration, the word 'department' should be deleted and the word 'division' inserted."

A follow up memo from October 28, 1957, "The contents of the memorandum regarding the above captioned program were discussed in detail with Mr. William Park, News Reel Editor and Mr. Douglas Duitsman, News Reel Staff Writer, who composed the script for the film by Special Agent John Cashel at Disney Productions, on October 25, 1957. The changes suggested were reviewed and made in the film script. Both Disney executives indicated that any subsequent changes which might be desired by the Bureau in connection with this program would be readily undertaken. It was their opinion that no retakes of scenes will be necessary in order to accomplish the suggested changes."

While all of this correspondence sounds fairly positive, the problems began when the Bureau was shown the scripts and rough unedited film, but not the finished films that they felt they needed to see and approve before release. A series of memos to Disney expressed concern that the Bureau had not seen the final cut.

Walt wasn't comfortable with others having final approval, a situation that would be revisited with *Mary Poppins* and P. L. Travers.

The situation escalated to the level of Hoover himself who wanted confirmation (which he received) that the Disney Studios had agreed that the Bureau needed to see the films for clearance before airing on television.

A memo from January 23, 1958 (one day before the broadcast) included the statement: "Obviously, the mishandling on the part of the Disney Studios and failure to live up to their agreement will be taken into consideration when future approaches are made to the Bureau by this outfit."

Apparently, Disney was to supply to the Washington Bureau the completed films no later than Monday, January 20, several days before the announced airing. The Bureau protested the situation with Disney's Washington representative, Hugo Johnson, who was also upset and shared his recent communications with the Disney Studios in Burbank urging them to send the films.

An official FBI memo from Friday morning January 24 indicated "Apparently our protest with Disney Studios took effect. Hugo Johnson, local manager Disney Studios, advised at 9:45 a.m. this morning that he was en route to the airport where he would pick up the film and would have it back to us no later than 10:45 a.m. this morning. We have arranged an immediate viewing of the film."

After all that turmoil, the FBI saw nothing at all objectionable in the films. A letter from Hoover on January 30, 1958 included the statement: "I thought that the whole series was exceptionally fine in that it gave very young people an excellent concept of the operations of the FBI."

Hoover even sent a note of praise to Dirk Metzger as did President Eisenhower.

However, a bond of unspoken trust had been strained and some at the agency felt angry at the perceived snub and on a later memo there is a scribbled comment by Tolson "no further cooperation".

Nearly two years later, the Bureau, which routinely monitored several publications that focused on what was going on in Hollywood discovered in a Hedda Hopper column that Disney was going to make a movie called *Moon Pilot*. Warning flags went up instantly. Early reports that the film would feature an "ineffectual" FBI agent body guarding the Air Force pilot who saw something odd in outer space during a space flight once again brought a flood of memos and clippings to add to Walt's FBI files.

Walt had no intention or desire to ridicule the FBI, but was just using his story sense to include the time honored device of having a bumbling representative of authority unable to thwart the hero of the story.

However, even though Walt changed the organization to the "Federal Security Agency," film reviewers weren't fooled. The review of the film in the *Washington Daily News* on April 26, 1962 said, "Air Force brass are mutton-heads, and the FBI is an ineffectual as the DAR."

Whatever became of the boy wonder Dirk Metzger?

Dirk became a Marine Corps officer after growing up, then went to law school and is still a practicing attorney. One of his skills is conflict management. It is a skill that was needed more than half a century earlier when both Hoover and Disney struggled for the ultimate control of the final cut and Walt fell out of favor with the F.B.I.

# CHUCK JONES: FOUR MONTHS AT DISNEY

On his 85th birthday celebration on Sunday, September 21, 1997, the legendary Chuck Jones spoke to a group of five hundred of his friends, family, fans, and colleagues. He recalled the many letters he had sent to Walt Disney in his early years, and how Walt personally replied to each one. Later, when he met Walt, Jones thanked him for those letters and Walt replied, "Well, of course, you're the only animator who ever wrote to me!"

It was a story that Jones told many times over the decades although some have wondered whether that story was apocryphal.

"Walt was a strange kind of guy, but he's still by all odds the most important person that animation has ever known. Anybody who knows anything about animation knows that the things that happened at the Disney Studio were the backbone that upheld everything else," stated Jones.

"When Warners shut down the [animation studio], I went to work at Disney's for a while. I couldn't stand it. [Walt Disney] asked me what kind of job I wanted and the kind of job I wanted was his. But I got to know him and like him," Jones told well-respected and well-liked animation historian Joe Adamson in a 1980 interview.

Jones worked briefly at the Disney Studios from July 13, 1953, to November 13, 1953. He recalled that experience in his autobiography, *Chuck Amuck* (Farrar, Straus and Giroux, 1989). Jack Warner at Warner Brothers studio decided to shut down the animation department. The studio executive felt that the future of filmmaking would be 3-D and that it was too expensive to make 3-D cartoons because the cost couldn't be recouped with rental fees. While Chuck Jones did have a contract, he didn't want to stay there if his team had been laid off and there was scant opportunity for future work.

"I called up Walt Disney and asked him if I could come over there for a while. He said, 'Sure, come on over.' I was there for four months. I worked on *Sleeping Beauty* and the beginning of the television show. But I couldn't adjust to waiting for Walt ... the Disney people were raised that way, and used to it. You'd finish a sequence, and then you'd wait, maybe for weeks. Five or six men, just sitting around waiting for Walt to come around. When he did come around, he'd already been there the night before when the plant was dark and looked at the boards, and everybody knew he'd seen the sequence, but they still had to show it to him as though he hadn't."

The culture and process at the Disney Studio was so different that Jones leapt at the opportunity to return to Warner Brothers when the opportunity presented itself without any regrets.

"Eventually, I felt I just couldn't take it any more, so I went in and talked with Walt. He said, 'Well, what do you want to do? We can work out something for you.' I said, 'Well, you have one job here that I want, and that's yours,' because he was the only one there who could make a decision. He said, 'I'm sorry, but I'm afraid it's filled.' So we shook hands and I left. By that time, Warner's had decided to start up again, because 3-D hadn't completely revolutionized the world. That was the only time I left Warner's until they closed it down again in 1962."

The artistic designer for *Sleeping Beauty* was painter Eyvind Earle and what he recalled about those months was "Way back when we did *Melody* and *Toot, Whistle, Plunk and Boom,* Walt had let Ward Kimball sort of take over and strive for a new look at Disney. He was put on *Sleeping Beauty* at the same time I was. I remember he had a special room up on the third floor, and with a newcomer to Disney's—the famous Chuck Jones, animator, director from some other studio—the two of them [Ward and Chuck] sat upstairs in their private room, and talked and talked and talked, and for many months did absolutely nothing at all. I have never been able to figure it out. I asked Ward Kimball once, 'Why aren't you doing anything?' And Ward Kimball answered me, 'You don't know Walt Disney', whatever that was supposed to mean."

When these comments were shared years later with Kimball, he responded, "I was just filling in between animation assignments. Walt had said, 'Why don't you go up and work on that sequence about the fairies changing colors' and so forth. I was a fill-in. That happened a lot. I could leave the animation department and go and work on things of that sort, as a story man. All we [Chuck and Ward] did was sit around. I think every time Eyvind came up there, Joe Rinaldi, he and myself and Chuck Jones would get into these gabfests. Chuck had just discovered one-upmanship, and he ran into his nemesis with Bill Peet, because Bill Peet wouldn't say much, but he was funny, and he could cut you to the quick. I started enjoying it, because I knew Chuck always wants to dominate the conversation, and Peet would cut his legs out from under him. Maybe that's one reason he didn't want to work there."

As Disney producer Harry Tytle recalled, "Chuck's brief stint with Disney in 1953 lasted only four months. During this short time, he earned no screen credits and, to the best of my recollection, made no significant contributions. Chuck has joked that the only job he wanted at Disney's was already filled by Walt. He and Walt were used to the being the biggest fishes in their respective ponds. Chuck was a talented innovator but at Disney's, as far as Walt was concerned, he was the new kid on the block and had to prove himself. This must have been a new and confusing role for Chuck."

Fortunately, like Kimball, Tytle kept a detailed journal diary of his time at Disney and thanks to those notations, a much fuller insight exists into the brief Disney experience of the co-creator (with writer Mike Maltese) of the Road Runner and Coyote, Pepe Le Pew and so many other classic Warner characters.

Here are some related excerpts from Tytle's diary at the time:

> "*June 10, 1953:* *This morning I was called into Walt's office. Chuck Jones at Warner Brothers had called Walt applying for a job. Walt asked my opinion of Jones. I said, to the best of my knowledge, he was a very nice fellow personally and considered to be on of the best directors on the outside. That he had done a lot of work for Warner Brothers across the years.*"

However, the first meeting with Chuck and Walt did not go as well as expected. Chuck did not understand that he was viewed as the "new kid on the block" and felt he could slide into the same position of authority that he had at Warners.

> "*June 15, 1953:* *At 9 a.m. we met with Chuck Jones. Chuck explained how he had been working, stating he would like to work here. That he was not under contract anymore and could be available to us in a month, after winding up what he had to do at Warners and taking a vacation. Walt knew what*

*Chuck's salary was. Peterson had gotten it for him and we had discussed it—so Walt pulled a cutie by saying he didn't know 'what your salary is, Chuck, but whatever it is, you must be worth it to Warners, and I will pay you the same.' Chuck, I believe, expected more because he mentioned something about working under scale. The one thing that I thought Chuck failed in was he made clear to those in the meeting that he dominated his unit, especially story, which is un-Disney."*

While Chuck respected Walt, Jones was used to doing things his own way and at the Disney Studio there was only one way and it was Walt's way as many other talented and independent artists learned that hard lesson over the decades.

*"**June 23, 1953:** Chuck Jones knows he is definitely coming in on the 13th. Although I do not think we should bring it up, he will probably ask about contract and we have no decision or directive as to Walt's thinking. Incidentally, Chuck was in today and Hal told me he didn't make out so well in his meeting with Walt. He had a sheet of typewritten suggestions he tried to hold forth, and Walt was not interested. Chuck is going to have to learn to work with Walt. I presume that he feels he was called in for his creative thinking and ability. He will soon have to learn that Walt sets the direction, the pace, and even the topic of conversation. Hal stated that Walt made the remark to him later on that Chuck had a lot to learn."*

Jones was placed with another independent and creative animator/director, Ward Kimball. This pairing seemed to stir up even more trouble and Kimball was well known for his ego and for prodding others into doing things.

*"**September 15, 1953:** I heard today, through Hal, that Chuck who was just put on **Sleeping Beauty**, and had never directed*

*for Disney's, requests the same salary as the other feature
directors. Hal is going to present this demand to Walt this
morning. It will be very interesting to see the outcome.*

*"**September 16, 1953**: [Walt] got into the Chuck Jones' deal
and asked me if I knew that Chuck has asked for an increase,
which he indicated he would have no part of. I told him that
I was very interested in what his reaction would be, that I for
one, feel as Walt does, Chuck should prove himself here first.
Walt got a little upset because I understand he feels maybe this
increase was instigated by Ward [Kimball]. He made it clear
again that nobody is indispensable, Ward included. It was the
organization that counted."*

Things quickly escalated to the point that Jones actively
pursued other offers and eventually left the Disney Studio.

*"**November 5, 1953**: Chuck hit Walt the second time, through
Hal, for an increase. Supposedly, he has an offer from
Sutherland for $500 and an offer to return to Warner Brothers.
Walt's remarks to Hal were 'Have Chuck make up his mind as
to what he wants to do. There is no increase until we find out
Chuck's ability—he has shown nothing to date'.*

*"**November 13, 1953**: The Chuck Jones situation came to
a head today....The story is that he left for New York this
evening, starts work at Warner Brothers again the first of the
year at a $40 increase, making the new salary $400. I had
heard in the morning that he was telling people that 'the place
here worked at too slow a pace'...."*

A letter from Chuck Jones to his daughter Linda dated
November 30, 1953 states in part: "At Disney's it was always
necessary to be certain places at certain times. God knows

why, nothing ever happened, so it was nearly impossible to work there without a timepiece. You could get along without talent, but not a watch. As you know I gave up time about a year before leaving here and I must say I never missed the damn stuff... I had not realized how much I missed the sweetness of my own solitude. At Disney's, aloneness or desire to be alone generates suspicion, you are always surrounded by people, drifting in and out, exchanging hackneyed pleasantries or just sitting, staring with baleful intensity at one's own navel. What a waste! What a waste of wonderful talent!"

Despite the fact that his brief tenure at Disney was not satisfying for either himself or Walt Disney, Jones still held the Disney Studios and Walt in the highest regard for the rest of his life. "Disney was not a good animator, he didn't draw well at all, but he was always a great idea man, and a good writer," Jones remarked.

In a 1975 interview with Greg Ford and Richard Thompson, Jones stated: "Disney's was to animation what Griffith was to live action. Almost all the tools were discovered at Disney's. They were the only ones who had the money, and who could and did take the time to experiment."

It was obviously better for everyone that Jones returned to Warners and created some more memorable cartoons and characters in his distinctive style and later formed his own animation studio. At the time Jones was at Disney, Walt was cutting back on the theatrical short cartoons, an area of strength for Jones, and concentrating less on animation and more on the creation of Disneyland... and after all, at the Disney Studio, there could be only one Walt Disney and Walt was doing that job pretty well himself.

## WALT'S WOMEN: TWO FORGOTTEN INFLUENCES

Despite Walt's joking complaints to reporters that he was surrounded by nothing but females in his life, it was apparent that Walt enjoyed women, not as objects of lust or fodder for humiliating humor or second class citizens, but as interesting people which was a very out of the ordinary approach during the time when Walt lived.

"He (Walt Disney) lived surrounded by women. Besides Lilly and the two daughters and the cook, there was often a female relative living with the Disneys. Walt complained wryly that even the family pets were female. But his grumblings seemed half-hearted. He appreciated femininity," wrote Bob Thomas in *Walt Disney: An American Original.*

There are countless examples of how Walt was cautious about his casual swearing around women and was always respectful and expected the same from his employees although that didn't always happen. He employed talented women in positions of authority and influence at the Disney Studio when it was uncommon at other studios.

As Diane Disney Miller remembered: "It puzzles me why people think that dad was 'shy', or 'uncomfortable' with women. Quite the opposite. He was very easy around women, and liked and respected them, with the exception of those who were pretentious or domineering, and I am aware of a few of those sorts that he complained about ... none family members! This should seem obvious, because of his well-documented close relationship with his sister, his mother, his Aunt Margaret, his sisters-in-law Louise and Edna, my mother's sister Hazel, her daughter Marjorie, his secretaries Dolores Voght, Tommie Willke and Lucille Martin who was not with him for too long before he died. The letters he received from old girl friends, and his responses, and Ruth's interview with Dave Smith are documentary proof of his genuine, natural, healthy appreciation of the women in his life."

In the interview that Diane refers to in her comment, Walt's younger sister Ruth told Disney Archivist Dave Smith that when Walt wanted to take a Manual Arts class at McKinley High School, all that was available was a cooking class so he took it. He was the only boy in the class.

Ruth remembered: "Oh, he was as happy as could be in there, because the girls were all making over him something terrible. The only boy! And he loved it. He used to come home and tell about it and all the fun he had there. He had a lot of friends everywhere and especially the girls. One time coming home from high school there in Chicago, my mother saw…we had such big snow that there were big, about four or five foot, banks on each side of the side walk, and here, coming down there, was a boy with a girl on each arm. She was just casually looking at him wondering 'you know, that boy was popular!' When he got closer, she saw it was Walt!"

Two of the most interesting women in Walt's life saw him nearly every day of his life, and don't get enough recognition for the positive influence they directly had on Walt.

Thelma Howard was the Disney live-in housekeeper and cook for thirty years beginning in 1951. Her nickname was "Fou-Fou," (sometimes spelled "Foo-Foo"), the closest one of the Disney grandchildren could come to pronouncing "Thelma". Walt just referred to her as "the real-life Mary Poppins."

She died just before her 80th birthday, on June 10, 1994.

Thelma Howard has actually been described as having been more like the feisty maid in the Ted Key comic panel *Hazel* than like the character of Mary Poppins because she was much gruffer than a spoonful of sweetness. Like Walt, she loved to smoke. She also loved to play gin rummy, and she was accepted fully as a part of the Disney family.

She was described by those who knew her as a handsome, quick-witted woman who loved football and the color pink and who baked a lovely boysenberry pie. She was a perfectionist in her work, making sure the Disneys were well cared for down to the tiniest details, and she was not hesitant to give orders.

"She was a combination of real loving and kind of crusty," said Jack Shakely, president of the California Community Foundation, "...a chain-smoking, no-nonsense type, but very loving, like TV's old 'Hazel' character."

She had her share of tragedy in her early life. She came from a poor family. Her mother died in childbirth when Thelma was just six years old, and her sister died in a fire in their kitchen years later. Like Walt, she was from the Midwest. Thelma was a native of Southwick, Idaho.

Shortly after graduating from high school, she left Idaho to attend a business college in Spokane, Washington. She hoped to become a legal secretary, but ran out of money and had to drop out. She stayed briefly with relatives in Northern California and in 1931 moved to Los Angeles, where she did office work and cleaned homes. Before working for the Disneys, she was married briefly and had a son, Michael, who was constantly in trouble.

Thelma always made sure that the fridge was always filled with hot dogs, because when Walt came home from work, he'd like to grab a couple. He'd give one to his pet poodle, and then eat the other two himself, even though they were cold and uncooked.

Despite acknowledging that Thelma was a great cook, Walt would often try to get her to visit *Biff's*, a diner-type restaurant near the Disney Studio, to try and duplicate some of their offerings. Grudgingly, she would make the trip to try and recreate the recipe for the pan fried potatoes (actually hash browns) they served that Walt loved so much or the silver dollar sized pancakes. On Thelma's days off, Walt and Lilly would go out to eat, usually at the Tam O'Shanter or the Brown Derby.

Walt's grandchild Chris Miller said, "My grandfather had an incredible rapport with her. They seemed to share everything, from a sense of humor to their notions about what was happening with the kids and what was best for them."

Walt felt very comfortable joking with her and teasing her and reportedly, Thelma was quite capable of giving as good as she got.

Howard's niece remembers visiting her aunt at the Disney home and staying in Thelma's quarters. When the Disneys were gone, they would spread themselves out, pretending the house was their own.

"We would sit at their big dining room table, and I remember she would act silly, like a schoolgirl. She would sit at one end, and I would sit at the other end, and we would shout like, "Could you pleeeeeeze pass the peas?', laughed her niece, Cheryl Wallace.

When she started as a housekeeper for the Disney family in 1951 at the age of thirty-eight, she'd get a few shares of Disney stock as a Christmas gift as well as for birthdays and special events. Walt advised her to hang on to the stock because it might become valuable one day. She lived frugally throughout her life, apparently not knowing the rising value of the stock actually made her a multi-millionaire at the time of her death.

Through numerous splits, her shares had grown to 192,755 shares. Between 1980 and 1993, the stock had increased in value tenfold and was valued at $8.39 million. Her property and savings pushed the total over $9 million.

She left nearly four and a half million dollars to poor and disabled children as well as nearly the same amount to her son, Michael. He was an only child from Thelma's brief marriage. At the time of her death, he was in his mid-Fifties and in a home for the developmentally disabled.

"She was told to hang onto it, and she did. She never sold a share of it," said Jack Shakely, president of the California Community Foundation, which assists the Thelma Pearl Foundation in dispensing the money. "I don't think she knew what it was worth. She had great faith in the Disneys and wouldn't part with it."

In 1981, Howard had retired to a modest two-bedroom bungalow in West L.A. Her health began failing. Her health continued to worsen and she was moved to a nursing home in Santa Monica by 1991 where she was not treated well, and a man claiming to be her husband (with no proof) was trying to gain control of her estate.

Around the same time, Diane Disney Miller became concerned because she hadn't received the usual Christmas cards from Howard and discovered her in the nursing room. Howard had kept a framed, autographed photo of Walt and Lillian Disney by her bedside and it had been recently stolen. Diane gave her another and Howard kept it hidden.

Howard was moved to another home where she had a private room. Miller sent fresh flowers every Monday and visited her often. When she died, Howard was living in a retirement home with beautiful gardens.

She was buried in Forest Lawn in a pink coffin and her grave overlooks the Disney Studios in Burbank, California. The foundation that bears her name has given out over four million dollars in grants since 1995.

"I guess there isn't any sucker bigger than the one who sounds off about the fair sex," moaned Walt when during an interview he was reprimanded for suggesting that women don't have a sense of humor. In fact, he stopped bringing Disney films home to screen for his family because he said that Lilly and Thelma didn't "laugh loudly enough" during them.

If Thelma Howard was like the fictional character Hazel, there was an actual Hazel in Walt's life as well. That woman was the Disney Studio nurse, Hazel George who he relied on for studio gossip as well as her keen story insight on proposed productions.

Walt's old polo injury resulted in considerable pain. Sometimes he wasn't even able to bend to get into his car. In a room next to Walt's office, a room Walt called his "laughing place," studio nurse Hazel applied hot packs and traction every evening, usually after five p.m., to ease the pain.

He spent this time to use Hazel as a sounding board for his plans, as well as to exchange gossip as he unwound from the pressures of the day. Often times, Walt would get philosophical, but Hazel's sharp wit never let him get maudlin.

"After I die, I would hate to look down at this studio and find everything in a mess," Walt moaned as he was getting his nightly massage.

"What makes you think you won't be using a periscope?" she replied.

"Smart ass," Walt muttered under his breath as he lay there.

Another time after she had deflated another of his stories, Walt said, "You know what my next project is going to be? An audio-animatronics nurse."

Hazel claimed in an interview that "Walt was more at ease with women than he was with men." He certainly was very much at ease with Hazel and appreciated her honesty and outspokenness. He also appreciated her discretion since during his sessions with her, he became very vulnerable and opened himself up in a way he didn't with others. Even after his death, Hazel was discreet about what Walt shared in those sessions.

Born Hazel Gilman on February 21, 1904 in Bisbee, Cochise County, Arizona, she was the oldest of three children. Her father was a copper miner. Perhaps due to the labor uprisings against copper miners in the area when she was thirteen, she ended up a ward of the juvenile court.

A brief marriage in 1928 resulted in a daughter and the quick disappearance of her husband, Mr. George. By 1930, Hazel was living with her divorced mother and younger brother in Los Angeles. She eventually graduated from a nursing college, and was later hired by the Disney Studio during the infamous strike of 1941.

"I felt that Walt's greatest talent was recognizing the potential in others," said George in an interview shortly before her death. "He really sought to bring out the best in people, whether they were artists, story people or accountants. He personally went through every day's work at the Studio. He didn't just ask someone how things were going. He found out himself. He was a very hard worker and a wonderful man. He encouraged me to get into writing lyrics for music at the Studio, as he knew that I wasn't really using my college degree in literature as a nurse. So I did, and he loved my writing. Walt was a special man, even today, I have a lot to thank him for."

Under the pseudonym "Gil George", she co-wrote over ninety songs for Disney. Her work included songs for films like *The Light in the Forest*, *Perri*, *Tonka*, *Westward Ho the Wagons*, and *Old Yeller*. She was also a frequent song contributor to the television shows including the original Disney weekly show, *Zorro*, and the original *Mickey Mouse Club*. For *The Mickey Mouse Club*, she was responsible for the song for Talent Roundup, the *Corky and White Shadow* serial, and several of the Jimmie Dodd "Doddisms" among other contributions.

She was a lyricist, collaborating mainly with her long-time companion, Disney Studio composer Paul Smith, but also worked with George Bruns and Jimmie Dodd occasionally to write songs for *The Mickey Mouse Club* show.

Incredibly, her contributions to the musical heritage of Disney are often overlooked in the various books and articles devoted to Disney music. In addition, her influence in the creation of Disneyland has never been fully explored.

Hazel was the one who suggested that to help him relax that Walt should go to the Chicago Railroad Fair with Ward Kimball. That experience helped Walt formulate his plans for Disneyland.

When Walt was considering building his "Mickey Mouse Park", Hazel became the head of the Disneyland Boosters and Backers Club to raise contributions from the studio employees for the project. That action helped convince Roy O. Disney to lend his support to Walt's dream of a theme park.

Hazel's songwriting career seems to have ended when Paul Smith retired from the Disney Studios in the early Sixties, although as a nurse, she continued treating Walt right up until he went into St. Joseph's Hospital.

Hazel passed away on March 12, 1996 (roughly ten years after the death of Paul Smith, whom she lived with and cared for in his final years) and fortunately several oral interviews with her survive, although they currently remain unpublished.

Bob Thomas, who authored the biography *Walt Disney: An American Original*, acknowledged that she provided him with the key to understanding Walt's personality.

"One thing that I learned from my long time friendship with Walt was that in most cases, he was strongly motivated by love," remembered Hazel. "He loved his family very much, and would tell me about his daughters' exploits, and about his wife Lilly. He really loved them dearly, and enjoyed telling me all the wonderful stories of what they were doing. He also loved kids in general and animals, especially his own little dog. He would often tell me stories about that wonderful little poodle. He never got tired of talking about animals."

Unfortunately, Hazel suffered from the effects of prolonged alcoholism (as did Paul Smith) and in her later years, her memories were not always reliable and there are some outrageous observations credited to her.

"She was a good friend to my dad and somewhat his confidante. My mother had the same sort of relationship, as some women do, with her hairdresser," recalled Diane Disney Miller who didn't meet Hazel until years after Walt's death. "I sent Hazel flowers every month until she was gone."

# ABOUT THE AUTHOR

Jim Korkis is an internationally respected Disney historian who has written hundreds of articles about all things Disney for over three decades. He is also an award winning teacher, professional actor and magician and author of several books about animation.

He grew up in Glendale, California, right next to Burbank, the home of the Disney Studios. His third grade teacher at Thomas Edison Elementary School was Mrs. Disney, the wife of one of Walt Disney's brothers. Upon discovering this fact, Jim took a large sheet of easel paper and drew a huge picture of Jiminy Cricket, his favorite Disney character at the time. He gave it to Mrs. Disney in the hopes that she would immediately take it to the Disney Studios where he would be offered a job and not have to learn his multiplication tables. He was not hired and still has trouble with math to this day.

As a teenager, Jim wrote down the names he saw on the credits of Disney animated cartoons and went to the Glendale-Burbank phone book and cold called some of them. Many were gracious enough to ask him to visit them with the resulting articles sometimes appearing in the local newspapers or various "fan-zines" and magazines. Over the decades, Jim pursued a teaching career as well as a performing career but was still active in writing about Disney for various magazines.

In 1995, he relocated to Orlando, Florida to take care of his ailing parents. He got a job doing magic and making balloon animals for guests at Pleasure Island. Within a month, he was moved over to the Magic Kingdom, where he "assisted in the portrayal of" Prospector Pat in Frontierland and Merlin in Fantasyland for the *Sword in the Stone* ceremony. He has pictures, videos and pay stubs to prove it.

In 1996, he became a full time salaried animation instructor at the Disney Institute where he taught every animation class including several that only he taught. He also instructed classes on animation history and improvisational acting techniques for the interns at Disney Feature Animation Florida. As the Disney Institute re-organized, Jim joined Disney Adult Discoveries, the group who researched, wrote and facilitated backstage tours and programs for Disney guests and Disneyana conventions.

Eventually, Jim moved to Epcot where he was a Coordinator with College and International Programs and then a Coordinator for the Epcot Disney Learning Center. During his time at Epcot, Jim researched, wrote and facilitated over two hundred different presentations on Disney history for Disney cast members and corporate clients including Feld Entertainment, Kodak, Blue Cross, Toys R Us, Military Sales and more.

He was the off camera announcer for the syndicated television series *Secrets of the Animal Kingdom*, wrote articles for Disney publications like *Disney Adventures*, *Disney Files* (DVC), *Sketches*, *Disney Insider* and more. He worked on special projects like writing text for WDW trading cards, on camera host for the *100 Years of Magic Vacation Planning* video, facilitator with the Disney Crew puppet show and countless other credits including assisting Disney Cruise Line, WDW Travel Company, Imagineering and Disney Design Group with Disney historical material. As a result, Jim was the recipient of the prestigious Disney award, *Partners in Excellence*, in 2004. Jim is not currently an employee of the Disney Company.

# ACKNOWLEDGEMENTS

I would like to take this opportunity to acknowledge not only those people who directly helped me with this book but those who have inspired or supported me over the years and deserve to see their name printed prominently in a Disney related book.

This book and this author have been greatly enriched by the generosity and enthusiasm of Diane Disney Miller whose many kindnesses truly honor the memory of her parents.

Many thanks to my good friend Didier Ghez whose passionate love of Disney history and his editing and publishing of the book series, *Walt's People*, is a constant inspiration.

Thanks to my brothers, Michael and Chris, and their families including their children: Amber, Keith, Autumn and Story who never really understood what their uncle does or why he does it. Uncle Jim loves you all very much. Please don't throw away Uncle Jim's Disney collection after he is gone.

Mark Goldhaber, Adrienne Vincent-Phoenix, Shoshana Lewin and the rest of the gang at www.mouseplanet.com. Your support has always been a blessing. Thank you so much.

Thanks to Chad Emerson and Ayefour Publishing for thinking this book might be a good idea and more importantly, making sure it got published.

Many thanks to Jennifer Solt of *24 Communications* for all her talented hard work and patience on the design of this book as is evident from cover to cover.

Many thanks to Lou Mongello, Jim Hill, Werner Weiss, Jim
Fanning, Greg Ehrbar, Michael Lyons, John Canemaker, Mark
Kausler, Michael Barrier, Paul Anderson, Dave Smith, Kim
Eggink, Brad Anderson, Wade Sampson, John Cawley, Kaye
Bundey

Marion and Sarah Quimby, Tom and Marina Stern, Jerry
and Liz Edwards, Kendra Trahan, Marie Schilly, Tommy
Byerly, Nancy Stadler, Lonnie Hicks, Michael "Shawn" and
Laurel Slater, Tom Heckel, Kirk Bowman, Jeff Kurtti, Amber
Walls, Ryan N. March, Michelle, Randy and Belinda Swiat, Phil
Debord, Todd James Pierce, Greg Dorf, Betty Bjerrum, Jeff
Pepper, Jerry Beck, Amid Amidi, Michael Sporn, Leonard
Maltin, Robin Cadwallender, John Culhane, Scott Wolf, Pete
Martin, Bill Cotter, J.B. Kaufman

Bob Miller, David Koenig, Kevin Yee, John Frost, Dave
Mruz, Rich Cullen, Mark Matheis, Danni Mikler, Tracy M.
Barnes, Sarah Pate, Tamysen Hall, Evlyn Gould, Tom Heintjes,
Bruce Gordon, David Mumford, Randy Bright, Jack and Leon
Janzen, Mickey Boyd, Malcolm and Mary Joseph (and their
children: Melissa, Megan, Rachel, Nicole, Richard)

Keith Seckel, Larry Lauria, Paul Naas, Mark Jones, Rachel
Nacion, Danielle Wallace, Tom Nabbe, Tim Foster, Arlen
Miller, Floyd Norman, Lock Wolverton, David Lesjak, Phil
Ferretti, Anne Smith, Jim Ryan, Howard Kalov, Jennifer Bacon,
Dana Gabbard, Dave Bennett, Margaret Kerry, Wanda Perkins,
Howard Green, Micki Thompson, Bob Thomas, Alex Maher,
Kathy Luck, Brian Blackmore, Kaye Malins, Heather Sweeney

And sadly some people that I have foolishly forgotten for
the moment. Their kindness and generosity like those names
listed here have lightened my journey through life and made

this book possible. I hope all of you, both acknowledged and temporarily missing, live happily ever after. I also hope that each one of you buy at least a dozen copies of this book because your name appears in it.

LaVergne, TN USA
29 November 2010
206653LV00001B/19/P